THE LIFE INDUSTRY

THE LIFE INDUSTRY

Biodiversity, People and Profits

Edited by
MIGES BAUMANN, JANET BELL,
FLORIANNE KOECHLIN and MICHEL PIMBERT

INTERMEDIATE TECHNOLOGY PUBLICATIONS 1996

Intermediate Technology Publications Ltd,
103–105 Southampton Row, London WC1B 4HH, UK

© Worldwide Fund for Nature and Swissaid 1996

A CIP catalogue for this book is available from the British Library

ISBN: 1 85339 341 X

Cover photograph: WWF/John E. Newby

Typeset by Dorwyn Ltd, Rowlands Castle, Hants
Printed in the UK by SRP, Exeter

Contents

Preface   vii

1. Introduction (*Janet Bell and Michel Pimbert*)   1

Part 1   The Tools of Control

2. Science, markets and power   25
   2.1 Changes in the genetic supply industry (*Jack Kloppenburg*)   25
   2.2 Genetic engineering and biotechnology in industry
       (*Janet Bell*)   31
   2.3 Biodiversity Newspeak (*Christine von Weiszäcker*)   53

3. The power and the glory   69
   3.1 The gene – that obscure object of desire (*Regine Kollek*)   69
   3.2 Patenting life – trends in the US and Europe
       (*Christine Noiville*)   76
   3.3 The changing face of patents   86

Part 2   The Practice – Bioprospecting or Biopiracy?

4. Green gold   95
   4.1 Equity issues in bioprospecting
       (*Charles Zerner and Kelly Kennedy*)   96
   4.2 The Body Shop model of bioprospecting (*Mark Johnston*)   110
   4.3 Indigenous peoples' responses to bioprospecting
       (*Marcus Colchester*)   114
   4.4 The losers' perspective (*Vandana Shiva*)   119

5. Human genes – the new resource   137
   5.1 The Human Genome Diversity Project   137
   5.2 Indigenous peoples' reactions to the HGDP
       (*Victoria Corpus and Alejandro Argumedo*)   145
   5.3 Glorification of the genes – genetic determinism and
       racism in science (*Alan Goodman*)   149

Part 3   Which way now?

   6.1 Choices   163

6.2 Reversals for diversity – a new paradigm
    (*Robert Chambers*)   173
6.3 Seeds of hope –   185
    A vote for conscience over capital   185
    Europe's moratorium on BGH   187
    A gene bank working with farmers   189
    The MASIPAG experience   190
    The butterfly rises (*Pat Mooney*)   192

Appendices
  About the authors   195
  Acronyms   197
  Glossary   199
  Organizations   205

Preface

The conservation of biological diversity in the context of rapid technological change and the commercialization of biological resources raises many fundamental scientific, economic, socio-political and ethical questions.

Most of the world's biological diversity is located in countries of the South. The North and its private industry is increasingly using these countries as reservoirs of biological and genetic resources to develop new products such as crop varieties, drugs, biopesticides, oils and cosmetics. The diversity of the living world – biodiversity – has become the raw material of the new biotechnologies and the object of patent claims.

The Convention on Biological Diversity aims to conserve the variety of genes, species and ecosystems which sustain life on Earth. This internationally legally binding instrument also seeks to facilitate the just and equitable sharing of benefits arising from the use of biological resources.

However, the negotiations around the Convention have highlighted major differences in interest and priorities among stakeholders. For example, Southern countries demand ready access to the new biotechnologies in compensation for the use of biological resources that originate within their territories. The Northern countries, for their part, insist on the recognition of intellectual property rights for their technologies and payment for genetic products derived from materials they have often obtained from the South. Indigenous peoples and other rural communities are also demanding that their knowledge of the uses of plants and animals, as well as their innovations and intellectual contributions to the maintenance and development of biodiversity, be acknowledged and rewarded. Meanwhile, the pharmaceutical industry is interested in the hereditary characteristics of indigenous peoples: patent claims on cell-lines of indigenous communities from developing countries are pending.

What are the likely impacts of these trends on the self-determination of peoples (and ultimately on human rights); biodiversity conservation; the relationship between science and society; the growth of the biotechnology industry; and development models in the North and the South? Can the conflicting perspectives of

vii

different social actors be reconciled? And, if so, under what conditions and with what implications for conservation and development?

The international symposium *Patents, Genes and Butterflies* offered a lively context in which these important questions and concerns could be discussed and relayed to a wider public by the media. The event was organized jointly by SWISSAID, WWF Switzerland and WWF International and was held on 20–21 October 1994 in Berne, Switzerland. The symposium brought together some of the leading thinkers on these issues as well as policy makers, journalists, industry representatives and grassroot activists engaged in the debate on the uses and abuses of biodiversity, both in the North and the South.

This book presents the contributions of the main speakers and also reflects the collective learning and sharing of views which took place during the symposium workshops. In editing these proceedings, we decided not to put individual names to ideas, arguments, information and analysis offered by the workshop participants. But to reflect the participative nature of the book's creation, some sections have been left unauthored.

Miges Baumann
Swissaid

Janet Bell
Editor

Florianne Koechlin
WWF-Switzerland

Michel Pimbert
WWF-International

1 Introduction

JANET BELL and MICHEL PIMBERT

In 1992, 20 years after the United Nations Conference on the Human Environment held in Stockholm, governments came together in Brazil for the UN Conference on Environment and Development. This 'Earth Summit' highlighted how important environment and development issues had become on the international political agenda. One of the aims of the summit was to establish the first global action plan for a sustainable future for the planet. It was the first time that many countries had accepted environment and development as important issues on the political agenda. The conservation and use of biological diversity, or biodiversity for short, were the hottest topics on the conference agenda, and hence the media was full of it at the time. To many people around the world reading the newspapers and watching TV, this was their first conscious encounter with 'biodiversity' – or at least with the technical term. To many others, who were probably too busy tending their crops and feeding their families to worry about politicians expounding earnestly in Rio de Janeiro about global environmental threats, biodiversity was not news. It had been an integral and highly valued part of their lives for centuries.

The conservation and sustainable use of biodiversity is now one of the most important challenges facing the planet, because if we destroy diversity we destroy life itself. But it is more than an environmental issue, even in the broadest sense of the term. As biodiversity declines and as it is transformed into a globally traded commodity, a whole host of other important issues – such as human rights and ethical concerns – are drawn into the debate. This book aims to help the reader understand the huge importance that biodiversity has for our lives and the changes that we will have to face as our relationship with the planet's biological wealth changes. The way biodiversity is conserved and used will have a fundamental impact on the food on our dinner plates, the medicines that we buy, the livelihoods of farming communities all over the world, the future of indigenous peoples, tropical forests and African savannahs, and the bank balances of multinational corporations.

What is biodiversity?

The word 'biodiversity' conjures up pictures of flowering meadows and colourful butterflies. Technically, biodiversity is often defined as

1

the diversity of life. It refers to the millions of different life forms found on earth, the genetic variation between them, and their complex ecological interrelations. As such, biodiversity is one of the planet's life-support systems. It embraces the differences between a dandelion and a dodo (species diversity), between green and red apples (different varieties), between eskimos and aborigines (cultural diversity) and between alpine meadows and coral reefs (ecosystem diversity).

Genetic diversity is the diversity of genes in the individual plants, animals and micro-organisms that inhabit the Earth. Species are made up of individuals with different characteristics inherited through their genes. The different characteristics expressed allow species to evolve gradually and to survive changing environmental conditions. Genetic diversity is the ultimate source of all biodiversity amongst species and ecosystems.

In many of the debates on the issue, biodiversity is viewed as an arithmetical construct, and biodiversity conservation is seen simply in terms of saving individual species (such as the rhino or the panda) or whole ecosystems (like wetlands or tropical forests). Increasingly it is being viewed even more narrowly, simply in terms of saving genes in whichever form is most convenient, which often means isolating them from their host organisms and ecosystems. But biodiversity is much more than genes. As Vandana Shiva points out in Chapter 4.4, biodiversity is a web of relationships which ensures balance and sustainability in ecosystems.

No one knows how many different life forms share the planet. Generally accepted estimates of the total number of species vary from 5 to 25 million. Yet so far scientists have been able to identify a total of only 1.5 million animal species and 300 000 plant species.[1]

The bulk of biodiversity is in the tropics, largely because recurrent ice ages slowed down the proliferation of life closer to the poles. Consequently, a mere 7% of the earth's surface holds between half and three-quarters of the world's biodiversity. Virtually none of this wealth resides anywhere near Europe or the United States. For example, one study found that a 15 hectare plot in Borneo supported more tree species than the entire United States.[2] The Amazon river was found to hold three times more aquatic species than the Mississippi river and ten times more than can be found in any European river. There is more biodiversity on one tiny island off the coast of Panama than there is in all of Great Britain.[3] Table 1.1 shows the huge differences in plant species in selected countries.

The importance of biodiversity

If we destroy biodiversity, we ultimately destroy not only individual species but our own lives, either directly or indirectly. For many

Table 1.1   Plant biodiversity: comparisons among selected countries and regions

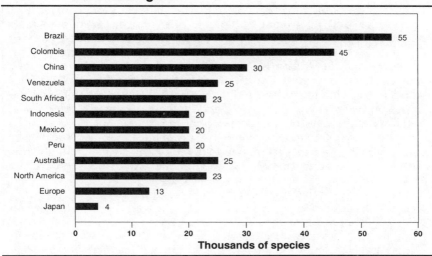

Source: David, S.D., *et al.*, (1986). Plants in Danger: What do we Know? IUCN, Gland, Switzerland. WRI/IUCN/UNEP, (1993). Guidelines for Action to Save, Study and Use Earth's Biotic Wealth Sustainability and Equitably. Upon citation in: Cunningham, A.B., (1993). Ethics, Ethnobiological Research and Biodiversity. WWF, Geneva, Switzerland. p. 5.

farmers and indigenous peoples in the South, there is a direct connection. Most traditional livelihoods depend on a very high degree of diversity, be it cultural, biological or economic, and are thus threatened by loss of biodiversity. For example, Mexico's Huastec Indian communities cultivate some 300 different plants in a mixture of small gardens, agricultural fields and forest plots. In a typical Indonesian village it is not difficult to find 100 or more different plant species, all used for specific needs: for food, medicine, building materials, fuelwood and so on. Practices developed over the centuries for collecting, harvesting and cultivating the resources needed for sustaining livelihoods are carefully adapted to prevailing, and often challenging, environmental conditions. This requires a deep and extensive understanding of plants, animals, ecosystems, climate, soils and other factors (see Box 1.1 and Table 1.2). Without these the communities would simply die.

In the North, diversity is equally crucial although most people are several steps removed from food production. Food and health systems are highly dependent on biodiversity. Without regular collecting expeditions to the forests, fields, markets and gardens of communities in the South, industrialized countries would not be able to produce the food that they do, and would not have the range of medicines that

3

Box 1.1: Diversity for sustainable livelihoods

In the village of Mogbuama in Sierra Leone, farmers produce rice, their main staple food, on a range of different plots. Mogbuama farmers have developed a range of rice varieties for these different conditions and for different uses. Every family requires some early ripening rice for food before the main harvest starts. This is planted where the swamp and valley soils meet, and is harvested before the river floods its banks. Rice varieties with a longer growing season and higher yields are planted higher up the slopes on free-draining soils, while flood-tolerant varieties planted down in the wetlands take longest to ripen, but require minimal labour input. Recent research counted 49 different rice varieties in use, each with specific qualities. Without this tremendous biological diversity, Mogbuama farmers would simply not be able to continue producing the food that they need.

It is well known that hunter-gathering communities, such as the !Kung San in Botswana and Indian groups in the Amazon, depend heavily on wild resources for their livelihood needs. Less well understood is that many farming households also rely heavily on the diversity of wild resources as sources of food, medicine, construction materials and income. Wild foods can supply a substantial portion of the diet, and a great diversity of wild species are utilized by rural farming communities (See Table 2).

they now possess. It is a popular misconception that the application of biotechnology will remove the North's dependence on natural biodiversity and that biotechnology will be a useful tool in conserving and enhancing biodiversity. Chapter 2 explodes these beliefs.

Infusions of new genetic material will continue to be important to agriculture and medicine worldwide. For example, it is estimated that Mexican wheat varieties currently contribute $2700 million crop production in industrialized countries[4]. One gene from a single Ethiopian barley plant now protects California's $160 million barley crop from the yellow dwarf virus[5]. The importance of maintaining a diverse gene pool to protect against plant diseases is illustrated in Box 1.2. It is impossible to predict what genetic characteristics may become valuable in the future, so allowing our genetic heritage to dwindle is highly dangerous. Climate change, for example, will demand new and adapted plant varieties and animal breeds – derived from natural organisms in order to cope with its impact.

Industries involved in the development of new products derived from natural raw materials (drugs, oils, perfumes, biopesticides, resins, dyes etc.) also rely heavily on bioprospecting activities, in other words the exploration, extraction and screening of biodiversity and indigenous knowledge for commercially valuable genetic and biochemical resources (This is explored in Chapter 4).

Table 1.2. Use of wild species for food and medicine by farming communities

Location	Importance of Wild Resources
Brazil	Kernels of babbasu palm provide 25% of household income for 300 000 families in Maranhâo State
China, West Sichuan	1320 tonnes of wild pepper production; 2000 tonnes of fungi collected and sold; 500 tonnes of ferns collected and sold
Ghana	16–20% of food supply from wild animals and plants
India, Madya Pradesh	52 wild plants collected for food
Kenya, Bungoma	100 species wild plants collected; 47% of households collected plants from the wild and 49% maintained wild species within their farms to domesticate certain species
Kenya, Machakos	120 medicinal plants used, plus many wild foods
Nigeria, near Oban National Park	150 species of wild food plants
South Africa, Natal/KwaZulu	400 indigenous medicinal plants are sold the area
Sub-Saharan Africa	60 wild grass species in desert, savannah and swamp lands utilized as food
Swaziland	200 species collected for food
Thailand, NE	50% of all foods consumed are wild foods from paddy fields, including fish, snakes, insects, mushrooms, fruit and vegetables
South west of USA	375 plant species used by Native Indians
Zaire	20 tonnes of chanterelle mushrooms collected and consumed by people of Upper Shaba
Zimbabwe	20 wild vegetables, 42 wild fruits, 29 insects, 4 edible grasses and one wild finger millet; tree fruits in dry season provide 25% of poor people's diet

Source: Scoones, I., Melnyk, M., and Pretty, J., 1992. *The Hidden Harvest: Wild Foods and Agricultural Systems – an annotated bibliography.* IIED, WWF-I and SIDA. IIED, London.

The loss of biodiversity and its causes

Our biological heritage is disappearing at an alarming and accelerating rate: whilst it is estimated that early this century the earth may have lost one species a year, we are currently losing between one and 50 species a day. Industrialized countries, in particular, have suffered huge losses in the genetic diversity of their crops and domesticated animals. For example, since the turn of the century 97% of the

Box 1.2: Diversity for food security

Native to the Andes, the potato was introduced from the New World to Spain and the UK in the late 1570s. For 250 years all the potatoes grown in Europe were descendents of these two introductions. In Ireland, the potato became the staple crop of the poor, and one third of the population was totally dependent on it for its food. When the potato blight, *Phytophtora infestans*, struck in 1845, it swept across the country wiping out the entire crop, because the genetically uniform potatoes had no resistance to the disease. Between one and two million people died of starvation. Andean potatoes, some of which had genes affording them resistance to the virus, came to the rescue, and these varieties soon replaced the blight-susceptible varieties in farmers' fields. Without them, potatoes would probably have disappeared from Northern consumers' dinner plates.

Similar crop uniformity led to the devastating Southern Corn Blight in the US: in 1970, American farmers lost 15% of their most important crop, worth $1 billion. Some Southern states lost half their harvest and many farmers went out of business. Two years later the highest yielding wheat variety the USSR had ever seen, which covered 40 million hectares of land from Kuban to the Ukraine, failed to survive the harsh Russian winter. At least 20 million tonnes – or 30–40% – of the winter wheat crop was lost and 27 million tonnes of grain were imported from the West. World grain prices soared by 50% in less than six months. This increased incomes for Northern grain producers but dramatically increased food costs for consumers. This affected the South particularly badly: between 1972 and 1973, grain imports to developing countries rose by 25%, but their cost doubled to $6 billion.

Source: Fowler, C. and Mooney, P. (1990). *The Threatened Gene.* Lutterworth.

varieties of 75 vegetable species in the US have become extinct.[6] Some scientists predict that if we continue current practices the world will lose a quarter of all our biological wealth by the middle of the next century.[7]

Many factors contribute to the loss of biodiversity. The destruction of tropical rainforests in the search for timber and minerals is partly responsible. So is the construction of large-scale projects which dam rivers and flood areas rich in biodiversity. Other immediate causes include the migration of farmers from overpopulated areas to fragile ecosystems, the pollution of wetlands, modern farming practices, and the over-exploitation of plants, animals and other resources to meet the ever-increasing demands of the rich industrialized countries (see Box 1.3).

A gross imbalance of wealth, power and natural resource utilisation is inherent in the modern world order. Industrial countries, which contain only 26% of the world's population, consume 80% of its

It has taken centuries of work for Andean peoples to develop more than 60 varieties of potato. (Kongelige Bibliotek, Copenhagen)

Box 1.3: How biodiversity is lost

Habitat loss and fragmentation

The number and size of relatively undisturbed ecosystems in the world have shrunk dramatically as global population and resource consumption have grown. For example, only 2% of the tropical dry forest along Central America's Pacific coast remains. Thailand lost 22% of its mangrove swamps between 1961 and 1985, due largely to prawn cultivation for export. Worldwide, dams have destroyed large sections of river and stream habitat, and coastal development has wiped out reef and near-shore ecosystems. A major proximate cause of tropical rainforest loss is the expansion of marginal agriculture, though in some regions commercial timber poses an even greater problem.

Introduced species

Introduced species are responsible for many recorded species extinctions, especially on islands. In these isolated ecosytems a new predator, competitor or pathogen, can rapidly imperil species that did not co-evolve with the newcomer. In Hawaii, some 86 introduced plants seriously threaten native biodiversity – one introduced tree species has now displaced more than 30 000 acres of native forest.

Over-exploitation of plants and animals

Throughout the world numerous forest, fisheries and wildlife resources have been over-exploited, sometimes to the point of extinction. Historically, both the great auk and the passenger pigeon succumbed to such pressure, and the Lebanon cedar that once blanketed 500 000 hectares is now found only in a few scattered remnants of forest. Many 'big game' animals, such as the Sumatran and Javan rhinos, have been hunted to the verge of extinction. Many extinctions are linked to the harvesting of food by people, but the quest for collectors' items, pets and curiosities has also obliterated some populations.

Pollution

Pollutants put pressure on ecosystems and may reduce or eliminate populations of sensitive species. Contamination can reverberate along the food chain: barn owl populations in the UK have fallen by 10% since new rodent poisons were introduced, and illegal pesticides used to control crayfish on the margins of one national park in Spain killed 30 000 birds in 1985 alone. Acid rain has made thousands of Scandanavian and North American lakes and pools virtually lifeless and, in combination with other kinds of air pollution, has damaged forests throughout Europe. Marine pollution has affected the Mediterranean and many estuaries and coastal seas throughout the world.

Global climate change

In the coming decades, a massive 'side effect' of air pollution – global warming – could play havoc with the world's ecosystems. Human-caused increases in greenhouse gases in the atmosphere are likely to produce a global temperature rise of 1–3°C during the next century, with an associated rise in sea level of 1–2 metres. It is estimated that each 1°C rise in temperature will displace the limits of tolerance of land species some 125 km towards the poles or 150m vertically into the mountains. Many species will not be able to redistribute themselves fast enough to keep up with the projected changes, and considerable alterations in ecosystem structure and function are likely. Many of the world's islands would be completely submerged if the more extreme projections for rises in sea level prove to be accurate – wiping out their flora and fauna.

Industrial agriculture and forestry

On-farm diversity is shrinking fast as a result of modern plant-breeding programmes. Similar trends are transforming diverse forest ecosystems into high-yielding monocultural tree plantations.

Source: Global Biodiversity Strategy, 1992. WRI, IUCN, UNEP.

Livestock breeds are disappearing even faster than crop varieties
(Ron Gilling/Panos Pictures)

energy and about 40% of its food. For example, the United States' consumption of fossil fuel is 33 times higher per capita than India's. In 1989, OECD* countries – home to only 16% of the world's population – accounted for 40% of the world's sulphur dioxide emissions and 54% of its nitrogen dioxide emissions. Sulphur and nitrogen oxides are key constituents of acid rain. In the same year, these countries produced 68% of the world's industrial waste and 38% of the gases that are thought to cause global warming.[8]

The excessive demands of the industrialized countries threaten biodiversity throughout the world, but the impact is particularly clear in the developing world, partly because these countries have so much biodiversity to lose, and partly because exploitative practices are often imposed by commercial forces from the North. The affluent North has come to depend on the developing South to provide it with cheap raw materials such as timber, cotton, cocaine, and plant and animal genes.

In addition, the biodiversity-nurturing practices of the Southern countries that began the long process of domesticating plants for agriculture are being seriously undermined. It was in part these very practices which created the impressive genetic mosaic of local crops, wild plants and animals, thus enabling the development of societies all over the world. Now new uniform crop varieties are replacing the myriad of species grown traditionally. For example, scientists predict that by the year 2000 Indian farmers will be growing 12 varieties of rice in place of the 30 000 that have been nurtured and cultivated over the centuries.[9]

Conservation strategies

Recognition of the world's shrinking biological heritage has prompted numerous reactions, both at international and national levels, as well as within local communities. Several international agreements and technical measures are being promoted to conserve the biodiversity left in the world's forests, wetlands, coastal waters and in farmers' fields.

The 1992 United Nations Conference on Environment and Development (UNCED) provided important guidelines and international legally-binding instruments for governments to tackle the more immediate and fundamental causes of biodiversity loss. Agenda 21 is a comprehensive action plan for the 1990s and beyond, adopted at the Conference by the international community. It presents a set of integrated strategies and detailed programmes to halt and reverse the effects of environmental degradation. The Conference's Convention

---

* The Organization for Economic Co-operation and Development

on Biological Diversity (see Box 1.4) and the Climate Convention can also potentially help decision-makers to re-orientate national policies towards more environmentally sound and sustainable development.

Box 1.4: The Biodiversity Convention

On December 29, 1993, a legally binding Convention on Biological Diversity came into force. It was heralded as the most important initiative ever taken to set the world on a course toward environmentally sustainable development.

The Convention is a global instrument committing signatory nations to work together towards conserving biodiversity, but it also recognizes national sovereignty and the right of countries to benefit from their biological resources. Further, it highlights the right of countries to have access to technologies, including new biotechnologies, that could assist the conservation effort or that may have use in the exploitation of biological resources.

The Convention was drawn up in preparation for the 1992 UN Conference on Environment and Development (UNCED). By October 1995, 128 countries and the EU had signed the treaty. Its negotiation has turned into a political battle between Northern and Southern countries. Southern states demand compensation for the use by other parties of biological resources that originate within their territories. One of the mechanisms proposed for achieving this is the provision of access to new biotechnologies to help in conservation or resource use. Some Northern states, however, see this as piracy and insist on intellectual property rights for their biotechnologies – without this recognition, they see innovation and research being stifled. It is largely concern over this issue that has to date prevented the US from signing the agreement.

Critics of the Convention point out that there are some important gaps in its coverage. According to Genetic Resources Action International, it excludes discussions on the fate of existing genebank collections (see Box 1.5), and yet these represent the South's genetic heritage with the highest commercial value to the North. As an agreement between nation states, it is hard to see how the voices and concerns of local communities will be addressed. It also favours bilateral biodiversity deals, stating that agreements should be made 'on mutually agreed terms'; this kind of deal is an inappropriate mechanism for dealing with issues of global concern.[10]

UNCED was only the start of the biodiversity convention process and the negotiations continue through annual meetings of the Conference of Parties. Progress is slow and tortuous, partly because the language is couched in vague and often ambiguous terms. The text is full of statements like 'as far as possible' and 'as far as appropriate', leaving it open to interpretation. The issues of rights to, and ownership of, genetic resources are proving the most problematic for negotiators. These are discussed in more detail in Chapter 4.

11

On the practical level, several complementary methods are being used to conserve biodiversity with different degrees of success. These methods can be divided into two broad categories: *in situ* conservation, which means conserving plants, animals and micro-organisms within their natural habitat; and *ex situ* conservation, which means maintaining living organisms out of their natural habitat, either as whole living organisms or as parts (cells, sperm, seeds, etc.)

Ex situ *conservation*

There are three main methods of *ex situ* conservation used for plants : genebanks, field gene banks and tissue culture. Zoos and cryopreservation are important means for *ex situ* conservation for animals.

Genebanks Genebanks are vast refrigerators where seed samples are stored under controlled humidity and temperature conditions. Under the recommended storage conditions, some seeds can survive for up to a hundred years, but regular checking for viability and damage is necessary. Samples of crop varieties must be grown out before the seeds begin to deteriorate so that a fresh generation of seeds can be obtained for continued storage. Wild species are more difficult to handle during this regeneration process as the conditions required to germinate them are often unknown.

Some 3.9 million seed samples are held in gene banks around the world but, given the challenges of keeping seeds viable, not all are healthy. Seeds lose viability if they are not grown out regularly; cold storage can affect the genetic material in the seed; and simple mismanagement, like a power failure, can endanger the materials stored. A 1989 evaluation of the US central seed bank disclosed the alarming information that of all the stored seed samples, only 28% had been recently tested and found healthy. The rest of the collection had not been tested for at least five years, contained too few seeds to risk testing, or was already dead.[11] In 1991, representatives of 13 national germplasm banks in Latin America announced that between 50% and 100% of the maize seed collected between 1940 and 1980 was no longer viable.[12]

The network of International Agricultural Research Centres (IARCs) is one of the most important *ex situ* repositories of agricultural bio-diversity, with some four and a half billion seeds from around the world (see Box 1.5).

Field genebanks Plant species that do not easily produce seed, and those with seeds that cannot be dried without injuring them (such as mango, cacao, avocado and nutmeg) are usually conserved in field genebanks. These include botanical gardens, arboreta, plantations

12

and other areas of land in which collections of growing plants have been assembled. Some of the most valuable conserved collections of bananas, plantains, coffee and oil palms were established long ago in field genebanks.

Tissue culture   Plant tissue culture involves growing plants in tubes in nutrient-rich jelly, and is well suited for mass cloning of a single species or crop variety. Crops and wild relatives that reproduce vegetatively (e.g. potatoes, cassava, sweet potatoes), or have seeds that cannot be dried without injuring them, can also be maintained this way.

Zoos   Zoos can contribute to the conservation of individual animal species, especially those that are critically endangered. Zoo collections sometimes include individuals of species which have entirely disappeared from the wild. These captive specimens therefore represent an important part of the remaining genepool which may be used in the future to supplement wild populations, or to build entirely new populations. Some well-known reintroduction projects involving zoo-born animals include the European bison in Poland, the Hawaiian goose in Hawaii, the golden lion tamarin in Brazil and the eagle owl in various European countries.

Perhaps the most important contribution zoos make to conservation is through their public education role. Zoos attract many more visitors than most natural history museums, botanical gardens and other comparable nature-orientated institutions. Worldwide, the existing 1000 or so zoos annually receive 600 million visitors – over 10% of the world's entire population. Living animals exhibited in zoos clearly have an enormous power of attraction.

Cryopreservation   Cryopreservation techniques – the short- or long-term conservation of sperm, egg cells and embryos in liquid nitrogen (at -196°C) – are used in combination with artificial reproduction techniques in zoos. Eland antelopes and baboons have been produced by transplantations of frozen and thawed embryos. Frozen and subsequently thawed sperm have been used to fertilize deer, apes and wolves, with young successfully produced from these artificial reproductions. Different zoos and zoo-related research institutions have already accumulated extensive collections of deep-frozen germplasm material from exotic animal species.

Genetic Engineering   Advances in gene manipulation techniques mean that, for commercial and therapeutic reasons, genes in any form are now an important focus for conservation strategies. These

Box 1.5: Robbing the poor to feed the rich?

The Consultative Group on International Agricultural Research (CGIAR) was set up in 1971 to support Green Revolution agricultural research and development. The Group is an informal coalition of donors (governments, intergovernmental agencies and private foundations) co-sponsored by the World Bank, the UN Food and Agriculture Organization (FAO) and UN Development Programme (UNDP).

Today there are 41 donors, almost all from the North, contributing nearly $300 million a year to 18 International Agricultural Research Centres (IARCs). The donors consist of governments, private foundations, banks (including the World Bank) and international organizations. Through the IARCs, the CGIAR provides investment and technical support for agricultural Research and Development, particularly focusing on the major food crops. At the outset its mission was to feed the world's hungry, and the goal of poverty alleviation still features strongly in the Group's Mission Statement.

The CGIAR has had three major impacts: firstly, it has built up major germplasm collections of certain crops like rice, maize and wheat; secondly, plant varieties developed at the IARCs underpin a significant part of world agriculture today; and thirdly, it has had a huge influence on the focus of agricultural research worldwide. There has, however, been a price to pay for these widely-touted successes, and those that have paid for it are the very beneficiaries the CGIAR was set up to help – poor farmers in the South. For example, a survey carried out in the Philippines showd that although farmers experienced a 70% increase in yields from IRRI rice varieties, this was offset by a 50% cut in the sale price for the rice and a 358% increase in farm expenses due to the chemical inputs the varieties required. The end result was a 52% drop in farm income.[13]

The IARCs provide free access to their collections for researchers, farmers and commercial interests. The vast majority of germplasm held in the IARCs comes from the farmers of the South: For example, more than 91% of the maize collections at CIMMYT, the IARC based in Mexico, and more than 93% of the rice collection at IRRI in the Philippines are derived from contributions from the South.

But while the CGIAR speaks proudly of the alleged benefits of its research and genebanks for farmers in developing countries, many critics argue that it is largely the North that has benefited from the IARC collections and that many farmers in the South are worse off as the result of the establishment of the IARCs. For example, the benefit of the CGIAR to Australian agriculture over the last 20 years has been estimated to be US$2.1 billion, and the direct benefit to Australian wheat in 1994 was at least US$ 97 million. In return, Australia gives the CGIAR $4–6 million per year.[14] Although industrialized countries are reluctant to reveal the benefits they have accrued from their 'aid' contributions, there is general recognition that flow of benefits is reversed. In 1994, US Secretary of State, Warren Christopher, stated that foreign germplasm contributes $7 billion annually to the US's $18 billion maize crop.[15] It is safe to assume that at least some of this can be attributed directly to the IARCs.

As for fairness in the South, since the late 1970s the CGIAR's Green Revolution has come under attack from many different quarters. By the late 1980s, several interrelated crises could be identified within the system. These related to difficulties that the CGIAR system had in adequately answering criticisms levelled at its philosophy and practices with regard to sustainability, environmental impact, and equity. After floundering for several years, an agreement was signed in 1994 to place the germplasm collections under the trusteeship of the FAO, which many hope will lead to greater protection of the collections from uncompensated exploitation by commercial interests.

developments signify a shift away from conserving ecosystems and organisms to conserving individual cells and genes. Since genes can now be isolated and stored outside the organism they derive from, *ex situ* conservation is taken a step further away from the natural habitat. The Human Genome and Human Genome Diversity Projects (see Chapter 5) have added yet another dimension to biodiversity conservation, and have put the spotlight on human genes as an important new resource.

In Situ *Conservation*

The *in situ* approach to conservation aims to preserve whole tracts of land and water so that ecosystems and diversity *among* species can thrive and continue to evolve. National Parks and other protected areas are the vehicles for this approach.

There are now close to 8500 major protected areas throughout the world. These are widely distributed across continents. Worldwide, the growth in national parks and protected areas has been relatively rapid over the last two decades. Protected areas now exist in 169 countries. Strictly protected areas (such as national parks and strict nature reserves) constitute 3% of the earth's surface. At least another 40 000 protected areas of various sorts have been established that do not meet internationally recognized criteria, but which contribute to biodiversity conservation. This brings the total protected land area up to almost 10%.[16]

According to the Fourth World Congress on National Parks and Protected Areas held in Caracas in 1992, each country should now designate a minimum of 10% of each biome under its jurisdiction (e.g. oceans, forests, tundra, wetlands, grasslands etc.) as a protected area. Many countries have already classified more than 10% of their

15

territories as protected areas. These include Costa Rica with 29%, Honduras with 22%, Bhutan with 22%, Botswana and Panama with 18%, Guatemala with 16%, Nicaragua with 14%, Central African Republic with 12%, Malaysia, Benin and Tanzania with 11.5%, Senegal with 10.8% and Rwanda with 10.4%.[17]

Conventionally, the establishment of protected areas has involved the displacement of local people, but increasingly moves are being made to involve local communities and to integrate their development needs into conservation strategies.

Some critics argue that many of the methods deployed to conserve biological diversity are biased towards a Western model where money and trained personnel ensure that technologies work and that laws are enforced to secure conservation objectives. During and after the colonial period, these conservation technologies, and the values associated with them, were extended from the North to the South – often in a classical, top-down manner. Western science and the ideology of conservation hang together through this top-down, transfer of technology, model. They are mutually reinforcing elements of the blueprint paradigm which still informs much of today's design and management of *ex situ* and *in situ* conservation everywhere (Table 1.3).

The politics of biodiversity

One of the reasons that biodiversity is becoming such an important issue is not so much because of its disappearance, but because of growing recognition of its increased economic value and potential due to developments in biotechnology. In the US alone, sales of plant-based drugs amounted to $15.5 billion in 1990.[18] Biodiversity has become a major focus of interest for governments and business alike, which recognize the rich pickings to be had from it (see Chapter 2). Consequently, biodiversity is rapidly being 'commodified', just like copper or gold. Biodiversity is no longer seen as a freely available resource and a great deal of effort is now being invested internationally into drawing up agreements for rights, ownership and access to genetic resources. Linked to this trend is the demand from countries in the South to share in the benefits of the commercialization of the world's genetic heritage, most of which comes from their back yards.

The commodification of biodiversity has caused a shift in the ownership of genetic resources from communal to private. This in turn has opened up a minefield of issues concerning intellectual property rights (Chapter 3), establishing monetary values for the resources and raising questions over the sharing of benefits from their sale and

16

Table 1.3. Biodiversity conservation and natural resource management paradigms: the contrast between blueprint and learning-process approaches

	Blueprint	Process
Point of departure	Nature's diversity and its potential commercial value	The diversity of both people and nature's values
Keyword	Strategic planning	Participation
Locus of decision making	Centralized, ideas originate in capital city	Decentralized, ideas originate in village
First steps	Data collection and plan	Awareness and action
Design	Static, by experts	Evolving, people involved
Main resources	Central funds and technicians	Local people and their assets
Methods, rules	Standardized, universal, fixed package	Diverse, local, varied basket of choices
Analytical assumptions	Reductionist (natural science bias)	Systems, holistic
Management focus	Spending budgets, completing projects on time	Sustained improvement and performance
Communication	Vertical: orders down, reports up	Lateral: mutual learning and sharing experience
Evaluation	External, intermittent	Internal, continuous
Error	Buried	Embraced
Relationship with people	Controlling, policing, inducing, motivating, dependency-creating. People seen as beneficiaries	Enabling, supporting, empowering. People seen as actors
Associated with	Normal professionalism	New professionalism
Outputs	1. Diversity of conservation, and uniformity in production (agriculture, forestry, . . .) 2. The empowerment of professionals	1. Diversity as a principle of production and conservation 2. The empowerment of rural people

Source: Adapted from David Korten in Pimbert and Pretty, 1995[17]

17

Box 1.6: GATT and biodiversity

The General Agreement on Tariffs and Trade (GATT) is a set of rules and a dispute-solving mechanism for trade negotiations. It was drawn up in 1947 in an attempt to try to avoid the kinds of trade conflicts that were partially responsible for the two World Wars. Then, as now, the conflicts were over access to raw materials and access to markets. GATT was originally a side agreement tagged on to the more substantial rules laid out by the International Trade Organization (ITO), which was set up at the same time.

GATT has been renegotiated several times since 1947, and it has turned into a very different beast. The 'Uruguay Round' of GATT, so-called because the negotiations first took place in Uruguay, began in 1986 and culminated in Morocco in 1994 with the formation of the World Trade Organization (WTO). The WTO is a 'super-GATT' – a formal, permanent organization instead of an agreement. The WTO is much more powerful than GATT, and is set to impose tight controls over the new, stricter and more inflexible rulebook governing trade negotiations.

GATT and the WTO will have several impacts on biodiversity conservation and management. Firstly, GATT is bad news for the environment because unilateral stances taken by one country against another for environmental reasons can be seen as a violation of free trade. At present, countries can overrule GATT, but this will not be possible with the WTO unless all the other members except the country in question agree to disregard the ruling. In theory, the WTO could be beneficial for the environment since it has the power to establish trade rules that penalize parties conducting activities that are detrimental to the environment. However, given that GATT is a *trade* agreement, not an environmental one, it is unlikely that these powers will be used effectively.

Secondly, intellectual property became a trade issue with the launch of the Uruguay Round, and the agreement encourages the global adoption of intellectual property rights, which will accelerate the process of commodification of biodiversity. The implications of GATT on the intellectual property issues related to biodiversity are discussed in more detail on p. 81 and in Chapter 4.4.

use (Chapter 4). The proposed GATT agreement is set to increase dramatically the momentum of the shift in ownership and control of biodiversity (see Box 1.6).

At the Earth Summit in 1992, governments addressed the need to manage the world's biological heritage more carefully. The Biodiversity Convention signed by 152 countries focuses on two main issues: steps required to stem the erosion of biological diversity and to address the thorny question of rights to, and compensation for, the use of genetic resources and indigenous knowledge (see Box 1.4). Reactions to the Convention have been mixed. Some welcome it as the first political commitment to biodiversity protection and because it provides the first framework for a global conservation strategy. Others, however, see it as a 'biological GATT', set to accelerate the shift towards privatization of genetic resources and control by the North. Pat Mooney suggests that it is a fast-track GATT, since the framework for the Convention will be implemented more rapidly than GATT itself.

It is clear that biodiversity will become even more pressing as an issue over the next decades. Its importance has long been recognized by farmers and indigenous peoples around the world, but their interests and concerns about biodiversity are changing. Many are now rejecting the North's moves towards monopolistic control of life forms and are calling for compensation for their knowledge and work which has nurtured diversity over the centuries. At the same time indigenous people are themselves threatened with extinction, which brings in new issues of concern, particularly since they are themselves becoming the objects of bioprospecting. Biodiversity is now well embedded into the political and business agendas. It is set to become more and more of an issue for consumers and producers all over the world as food and drug production moves from forests, fields and lakes into the laboratories, along with human reproduction itself.

In this fast-changing debate no one questions the need to conserve biological diversity. Political disagreements revolve around questions like, 'Conservation and use for whom?', 'For what?', 'In whose interests?', and 'With what effects at local, national and international levels?' These are difficult questions for conservationists, development planners, staff of non-governmental organizations and other decision-makers involved with the conservation and sustainable use of biological diversity in international, national and local forums. Depending on how these questions are answered, either existing trends in *ex-* and *in-situ* conservation could be reinforced or new approaches could be explored to encourage more diversity, and more decentralization and democracy in the conservation and management of biological resources.

The commercialization route to conservation is being promoted by others besides commercial interests alone. For example, both the World Bank's private sector lending arm, the International Finance Corporation (IFC), and the World Bank-controlled Global Environment Facility (GEF), have begun talks with potential investors about the possibilities of selling biological diversity for profit.[19] The proposed biodiversity venture capital fund would work on a planetary scale. So far three possible areas have been identified for funding: ecotourism (marketing tourism in protected areas to wealthy tourists); the screening and study of species in protected areas and tropical ecosystems for natural product development (such as medicines, perfumes, waxes, biopesticides); and the commercialization of existing knowledge of traditional medicines.

This new approach is not fanciful: such moves have already begun. For instance, in an August 1995 advertisement in the *Financial Times*, the Zambian Government advertised tender leases to foreign investors for 25 biodiversity-rich sites (ranging from five to 105 hectares) in several Zambian national parks. This particular advertisement focused on attracting investors for the tourism industry, but this kind of initiative sets convenient precedents for possible bioprospecting agreements. China is already taking the next step.[20]

For those who support alternative approaches, resisting uniformity, control and centralization implies a profound shift in conservation and natural resource management strategies. It implies moving from a top-down, blueprint approach towards a bottom-up, people-centered, process-orientated approach (See Table 1.3). It requires that outside institutions (public sector, NGOs, international bodies) no longer view themselves as 'implementors' (who are responsible for planning, implementing, managing and evaluating projects *for* local people), but 'enablers' (who help local people to plan, implement and manage their own projects).[21]

On-farm conservation offers an example of a more participatory, process-orientated approach to the management of biological resources. This approach has been the backbone of agricultural development since farming began, but is only now becoming widely recognized as important in the light of the problems with gene banks and other *in situ* mechanisms. This conservation mode builds on rural people's knowledge and their abilities to experiment, analyse, evaluate and extend technologies. Local institutions and groups (farmer research groups, credit management groups, consumer clubs and so on) help to co-ordinate community action among and within villages. External professionals and institutions behave in a more enabling manner, facilitating a process of local empowerment through changes in working relationships and policies that determine *who* conserves and uses biodiversity, *how* and *for whom*. But simply adopting a participative approach to the management of biodiversity does not magically remove the conflict farmers face between conserving varieties and maximizing their income under the current economic system.

These reversals from the normal are more fully explored in Chapter 6 and could have major implications for the way that conservation and development are practised in the future.

References

1. Damlamian, J. (ed.) (1994) Biodiversity: Science, Conservation and Sustainable Use. *Environment and Development Briefs*. UNESCO.
2. RAFI (1993) *Who is who in Biodiversity*. Ottawa.
3. UNDP (1994) *Conserving Indigeneous Knowledge: Integrating Two Systems of Innovation*. New York.
4. UNDP (1994). *ibid*.
5. CIIR (1993). Biodiversity – What's at Stake? *CIIR Comment*.
6. Fowler, C. and Mooney, P. (1990), *The Threatened Gene*. Lutterworth, Cambridge.
7. CIIR (1993) op. cit.
8. OECD (1991) *L'Etat de l'Environnement*. Paris.
9. CIIR (1993) op. cit.
10. GRAIN (1994) Intellectual Property Rights for Whom? *Biobriefing No. 4*. GRAIN. Barcelona.
11. Findings of a three-month investigation of Associated Press (AP), reported in *Agrinews*, Vol. 14, No.14. (1989).
12. Council for Tropical and Subtropical Agricultural Research (ASTAF, 1991), *ASTAF Circular 28:17*.
13. Modina, R. and Ridao, A. (1987). *IRRI Rice, the Miracle that Never Was*, ACES Foundation, Quezon City, the Philippines.
14. GRAIN (1994) A System in Crisis. *Seedling*, 11(2): pp 11–19.
15. Stated in a letter of August 16, 1994 to 'Mr. Leader' of the US Senate. The letter is supported by the Secretary of Agriculture and the Secretary responsible for the Environmental Protection Agency and calls for the Senate to ratify US participation in the Convention on Biological Diversity. Quoted in 'Declaring the Benefits', *RAFI Occasional Paper Series, Vol. 1, No. 3*, October 1994.
16. McNeely, J.A. (1994) Protected Areas for the 21st Century: Working to Provide Benefits to Society. *Biodiversity and Conservation 3*. pp 390–405.
17. Pimbert, M.P. and Pretty, J.N. (1995). Parks, People and Professionals. Putting Participation into Protected Area Management. *UNRISD–IIED–WWF Discussion Paper no. 57*. UNRISD, Geneva.
18. Reid, W.V., Laird, S.A *et al.* (1993). A New Lease on Life. In: *Biodiversity Prospecting*, World Resources Institute, Washington.
19. Chatterjee, P. (1994) *Bankcheck*, January, pp. 3–23.
20. Ghimire, K. and Pimbert, M.P. (eds.) (1996). *Social Change and Conservation: Environmental Politics and Impacts of National Parks and Protected Areas*, Earthscan and Unrisd, London.
21. Pimbert, M.P and Pretty, J.N. (1995). op. cit.

PART 1

The tools of control

2 SCIENCE, MARKETS AND POWER

2.1. Changes in the genetic supply industry

JACK KLOPPENBURG

Whose reality counts?

The history of the genetic supply industry is both fascinating and instructive. The analysis of history can tell us a great deal about the present and the future: seeing where we are coming from can help us see where we are headed. And because our understanding of history materially shapes what we do in the present and how we envision our future, contending interests struggle to shape how history is written. History therefore represents a social struggle.

I recently came across a six-page advertisement in the *New York Times*, the first page of which read like this :

1944, Bretton Woods : the IMF and the World Bank

1945, San Francisco : the United Nations

1994, Marrakesh : The World Trade Organization

History knows where it's going

It's in Morocco that 124 countries are signing the GATT agreement

Now that's a different view of history from the one I have. The corporate interests that placed the advertisement assert that the International Monetary Fund was just out there waiting to be discovered as part of a natural evolutionary flow, that it's the most natural thing in the world for countries to sign up to GATT and join the 'Marrakesh Express' on a fast track to the future. 'History knows where it's going', they say. But this statement obscures the reality of the struggle through which history is created and written. The people who placed this advertisement want us to believe that their view of the future is the only view.

The advertisement makes the formation of the World Trade Organization (WTO) look natural and inevitable, just as the pharmaceutical company Monsanto would have us believe genetic engineering is a 'natural science'. But how 'natural' is transferring fish genes into tomatoes, or chicken genes into potatoes?

Taking sides

I don't see history that way. I see it as a social creation, the result of the bump and grind of people with different interests, and with different and often conflicting ideas about what the present and future should look like. The formation of the World Trade Organization was not inevitable. Genetic engineering is not inevitable. In the history of plant breeding there were choices to be made, options that were shut down and paths that weren't pursued. When considering history, there are sides to be taken and it is important to recognize which side you are on.

I know which side I am on. I am not on the side of Monsanto, and I am not on the side of the WTO or the North American Free Trade Agreement. I am not on the side of those who want to see this wonderfully diverse world flattened biologically and socially to accommodate the free flow of capital and commodities. I am not on the side of those who would make plants and American Indians raw materials for the gene industry. I am not on the side of those who want to continue to cut up the world and parcel it out for sale. This process must be seen as part of the larger historical process of global commodification in which nothing is sacred and anything can be bought and sold.

Development of the genetic supply industry

A number of constants have supported the development of the global genetic supply industry:

○ *Commodification of genetic resources.* This process of commodification is nothing new – it has been a constant throughout the development of the genetic supply industry.

○ *Imperialist vision.* Northern capitalist nations use military and political force to create and enforce the conditions in which business and intellectual property rights can operate. The projection of military and political power was a precondition for United Fruit's cultivation of bananas in Guatemala in 1935, and it remains a precondition for obtaining oil or genes today. Northern states – acting unilaterally or jointly in international forums such as the WTO – continue to use military and political power as the essential foundation for the acquisition of genes.

○ *Scientific version of the imperialist vision.* This is the Northern scientists' assumption that they can go wherever they like and take whatever they wish. *The World Was My Garden*, is the title that David Fairchild, one of the US Department of Agriculture's principal plant explorers, gave to his autobiography in 1945.[1] The attitude encapsulated in the title of his book continues to pervade scientific attitudes today, as the planet is combed in the name of the twin gods of science and Mammon.

○ *Simultaneous and complementary appropriation of genetic and cultural information.* Access to genetic resources has frequently been facilitated by access to local and indigenous knowledge. It is not just the rainforest, but also Indians and peasants who have something that we want. Methods of extracting information may be kinder and gentler now – trust has often replaced guns as the instrument of persuasion – but neocolonial explorers are still searching the jungles for riches. The end result is the same. Northern corporate interests get what they want.

○ *Defaulting on the genetic debt.* Northern industries have realized enormous gains from the genetic and cultural information collected by corporate and academic scientists. The vulnerable, thoroughbred strains of modern agriculture on which the North is dependent are constructed from the germplasm, seeds and tubers produced and reproduced by farmers and indigenous peoples of the South. The same is true for many drugs. The genetic resources gleaned by science and industry are not simply the gift of nature – they contain centuries of labour by the people from whom these resources are appropriated. Not only has this labour been uncompensated in the past, it is only recently that it has even begun to be acknowledged. Genetic resources leave the fields of farmers and indigenous peoples as 'common heritage', but once they pass through corporate and academic laboratories they become commodities that must be paid for.

Are plants and Indians becoming raw materials for industry? Of course they are – they have been commodities for centuries already. These five historical constants have assured the supply of these raw materials and shaped the distribution of benefits. The last constant is the only one that may be changing slightly: there are now initiatives afoot to offer cash compensation to the stewards of the South. But does paying them make everything all right?

Trajectories of change

To answer that question we have to look at a number of changing historical trajectories:

o The corporations involved in the extraction of genetic and cultural resources are growing in size and power. Through mergers and buy-outs, they are creating more and more powerful entities with an enlarged interest in the control of genetic resources. Seed companies are being consumed by the petrochemical giants. These transnational corporations are looking to expand the reach and breadth of the existing global markets for agricultural and industrial products.

o Through pressure from business interests, intellectual property rights are being continually strengthened. But it has been a hard struggle – it was not inevitable that plants should be patentable. It has taken 100 years of pressure from business to get to where we are today (see pp. 78–9). The struggle continues in GATT and other forums.

o Biological diversity is being lost as the world industrializes. Concern began in the 1970s as Green Revolution seed varieties replaced local varieties. In the 1980s rainforests were the big issue. In the 1990s the focus has broadened out to biodiversity as a whole. Why? Because underpinning the organismic world is the reductionist world of DNA and it is now clear that we are losing diversity just at the point when we can really manipulate it to feed our needs and desires. An advertisement from Pioneer Hi-bred, one of the largest seed companies in the world, asks the question, 'Biotechnology – science or alchemy?' Actually it's both. The alchemists sought to change base metals into gold: biotechnology turns base life into money. All biodiversity is now seen as being potentially useful and potentially lucrative. Who knows where the cure for cancer lies? So everything must be checked out – insects, bromeliads, marine life, even humans, especially the endangered ones. The DNA molecule has become highly valuable and now forms the trunk of the 'money tree'.

o Conservationists are cutting deals with industry. The anthropocentric and utilitarian rationale of the 'price it to save it' method does not sit well with all conservationists. But increasingly conservation biology is embracing such an approach. In his book, *The Diversity of Life*,[2] E.O. Wilson talks of 'unmined riches' and describes what he calls the New Environmentalism:

> The race is on to develop methods, to draw more income from the wildlands without killing them, and so to give the invisible hand of free-market economics a green thumb.

Whose side is he on? Whose side are you on?

○ Genetic resources are being politicized. In the South, states, bureaucrats, scientists, farmers and indigenous people are beginning
to realize the potential wealth to be gained from their lost treasure.
The tug of war for their share of the benefits began with the Seed
Wars at the FAO in the 1970s and has spread to many other forums,
such as the Biodiversity Convention.

○ Business is now willing to pay for access to genetic information.
Companies were not willing to play by their own rules of the
market in the past. They preferred piracy to payment. But now they
are beginning to see that it is in their own interest to pay for their
raw materials and they are making a virtue out of necessity. The
pharmaceutical company, Merck and Co, broke into this new territory with its deal in Costa Rica (see p. 100). This is the new model
for bioprospecting for the green gold of genetic resources: bilateral
deals, contracts for genes, and corporations in control. Ultimately,
this is all that the Biodiversity Convention is about. It legitimizes
and institutionalizes the *status quo*: 'What's good for the world is
good for industry' is how Genetic Engineering News reported on
the drawing up of the Convention. President Clinton's letter of
interpretation reduces the treaty to it's essence: that is, 'we'll pay'
but 'on mutually agreed terms'.

Bioprospecting is increasingly being embraced by governments, industry and even NGOs as the way ahead. But these deals are characterized by inadequate compensation, inadequate consultation with
the stewards of the resources, and the extension of the reach of the
global market. I know of no case of bioprospecting that I would
regard as just, in the sense of informed consent by all parties and
adequate compensation for all parties.

So, what do we have to show for fifteen years of biotechnology
research, a billion dollars of research expenditure by the agricultural
biotechnology companies, and countless hours of scientific labour?
There is bovine growth hormone, which cost more than $500 million
to develop and which is so *socially* unsustainable that the European
Community has taken the unprecedented step of proposing to ban its
use on *economic* grounds. And there is the Flavr Savr, a $25 million
genetically-engineered tomato with a mere 3–5 day shelf-life advantage over existing commercial tomato varieties. I have no doubt that
industry will eventually have a great many biotechnological products
on offer, but developing them is far more difficult and orders of
magnitude more expensive than anyone had anticipated. The irony is
that we have many examples of sustainable agriculture before us
now, but they are largely ignored as scientists pursue their genetic

philosophers' stone. It is time to stop looking for new tools and learn to use well the ones we have already.

Corporate and academic biotechnologists have recently begun to focus on human genetic information as a raw material. The leading journal *Science* reports on a programme of bioprospecting that targets our own species: 'Geneticists want to collect DNA from such groups as the Arewete. Just 130 members of this tribe remain on the Xingu River in Brazil'. What kind of sensibility is it that would rather have the genes than the people themselves? The $70 million deal that Hoffman la Roche has just agreed with the Millennium company for work on the mapping of the human genome may give us a clue (see Chapter 5). Seeing our own species as a commodity, can we fail to see everything else in the same way? And if the commodity value is low, does that justify the disappearance of that bird, tribe or micro-organism?

Reversing the imperialist impulse

There are alternatives. Our strategy must be one of reversals (see Chapter 6). The principal challenge before us is to reverse the imperialist impulse. We must start not from the need of the industrialized countries for more productive crop varieties, but from the needs of Southern farmers; not from the need of the industrialized world for drugs, but from the need of indigenous people to survive.

Achieving such reversals will not be easy. For the 'New Conquistadors', the world is still their garden, and reversals of intellectual property rights are seen as piracy. Observe the vision of the future as portrayed in Monsanto's promotional materials: On a montage of mountains, fields and blue skies, a god-like face peers down through the clouds. Below, it reads 'A new environmental era where the aims of commerce and ecology are integral to a sustainable corporate future'. A recently published article by two Monsanto executives is titled *Planetary Patriotism* and embraces the notion that treating the environment gently while meeting a growing demand for food 'requires a sustainable agriculture.' But in 1992 Monsanto was the second biggest polluter in the United States. Are they planetary patriots or sophisticated scoundrels?

If you question their patriotism you'll see how fast the corporate fist comes out of the public relations glove. As described in Box 2.1 (page 38) Monsanto is marketing one of the first products of genetic engineering: bovine growth hormone, or rBGH, despite a frosty welcome from many farmers and consumers. A dairy in Iowa decided to label its milk rBGH-free and was immediately sued by Monsanto.

But there are other ways, other choices, other paths than the ones presented by corporations. Until we learn to cherish, preserve and respect each other, we will never learn to do the same for other species.

References

1. David Fairchild (1945), *The World was my Garden: Travels of a plant explorer*, New York, Scribners.
2. E.O. Wilson (1992), *The Diversity of Life*, Harvard Press, Cambridge, MA.

2.2. Genetic engineering and biotechnology in industry

JANET BELL

Broadly defined, biotechnology refers to any technique which uses living organisms to make or modify a product. It includes the spectrum of new and old technologies, from the beer-brewing techniques developed by the Sumerians in the Middle East in 7000 BC to the high-tech gene transfer techniques that graft chicken genes into potatoes today. Traditional biotechnologies are used in the production of many common foodstuffs, such as cheese, salami, yoghurt, beer and bread. These all rely on the addition of genetic material in the form of living organisms (bacteria or yeasts) to milk or grains in order to transform them into new products.

Commercial biotechnology today comprises a range of different techniques including tissue culture, cell fusion, enzyme and fermentation technology, embryo transfer and, increasingly, genetic engineering. The techniques make it possible to modify more and more profoundly the process of life itself. The history of the new biotechnologies is a short one, born in university laboratories and public research institutions, and only transported to the corporate sector in the late 1970s and early 1980s. However, industry's brief involvement has had a fundamental impact on the priorities and direction of agricultural and medical research around the world, and it is also set to change the nature of production systems for a vast number of essential products such as foods, chemicals and medicines.

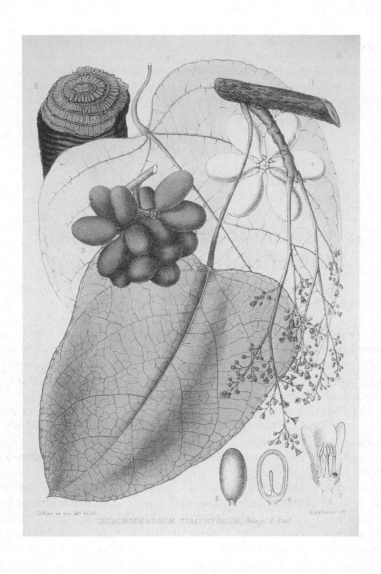

Tubocurarine, an important muscle relaxant drug used in open heart surgery, is derived from the curare vine from the South American rainforest.
(WWF/Royal Botanic Gardens, Kew)

Genetic diversity has always been a key raw material in agricultural and medical research. At least 7000 medical compounds in the Western pharmacopoeia are derived from plants, and plant-derived products account for a conservative estimate of $40–50 000 million in pharmaceutical sales globally.[1,2] Roughly one-half of the gains in US agricultural yields from 1930 to 1980 can be attributed to genetic diversity's contribution to crop breeding activities.[3] But whereas previously only close relatives of crops could be used in breeding programmes, now the genes from the world's entire genetic pool can be used.

The pharmaceutical industry

Natural products are back in fashion in the pharmaceutical industry. There are three main reasons for this. Firstly, the development of more efficient screening techniques has increased 100-fold the speed with which chemicals can be tested. Although only about one in 10 000 chemicals yields a potentially valuable 'lead', these new techniques have made large natural product screening programmes affordable.[4] Secondly, companies have realized that by tapping into the traditional medicinal knowledge of indigenous communities they can greatly increase the probability of finding a commercially valuable drug and thus dramatically reduce research costs. And thirdly, there is a growing demand in industrialized countries for 'natural' medicines.

Recent policy decisions made by the US National Cancer Institute (NCI) give an indication of the importance now attached to medicinal plants. In 1980, NCI suspended a 20-year programme of collecting medicinal plants. In 1986, it renewed and enlarged the programme when the opportunities presented by the new biotechnologies became apparent. Between then and the end of 1992 the NCI paid for the collection of 23 000 plant samples of 7000 species, almost all of which came from the South.[5] Table 2.1 outlines some of the main actors and their current bioprospecting interests.

One of the fastest-growing applications of genetic engineering is gene therapy, which involves manipulating a person's genetic make-up for therapeutic purposes. Along with plants and animals, human genes are now an important resource for industry (see Chapter 5). Two-thirds of all biotechnology companies are focusing on the medical applications of biotechnology, and only one in 10 is applying biotechnology to food and agriculture. Nevertheless, the application of biotechnology to food and farming is likely to have a much more profound impact on people's livelihoods, lifestyles and the environment than other applications of biotechnology, at least in the medium term.

Table 2.1. Selected companies and their bioprospecting activities

Company	What collecting?	Where?	Use of indigenous knowledge/people or territories	Additional information
American Cyanamid	Arid land plants for crop protection agents and pharm. R&D	Mexico, Chile, Argentina	Priority given to plants with rich ethnobotanical background	ICBG agreement with: Uni. of Arizona, Institute of Biol. Resources of Buenos Aires, National Univ. of Patagonia, Catholic Uni. of Chile, National University of Mexico, Purdue Uni.., Louisiana State University
AMEAD Corp. (American R&D Consortium)	Drug discovery from marine organisms	Australia		Collaborating with Australian Inst. of Marine Science
Andes Pharmaceuticals (USA)	Drug development from plants	Bolivia, Colombia, Ecuador	Uses indigenous knowledge, specific collecting areas unknown	Claims intention to name individual healers as co-inventors on patents and will look for ways to compensate indig. communities through representative orgs. when knowledge collectively held
Boehringer Ingelheim	Plants, microbes			Agreements with Uni. of Illinois and NY Botanic Garden to obtain plants
Bristol Myers Squibb	Insects and related species	Costa Rica dry tropical forests		US govt.-supported ICBG agreement with InBio and Uni. of Costa Rica
	Rainforest plants esp. *Ancistorciadus* (for anti-HIV activity) and anti-malarials	Cameroon (Korup) and Nigeria (Oban Hills)	Ethnobotanical info. from traditional medical practices will be used to prioritize plant collection	US govt.-supported ICBG agreements

Company	Resources	Location	Terms	Notes
	Fungi, microbes, plants, marine organisms			Ranked 2nd largest Pharm. co. in the US. Contracts with third parties to collect specimens, incl. Scripps Institute and Oncogen
	Rainforest plants for drug devt; non-medicinal plants for sust. harvest	Surinam	Uses of plants by indig. people to be documented. Specific terms of benefit-sharing agreement not made public. CI will set up 'Shamans Apprentice' prog. & ind. people fund	US. govt-sponsored ICBG agreement with Virginia Polytechnic and State Uni. of Blacksburg, Missouri Botanical Garden, National Herbarium of Surinam, Bedrijf Geneesmiddelen of Surinam, & Conservation International (CI)
Glaxo Group (UK)	Plants, fungi, microbes, marine organisms	Asia, Latin America, poss. elsewhere		Materials obtained from Kew Royal Botanic Gdns, Biotics Ltd, Uni. of Illinois, National Cancer Institute, contracts with Carnivore Preservation Trust to collect plants in Laos
Johnson & Johnson (USA)	Novel chemical compounds			Funds chemical prospecting at Cornell Uni. and training of Southern scientists in prospecting
Magainain Pharmaceuticals (USA)	African reptiles, marine fish and organisms			Developing human drugs from African clawed frog and antibiotic steroid from dogfish shark
Marine Biotechnology Institute (Japan)	Marine organisms	Micronesia		Consortium of Japanese govt. and 21 Japanese Corporations
Maxus Ecuador, Inc. (subsid. of Maxus Petroleum, USA)	1200 plant species gathered, 18 new to world	Ecuador – primary trop. rainforest	Plant collection and inventory traverses Yasuni Natl. Park and Waorani ethnic reserve	Contracts w/ Missouri Botanic Garden for plant collection & inventory during construction of 120-km road in tropical moist forest

continued over

Table 2.1. (cont.)

Company	What collecting?	Where?	Use of indigenous knowledge/people or territories	Additional information
Merck and Co.	Fungi, microbes, marine orgs., plants	Latin America	Indig. knowledge from Urueu-wau-wau of Brazil; holds patent on anticoagulant derived from their plant material	Major pharmaceutical corp. Contracts with NY Botanic Gardens, MYCOSearch; high-profile contract with InBio (Costa Rica)
Parcelsian Inc. & Pacific Liaisons (USA)	Plants, food	China	Focusing on traditional medicinal plants	Pacific Liaisons has provided >1000 samples of trad. Chinese medicinal compounds to major US p'ceutical co. Will launch in-house screening
Pfizer, Inc. (USA)	Plants	USA	Plant collection based partly on existing ethno-botanical leads	3-yr, $2 million research in collab. with NYBG
Pharmaco-genetics (USA)	Natural products for drug development	Latin America	Hopes to rely entirely on leads for indig. people. Interest in developing line of cosmetics based on indig. people's products	Founded 1993; partly owned by non-profit Pan American Development Foundation that works with rural and indigenous groups in Latin America. Will use these connections to organize plant collection and identification activities
PharmaMar (Spain)	Bioactive marine materials for AIDS and cancer	Worldwide		PharmaMar researchers travel aboard the ships of Pescanova, one of the largest fishing fleets in the world

Adapted from *Pirating Indigeneous Plants, RAFI and Indigenous Peoples' Biodiversity Nework*, RAFI Occasional Paper Series Vol. 1, No. 4, November 1994

Genetic engineering in agriculture

Genetic engineering speeds up dramatically the process of breeding for desirable traits in plants and animals – improvements that would take up to 20 years in conventional breeding can be achieved almost overnight. It also enables the creation of life-forms that would never come into existence in nature, as genes from completely different species can be exchanged and transplanted (see Table 2.2). In this way, genetic engineering provides us with the means not just to accelerate evolution, but to supersede it altogether.

Table 2.2. Sources of new genes in transgenic crops

Crop	Source of new genes	Purpose of engineering
Potato	Chicken	Increased disease resistance
	Giant silk moth	Increased disease resistance
	Greater waxmoth	Reduced bruising damage
	Virus	Increased disease resistance
	Bacteria	Herbicide tolerance
Corn	Wheat	Reduced insect damage
	Firefly	Introduction of marker genes
	Bacteria	Herbicide tolerance
Tomato	Flounder	Reduced freezing damage
	Virus	Increased disease resistance
	Bacteria	Reduced insect damage
Tobacco	Chinese hamster	Increased sterol production
Rice	Bean, Pea	New storage proteins
	Bacteria	Reduced insect damage
Melon, Cucumber, Squash	Virus	Increased disease resistance
Sunflower	Brazil nut	Introduction of new storage proteins
Alfalfa	Bacteria	Production of oral vaccine against cholera
Lettuce, Cucumber	Tobacco Petunia	Increased disease resistance

Information compiled from applications to the US Department of Agriculture to field test engineered plants (Union of Concerned Scientists, 1993)

The first genetically engineered foods are just beginning to enter our lives. Scientists have succeeded in producing engineered versions of most of the world's major food and fibre crops – including rice, potato, soybean, corn and cotton – as well as numerous fruits, vegetables and trees. More than 60 plant species have been engineered in

Box 2.1: BGH – Genetic genius or udder insanity?

In November 1993, the US Food and Drug Administration (FDA) approved the use of bovine growth hormone (BGH, also know as bovine somatotropin or BST). BGH is the first product of genetically engineered bacteria intended for use in production agriculture. Originally isolated from cows, the genes for bovine growth hormone are inserted into bacterial genes. The bacteria, which express the inserted genes as their own, act as a mini-factory for the hormone, and synthetic BGH (known as rBGH) can be harvested from the bacterial soup and injected into cows.

The commercial version of BGH, a drug called Posilac, which induces dairy cows to increase their production of milk by up to 25%, had been under review at the FDA for more than a decade.

Despite objections from the Consumers Union and other public interest organizations, and the lack of long-term tests, the FDA judged the milk from rBGH-treated cows to be safe for human consumption. However, the effect on the cows themselves can be significant. Posilac's official label identifies a number of potential adverse effects of the hormone treatment, including reduced pregnancy rates, an increase of nearly 80% in udder infections, and the occurrence of cystic ovaries and disorders of the uterus. The main concerns for humans are the poorer nutritional quality of the milk and the increased use of antibiotics that will result from the increase in udder infections. This will affect not only the animals, but will move up the food chain into humans through meat and dairy products.

There is huge controversy over whether there is a real need for rBGH in the first place. US dairy farmers already produce a massive surplus of milk and dairy products. In Texas, California and other Southern states, milk processors are dumping milk as a result of rBGH use. 'Genetically engineered BST does not enhance the quality or nutritional value of milk, nor does it make milk less expensive, more widely available, or more conveniently packaged' notes a Tufts University report. 'Rather it simply profits the manufacturers who sell it to dairy farmers.' Bruce Krug, a small dairy farmer says that 'It's capitalism in reverse. Monsanto and the other companies created the idea with biotechnology, and they're selling it into a market where there is already a surplus of milk and consumer resistance.' Consumer demand for milk has been going down over the years and many small family farms may lose their farms to rBGH.

The FDA rejected pleas from concerned groups for products to be labelled as containing rBGH, but did allow voluntary labels from producers stating that milk is *not* derived from hormone-treated cows, providing such labels are true and not misleading. However, the biotechnology company Monsanto filed law suits against a dairy co-operative in Iowa that refused to buy milk from farmers who use rBGH, alleging that the co-op was falsely implying that regular milk is safer than rBGH-derived milk. It also sued a Texas company that advertised its products as 'rBGH-free'. These lawsuits were not vigorously pursued, however, and opponents of rBGH consider them to have been scare tactics to coerce support from the dairy industry.

The public campaign against rBGH is growing. More than 50 school districts have enacted resolutions banning rBGH from their lunch pro-grammes, including Los Angeles, Berkeley, Chicago and New York City. Public milk dumpings have taken place in more than 100 cities, and the National Farmers Union has called on farmers and consumers to boycott *all* Monsanto products. It is too early to assess the economic impact, but according to the most respected opinion poll in the US, the Gallup Poll, public awareness of the issue was up to 70% in December 1994, as com-pared with 28% when rBGH was launched at the beginning of that year.

(Source: The Pure Food Campaign, Washington DC)

this way, most of which have moved from the laboratory to the field testing stage, and are now starting to reach the market place. In May 1994, the first of these, a genetically engineered rot-resistant tomato, was launched into US supermarkets. In spring 1994, the first commer-cial transgenic organism entered European markets: a herbicide-resistant tobacco plant.

It's not just crops and fruits that are the focus of new age bio-technology. Genetically engineered bovine growth hormone (rBGH) , which increases milk production in cows, was approved in the US in 1993. While the milk produced has been judged safe for humans, the health impact on the cows can be significant (see Box 2.1).

These first product launches illustrate the priorities of research and development in biotechnology. These were: a delayed ripening tomato that benefits food processing and transportation firms rather than consumers; a growth hormone that has a serious deleterious effect on animal health; and a tobacco plant that encourages in-creased use of a weed killer known to be a health hazard to plants, animals and humans.

Research priorities in the agrochemical industry

Biotechnology is often touted as promising tremendous benefits in the form of healthier food and low-chemical agriculture, and even as the solution to the problem of world hunger. Through genetic engineer-ing, plants can be made to fix nitrogen, thereby reducing the need for nitrogen fertilizers, and to protect themselves against the pests that plague them, thereby removing the need for environmentally-damaging chemical pesticides. Food crops engineered to be more drought-resistant could improve food security in arid regions.

Too much of a good thing? Industry says genetically engineered pesticides will reduce chemicals in farming: the evidence so far shows the reverse.
(Liba Taylor/Panos Pictures)

While some investment is going into these potentially useful fields, research priorities appear to be skewed away from the needs of the environment, farmers and consumers, and geared heavily towards corporate interests. So far, the lion's share of genetic engineering activity in crops is devoted to the production of crops tolerant to chemical weed killers, technically known as herbicides. Between 1986 and 1992, 57% of field trials of transgenic crops were for herbicide resistance. Such crops can withstand both high doses and new kinds of chemicals, which is likely to lead to *increased* rather than decreased herbicide use in agriculture.

Not surprisingly, chemical companies and their collaborators are the major sponsors of this work. For example, the US biotech company, Calgene, in collaboration with the multinational chemical company Rhone-Poulenc, is seeking US approval to market cotton genetically engineered to be resistant to Rhone-Poulenc's herbicide bromoxynil. Ordinary cotton is killed by the herbicide, which also causes birth defects in animals and has been classified as a developmental toxicant for humans. Widespread adoption of this new cotton could double or triple the current use of bromoxynil in US agriculture alone.[6]

Desclieu had to share his strictly rationed drinking water with his coffee seedlings when he took them to the Americas.
(Mary Evans Picture Library)

The agrochemical industry feels an urgent need to boost sales, which reached $25 200 million worldwide in 1992. In 1992 only Monsanto, Du Pont and American Cyanamid could boast an increase in sales over 1991.[7] In 1993, only four of the top ten companies saw any sales growth (see Table 2.3).[8] The slowing of sales growth has been attributed to recession, increased research costs due to increased environmental controls over product development, and farm policy reforms in the North. Consequently, companies are looking to the rest of the world, and Asia in particular, to boost their foundering profits.

Aside from herbicide-tolerance, other applications include reducing food-processing costs, improving the transportability and increasing the shelf life of foods, and improving pest resistance. Selecting for processing traits follows traditional plant breeding down the path that has brought us tough but tasteless tomatoes and apples that today dominate the grocery shelves. Even the more laudable pursuit of pest resistance, which offers potential benefits to both farmers and consumers, can create more problems than it solves, as illustrated by the case of Bt toxin (Box 2.2). The

41

Table 2.3. Global agrochemical sales and ranking of the top ten companies, 1993

1993 Ranking (1992)	Company	1993 Sales ($ million)	% Change 1993/1992	% Change 1992/1991
1 (1)	Ciba Geigy	2790	−5.1	−0.3
2 (4)	Du Pont	2014	+4.4	+9.2
3 (2)	Zeneca (ICI)	1950	−4.3	−20.0
4 (6)	Monsanto	1936	+17.5	+6.2
5 (5)	Bayer	1790	−6.8	−11.5
6 (3)	Rhone-Poulenc	1756	−9.4	−12.5
7 (7)	DowElanco	1604	+1.5	−0.6
8 (8)	Hoechst	1335	−0.3	−9.9
9 (9)	BASF	1149	−3.0	−14.7
10 (10)	Am. Cyanamid	1100	+10.0	+11.1

Sources: AGROW No 214, August 19, 1994; Seedling, December 1993

introduction of Bt toxin genes into plants took several years and cost between $1.5 and $3 million.[9] In early 1995 the US granted limited registration for genetically-engineered Bt corn, cotton and potatoes. Yet the future of Bt toxin is already being threatened by the very feature that makes it so effective.

Pest resistance may be a useful application for genetic engineering, but there are often better ways of accomplishing the same goal: working with nature is often more effective than trying to stamp on it. This is the foundation on which agroecology is built. The agroecological approach addresses the health and dynamism of the whole farming ecosystem, rather than focusing on the output of a particular crop or attacking a single pest. Its strategy is defined by closely examining the relationships between the different elements, living and non-living, of the ecosystem and following a path that achieves the productive ends desired without compromising or un-balancing the ecosystem.

Agroecology encourages the use of techniques such as intercropping and integrated pest management, which do not aim to eradicate pests altogether, but to keep their populations low or to tempt them away to a more appealing food source. Crop rotations and inter-cropping may, for example, be more effective in controlling a range of pests by breaking the cycles through which they achieve destructive population levels. Rotations are effective against a wide range of pests, whereas chemical pesticides and genetic manipulations tend to be pest-specific, requiring a complex cocktail of elements to protect a plant fully. The agroecological and biotechnological approaches to agriculture are summarized in Table 2.4.

Box 2.2: Bt Toxin: Miracle or menace?

Over the last forty years of agricultural research, scientists have found themselves embroiled in a tail-chasing game in their pursuit of crop pests plagued with problems of resistance development, or finding that removal of one pest simply provided a niche for another. *Bacillus thuringiensis* (Bt) toxins promised to be different. This group of toxins selectively kills serious pests such as caterpillars, beetles and fly larvae, while sparing humans, spiders and most beneficial insects. One of the advantages of Bt is that, unlike most chemical pesticides, commercial Bt sprays contain a mixture of toxic proteins, and so the odds were thought to be minute that an insect would be resistant to all the toxins included.

The most exciting characteristic of Bt toxins, for agricultural scientists, is that they are produced by the *Bacillus thuringiensis* bacterium rather than by synthetic laboratory processes. This opens up the possibility of transplanting the gene coding for the toxin into crop species to provide an internal defence mechanism against the prevailing pests. In doing so, it was thought that the toxin would be a more effective weapon against the pests, because it would be produced continuously by the plant. Industry has been quick to recognize the potential Bt offers, and Monsanto expects to have genetically engineered cotton and potato plants producing Bt toxins within three or four years.

However, the very feature that makes Bt so efficient at killing pests is also its weakness. The fact that it kills all pests without resistance to the toxin means that *only* resistant strains survive. Without competition from non-resistant strains, they propagate even faster than they would with less potent pesticides. A second factor that contributes to the threat of unmanageable resistance in Bt is that it is already used very widely as a pesticide spray, and its insertion into a wide range of cultivated crops will accelerate the problem of resistance.

Various resistance management strategies are being investigated. The first is to use high enough doses of insecticide to kill even somewhat resistant insects. Another is to alternate between different Bt toxins, giving pests at most a few generations to adapt to one toxin before confronting them with another. A third approach involves using Bt toxins as one component of an integrated pest management programme (IPM). This approach keeps pest populations down, not with a single blow from one agent but by using a variety of complementary techniques such as crop rotation, introducing natural predators, planning planting dates to miss periods of peak pest development, and using Bt and other pesticides only sparingly.

Most experts agree that the most promising approach is to grow toxin-free plants alongside the genetically engineered variety. Refuge areas would allow pests that are still susceptible to Bt toxins to survive and contribute their genes to the next generation. Refuges pose a problem in the real world, in that farmers may be reluctant deliberately to feed some of their current year's harvest to pests for the intangible benefit of delaying resistance at some unspecified time in the future.

Table 2.4. Biodiversity as a productive force: two agendas

Problem	Biotech	Agroecosystem design
Pests and diseases	Single-gene resistance; engineered bio pesticides	Genetic diversity; indigenous varieties; intercropping, insecticidal plants; crop rotation
Weeds	Pesticide-tolerant genes	Early soil coverage; intercropping; cover crops; allelopathic crops
Plant nutrients	Engineered nitrogen-fixing crops and microbes	Soil conservation techniques; multiple cropping with legumes; integrated animal and crop agriculture (dung); composing; green manure
Yield	Yield increase for monocropping	Polycropping; one crop for multiple functions; use of associated crops and animals (weeds, fish, snails, etc.)

Feeding the world

Biotechnology is often presented as the answer to feeding the world's burgeoning population. But very little research and field testing is allocated to meeting this challenge. Given the expensive nature of the technology, this is not surprising. Biotechnology companies cannot develop products for people who cannot pay for them: most of the world's hungry are too poor to buy traditionally produced crops, let alone biotech's designer collection.

One partial solution is to provide developing countries with the genetic engineering tools they need to create their own transgenic crops. This approach is being considered by the parties to the Bio-diversity Convention as a way of compensating the South for the contribution of its genetic heritage to the benefit of Northern countries, companies and consumers. Agreeing terms and conditions of such exchanges is a great challenge, however, and industry is likely to try to ensure that it retains a strong influence in the application of such technologies and to share the benefits that derive from them.

In 1992, Monsanto gave Mexican scientists virus-resistant genes from potatoes for introduction into local potato varieties. The agreement was made on the condition that the transgenic potatoes were only to be sold for consumption in Mexico, where potatoes are a small part of the diet. According to Monsanto, 'We are aiming to help the subsistence farmer to feed his family – they don't export potatoes,

44

they eat them. We wanted to leave the door open for us to participate in the marketplace with Mexican farmers who are in it for profit[10]'.

Given the limited interest shown by companies and universities in crops that would help Southern communities, genetic engineering is likely to play a minor role, at best, in the coming crisis of food production. The resources available for research into crops like cassava and sorghum will continue to be small compared to those devoted to corn, cotton and soybeans. Many of the IARCs (see p. 14) are struggling to decide how many of their resources should be devoted to genetic engineering techniques, given the high investments required which can often be made only at the expense of other areas of research. At IRRI, for instance, four new biotech laboratories are being set up to work specifically on rice. Bt toxin is a major focus of research, but some staff fear that the toxin may not ultimately be useful in farmers' fields because of the resistance problems described in Box 2.2 (p. 44). Critics argue that Bt research is being undertaken widely in the public and private research arenas, and that IRRI would be better advised to examine ecological approaches to rice-stem borer control, which are largely being ignored.[11]

Even where research does yield new varieties of crops that show promise for Southern farmers, productivity is only one factor in the complicated equation of world hunger. Trade, agricultural subsidies and unsustainable agricultural practices are also important causes of hunger. Developing higher-yielding crops without addressing these other issues will ultimately have little impact.

According to the US-based Union of Concerned Scientists, 'The notion that the products of genetic engineering can somehow single-handedly solve the problems of world hunger is a dangerous misconception. Genetic engineering may have a role to play in meeting the challenge of world hunger, but it will not serve as a technological 'fix' nor compensate for decades of environmental abuse and misguided agriculture.'[12]

Another consequence of commercial biotechnology is the dissection of organisms into their genetic components and their removal from the natural world altogether. There is increasing interest in transferring the production of commodities from the fields, forests and plantations of the South to the laboratories of the North. This has two major ramifications. Firstly, it reduces the perceived value of the indigenous plant or crop, reducing the need for its conservation, which has broader implications for biodiversity as a whole. Secondly, it shuts down important export markets for Southern commodities, thus threatening the livelihoods of millions of plantation workers and farmers. Commercial production of the West African sweetener, thaumatin, is a good example of the impact such production switches

Industrial soap production could soon replace local production, leaving these children without any buyers for their palm oil soap.
(WWF/D. Halleux/Bios)

can have, at least in the short term. Likewise, commercial production of vanilla may before long eliminate the need for both the vanilla orchid and the vanilla farmer. There is a wide variety of high-value plant-derived products that could be affected in this way. Calgene has engineered a variety of rape-seed (canola) which contains a high content of laurate, a fatty acid used in the manufacture of soaps and detergents. The traditional sources of laurate are palm kernel and coconut oils, which are an important export for Southeast Asian nations. Thus these countries may soon start to lose income they depend on. Farmers in the state of Georgia in the USA are already growing the first commercial transgenic rape-seed crop.[13]

In some cases, however, given the ever-decreasing prices of (and diminishing returns from) the major commodities like sugar, cocoa and coffee, exclusion from the global market could be a blessing in disguise for Southern countries. This situation could provide an opportunity to redirect food production strategies towards meeting local needs, rather than overloading the North's dinner plate.

It is not just Southern farmers' livelihoods that are threatened by biotechnology. If industrial agriculture follows its current course, Northern farmers will also be threatened as food production shifts to laboratories. Huge industrial vats of bacterial soup producing sugars, oils and cellulose are already providing the raw materials for the synthetic food industry, while research focuses on new 'food alchemy',[14] the packaging of industrial chemicals into mouth-watering delicacies, and exploring the 'gustatory perception of smell' or taste. Instead of global markets for maize, cocoa, coconut oil or soybeans, we will soon be dealing with market prices for starches, oils and proteins.

Environmental risks of transgenic crops

Genetically engineered crops are not necessarily inherently dangerous, but the introduction of new traits (such as resistance to cold, drought, etc.) through genetic engineering will necessarily result in unpredictable interactions with the environment into which the plant is introduced. Transgenic plants are likely to be less predictable than those produced by traditional breeding techniques, because the genes introduced are from a completely different species rather than from a related variety. New genes may not be subject to the same mutual constraints as those that have evolved as a group.

Another risk arises from the nature of the new trait introduced. Many transgenes control traits that are ecologically advantageous to plants. Resistance to cold, disease or herbicides enables plants to overcome obvious limits on population growth, which can affect the

Plant cloning is widely employed as a method of plant propagation around the world. Genetic engineering techniques are unlikely to reach laboratories like this owing to their high cost. (Sean Sprague/Panos Pictures)

balance of the local ecosystem. In addition, transgenes producing toxins may affect a wider target audience than desired. For example, a genetically engineered plant virus containing a scorpion-derived toxin gene is being field tested in the UK. It is intended to kill the cabbage white butterfly larva, but its host range is known to be wide, and includes rare and protected moth and butterfly species.[15]

New genes introduced into a plant are subject to the normal rules of genetic drift that occur in the process of natural selection and reproduction. And since the introduced traits tend to be determined by one or two genes (reflecting biotechnology's current limitations), they can readily be transmitted into wild populations. Thus, the new genes join the gene flows that occur throughout the whole ecosystem in which the plant lives.

Movement of these genes into wild relatives of crop plants with which the crop can cross-fertilize is almost bound to occur. Many of the genes introduced will come from animals and micro-organisms which would never have found their way into plants by natural processes. Currently the impact of this on ecosystems is extremely poorly appreciated or understood.

Health risks of genetic engineering

Some genetically engineered organisms are made with viral or trans-poson vectors that have been artificially modified to become less species-specific. Since viruses and transposons can cause or induce mutations, there is concern that enhanced vectors could be carcinogenic to humans, domestic animals and wild animals. There are also fears that once-familiar foods may become allergenic or meta-bolically destabilizing through genetic engineering. Allergenic effects could be carried by the transgene or be stimulated by imbalances in the chemistry of the host plant or organism. Strong evidence for a causal link has already been observed in the US and other countries related to an epidemic of eosinophilia-myalgia syndrome (EMS). By June 1992, 1512 cases and 38 deaths had been reported. This disease is caused by a hyper-sensitivity reaction of the immune system which appears to have been linked to ingestion of a batch of genetically engineered L-tryptophan, an amino acid found naturally in various foods.[16]

Innocent until proven guilty

Assessing the risks of releasing genetically modified organisms (GMOs) is extremely difficult since the flow of novel plant, animal and microbial genes into agricultural and wild ecosystems defies any nat-ural processes. Following historical legal precedents, regulation fa-vours placing the burden of proof on proving the harmful impact of GMOs rather than their benignity. Many NGOs argue that the burden of proof should be reversed for GMOs because the stakes are so high. Unlike faulty computers or washing machines, GMOs cannot be re-called if they go wrong. Past experiences with cases like DDT and thalidomide do not engender strong faith in leaving risk assessment in the hands of industry.

Moving towards a biosafety protocol

Since the mid-1980s, most industrialized countries have adopted regu-lations concerning the safe handling and use of genetically engin-eered organisms. Some, such as the US, simply adapted their regulatory framework by adjusting it to the special risks linked with the new genetic engineering techniques. Others, like the European Union and most of its member states, established new laws covering the contained use as well as the deliberate release of GMOs. In the South, however, biosafety regulation is virtually non-existent. As a consequence, an increasing number of companies from the US and Europe are choosing to conduct releases of GMOs in countries which

Table 2.5. Field tests with transgenic plants in Latin America (1989–92)

Year	Country	Company	Crop	No. of trials	Trait
1989	Guatemala	Asgrow (USA)	Squash	1	Virus resistance
	Puerto Rico	Monsanto (USA)	Soybean	1	Herbicide tolerance
1990	Mexico	Calgene (USA)	Tomato	1	Long shelf life
	Puerto Rico	Monsanto (USA)	Soybean	1	Herbicide tolerance
1991	Mexico	Campbell/Sinaloa (USA)	Tomato	1	Bt insect tolerance
	Argentina	Calgene (USA)	Cotton	2	Herbicide tolerance and Bt insect resistance
		Ciba-Geigy (CH)	Maize	1	Marker gene
		Monsanto (USA)	Soybean	1	Herbicide tolerance
	Dominic. Rep.	Monsanto (USA)	Soybean	1	Herbicide tolerance
	Costa Rica	Monsanto (USA)	Soybean	1	Herbicide tolerance
	Chile	Calgene (USA)	Tomato	1	Long shelf life
		ICI/PetoSeed (UK/USA)	Tomato		
	Bolivia	Calgene (USA)	Cotton	2	Herbicide tolerance and Bt insect resistance
	Puerto Rico	Monsanto (USA)	Soybean	1	Herbicide tolerance
1992	Argentina	Calgene (USA)	Cotton	2	Herbicide tolerance and Bt insect resistance
		Monsanto (USA)	Soybean	1	Herbicide tolerance
		Ciba-Geigy (CH)	Maize	1	Marker gene
			Canola		
			Sugar beet		
	Mexico	Campbell/Sinaloa (USA)	Tomato	2	Bt insect resistance and long shelf life
		CINVESTAV	Potato	1	Virus resistance
		Calgene (USA)	Tomato	1	Long shelf life
	Costa Rica	Monsanto (USA)	Soybean	1	Herbicide tolerance
			Cotton	1	Herbicide tolerance
			Maize	1	Herbicide tolerance
	Puerto Rico	Monsanto (USA)	Soybean	1	Herbicide tolerance
	Belize	Monsanto (USA)	Soybean	1	Herbicide tolerance
			Cotton	1	Herbicide tolerance
			Maize	1	Herbicide tolerance
	Bolivia	Univ of Venezuela/ CIP	Potato	1	Cold tolerance

Source: *Seedling.*, Dec. 1994, after Jaffe (1993)

have no regulations in place (see Table 2.5). For example, Calgene tested its 'Flavr Savr' tomato in Mexico and Chile, and insecticide-producing cotton plants in South Africa. Monsanto conducted field trials of its genetically engineered soybean in Puerto Rico, Costa Rica, Argentina and Belize.[17] As can be seen from Table 2.5, the products being tested do not deal with the pressing problems of agriculture in those countries.

Only two developing countries, India and the Philippines, have any sort of biosafety system in place. Such a regulatory void can lead to biotechnological colonialism, whereby Southern lands are used to carry out field tests in conditions that would never be allowed in the North. Simply extending the regulations from the North to the South is not enough, because the impact of GMOs depends on the agroecological environment. Genetically engineered cold-tolerant potatoes may be approved in the US if it can be shown that there is no danger of gene flow to wild relatives. By contrast, the presence of many local varieties and sexually compatible wild potato relatives in Peru (a centre of diversity for potatoes) means that transgenes are more likely to move from the engineered crop to wild relatives.

The need for internationally harmonized safety regulations was recognized in the Biodiversity Convention. An expert panel appointed to address the issue recommended the adoption of a legally binding instrument. A few developed country representatives, led by the US, opposed the creation of any protocol, adopting the industry position that such action should be based on 'sound scientific evidence' rather than what they consider to be 'misrepresentations and distortions'.[18] The vast majority of countries, however, strongly supported the development of a biosafety protocol.

At the second meeting of the Biodiversity Convention's Conference of the Parties, in late 1995, Northern delegations were pushing to limit the protocol to dealing with 'transboundary transfer of LMOs [living modified organisms],' while Southern delegations were in favour of a protocol on biosafety in the field of the safe transfer, handling and use of LMOs. It was agreed that there would be a biosafety protocol and, although the precise terms of reference were still to be determined, it appeared that the North had won out. The conference called for a negotiation process to develop in the field of safe transfer, handling and use of living modified organisms, a protocol on biosafety, specifically focusing on transboundary movement of any LMO resulting from modern biotechnology that may have adverse effect on the conservation and sustainable use of biological diversity.[19]

References

1. UNDP (1994): *Conserving Indigenous Knowledge*. New York.
2. Reid, W.V., Laird, S.A. *et al.* (1993). A New Lease on Life. In: *Biodiversity Prospecting* (Eds Reid, Laird *et al.*). World Resources Institute, Washington, D.C.

3. Office of Technology Assessment (1987). *Technologies to Maintain Biological Diversity*. Washington, D.C. US Congress, US Government Printing Office.

4. McChesney, J. (1992). *Biological Diversity, Chemical Diversity and the Search for New Pharmaceuticals*. Paper presented at the Symposium on Tropical Forest Medical Resources and the Conservation of Biodiversity, Rainforest Alliance, New York, January 1992.

5. UNDP (1994). *Conserving Indigenous Knowledge*. New York.

6. Rissler, J. and Mellon, M. (1993) *Perils Amidst the Promise – Ecological Risks of Transgenic Crops in a Global Market*. Union of Concerned Scientists, Washington, D.C.

7. From *Chemistry and Industry*, 15 November 1993. Quoted in *Seedling*, December 1993. GRAIN, Barcelona.

8. Anon. (1994). Ishihara Joins Japanese Leaders in 1993 Sales Ranking. *AGROW, No. 214*, 19 August.

9. Collinson, M.P. and Wright, K.L. (1991). Biotechnology and the International Agriculture Research Centers of the CGIAR. 21st Conference of the International Association of Agricultural Economists, Tokyo, August 1991. Quoted in: Reid, W.V., Laird, S.A. *et al.* (1993). A New Lease on Life. In: *Biodiversity Prospecting* (Eds. Reid, Laird *et al.*). World Resources Institute, Washington, D.C.

10. Schmidt, K. (1995). Whatever Happened to the Gene Revolution? *New Scientist*, January 1.

11. Personal communication from Renée Vellvé of GRAIN.

12. Rissler, J. and Mellon, M. (1993) *Perils Amidst the Promise – Ecological Risks of Transgenic Crops in a Global Market*. Union of Concerned Scientists, Washington, D.C.

13. Schmidt, K. (1995). Whatever Happened to the Gene Revolution? *New Scientist*, January 1, pp 21–25.

14. Orr, D.W. (1992). *Ecological Literacy: Education and the Transition to a Postmodern World*. SUNY Press, New York.

15. Coghlan, A. (1994). Will the Scorpion Gene Run wild? *New Scientist*, June 25.

16. Egziabher, T.B.G., Goodwin, B. *et al.* (1994). *The Need for Greater Regulation and Control of Genetic Engineering*, A Statement by Scientists Concerned about Current Trends in the New Biotechnology. Third World Network, Penang.

17. Jaffe, W.R. (1993): 'Implementation of Biosafety Regulations: The Experience in Latin America', in *African Regional Conference for International Co-operation on Safety in Biotechnology – Proceedings*, pp 148–150.

18. GRAIN (1994). Threats from the test-tubes. *Seedling*, vol. 11, No. 4, December.

19. United Nations Environment Programme (1995). Convention on Biological Diversity / Conference of the Parties / 2 / Committee of the Whole / L.22

2.3. Biodiversity Newspeak

CHRISTINE VON WEISZÄCKER

In his book *1984*, written in 1948, George Orwell described plausible but most unpleasant social and political developments. Orwell's Utopian Society of 1984 demonstrates the interrelationship between the struggle for power and the control of language and historiography. Anyone who wants totalitarian control over people has to obtain a monopoly over defining and re-defining the meaning of words and over writing and rewriting history. In Orwell's Utopia the Ministry of Propaganda is called Ministry of Truth. Torturing by the secret police takes place in the Ministry of Love. The new controlled language is called Newspeak, which aims to abolish the old vernacular, called Oldspeak. Oldspeak is a term of abuse for the people's language, i.e. for the vernacular.

We are now more than ten years beyond 1984 and, fortunately, we do not have to live under totalitarian rule of the type Orwell described. We do, however, live in a time when the 'battle for the meaning of words'[1] has become prevalent and decisive. Moreover, today's Ministries for Research and Technology demonstrate strong tendencies towards becoming Ministries for the Production of Public Acceptance of Certain Research Projects and Technologies, which by their very structure do not promote a technology policy worthy of a democratic society.

The coining of words is a key tool in political conflicts. This paper will examine how the new verbal Siamese twins of 'biodiversity' and 'biotechnology' are shaping research and technology policy in academia, politics and business.

Scientific discourse has changed markedly since the 1970s. The relative decrease in public funding for universities has resulted in a growing concentration on certain key topics of research, sometimes aptly termed 'precompetitive' research[2]. Basic research, applied research and product development are converging in terms of time, personnel and structure[3]. Thus, university research has acquired a close similarity to research in normal business, which is geared to economic competition. Unfortunately, this also means that universities are being drained of their independent critical qualities.

Among the different forms of political negotiations over technological pathways, one has gained prevalence at the moment. This 'promotion of public acceptance' – sometimes also called 'acceptance PR' or 'acceptance production' is based on a purely strategic assessment and is meant to keep environmental stakeholders from instigating sanctions against government or industry policies. 'Acceptance promotion' optimizes justification without changing the reigning criteria and standards of decision-makers. It is a tool with which powerful decision-makers gain public acclaim (or at least resigned acceptance), and which guarantees the smooth running of their plans without calling into question their own criteria and decision-making priorities. This approach currently dominates over other, less cynical, forms of political negotiation, such as 'risk limitation' based on the precautionary principle, or 'global regionality for the environment'. The latter combines co-operation against ecologically destructive global structures with the promotion of differentiated and diverse solutions at local and regional levels.[4]

The verbal symbiosis between 'biodiversity' and 'biotechnology' is in line with the dominant trends in science policy and technology policy. The common use of the prefix 'bio-' and the rhythmical parallels between the two words suggest a natural harmony and logical coherence between them. A verbal screen of confused notions is being put into place, however. It encourages the merging of basic and applied research, thus weakening the important critical function of scientific discourse. It encourages the concentration of funds and personnel into one branch of biology. It acts as a perfect tool in the creation of acceptance by suggesting that whoever is in favour of preserving wild species must also be in favour of biochemical companies and their investments in genetic engineering. This is a public relations ploy aimed at the large constituency of environmental activists and people who enjoy the beauty and diversity of creatures in the world.

'Biotechnology' is most often used as a synonym for 'genetic engineering', a term which incites public alarm. The term 'biotechnology' does not incite the same alarm. There is a price, however, since it obliterates the technological, social and economic differentiation between traditional crafts using plants, animals and micro-organisms on the one hand, and a new 'mega-technology'[5] on the other. This megatechnology is promoted by a triple power alliance consisting of:

o the new scientific fraternity which uses the methodology of genetic engineering

o governments which heavily subsidize the quest for technological supremacy

o multinational chemical companies.

Philip Regal, Professor at the College of Biological Sciences at the University of Minnesota, says that there are really four biotechnologies: Firstly, biotechnology is a material technology for chemically rearranging DNA; secondly, biotechnology is a policy of several industrialized and other countries; thirdly, biotechnology is an ideology – a vision of the future; fourthly, biotechnology is an area for economic and career investment.[6]

In debates about genetic engineering its critics are often asked: 'Admittedly, you have rational arguments concerning single cases of deliberate releases, special production processes and certain questionable applications, but you must commit yourself and tell us clearly whether you basically believe in genetic engineering? Do you confess a fundamental faith in this technology? You must not evade this essential question!'[7]

So this technology calls for a basic belief and the confession of a fundamental faith. If you replace 'genetic engineering' in these sentences with 'metallurgical processes' or 'laser technology', it becomes evident how new, shocking and inadmissible this call really is. Nobody ever asked us to believe in 'metallurgic processes' or to confess our faith in 'laser technology'. Technologies are means to ends. At best, suitable means to carefully chosen ends. It is particularly strange for beliefs and confessions to turn up in the context of science and technology. Willingness to look at phenomena critically is what marks the difference between Galileo and the Holy Inquisition. Why are we suddenly urged to believe fundamentally in a technology?

There are certain mega-technologies that do not allow the normal scientific procedure based on trial and error. Professor Wolf Häfele, one of the fathers of the fast breeder reactor in Germany, gave an outspoken and clear analysis of this in the context of nuclear power. He classified nuclear power as a technological venture which enters into the domain of 'hypotheticality'.[8] This means that this technology leaves the domain of classical experiments with their spatial and temporal containment. Häfele calls it a technological adventure 'of the order of magnitude of the history of mankind'.[9] Incidentally he – unlike others who reacted to this insight – professed faith in this adventure.

Hence the preoccupation with faith and belief. It could well be that modern biotechnology will also lead us into another adventure of the order of magnitude of the history of mankind. It certainly shows some elements of hypotheticality:

○ Its scientific and technological impacts and hazards can spread themselves both spatially and temporally, potentially through the entire biosphere. Releases of genetically manipulated organisms are irreversible and cannot be recalled.[10] Releases are not scientific experiments in the classical sense.

55

○ The choice of scientific and technological pathways is not scientific. Increasingly, these choices take on the character of a bet on the future, of a self-fulfilling prophesy, of belief and make-believe.

○ The impetus of research and development becomes directed towards so called 'key technologies' to the disadvantage of other technological options.

○ Modern biotechnology is expensive, requiring and causing a concentration of investment and power. The very powerful constellation of biotechnological stakeholders in research, industry and governments does not only promote the engineering of genes but can forcefully push and engineer market successes of certain products. This poses problems in the patent debate, since patents can be defined as non-monetary state subsidies. It also poses problems in the debate on the general labelling of genetically engineered food, euphemistically called 'novel food'. Without labelling, forced consumption enters the 'market'. A third area of concern opens up if governments do not demand an adequate liability and insurance coverage for this risk-technology. Bets on the future of biotechnology seem like bets on horses at a racetrack where it is permitted to bribe the jockey, to dope the horse and to change the rules during the race.

If these observations are correct, the demand to confess one's technological faith becomes less of an absurdity. It becomes an icon of the technological realities of today.

Are these realities an advance or a setback? Are they desirable or not? Is there coercion towards technological fundamentalism? How does an 'experiment of the order of magnitude of the history of mankind' fit in with some of the cultural inventions that we are proud of? How does it fit with democracy, with the protection of minorities, with equality of opportunity and freedom of choice?

I do not see any international forum in which there are adequately comprehensive, sufficiently long-term and serious exchanges of views and negotiations on this technological mega-adventure involving the present generation of humanity, let alone future generations. I do, however, see many instances of experts condemning the public to mutism, confusion and resignation. This is part and parcel of devious pre-emptive acceptance promotion. Some international negotiations of the last few years have not met the standards of debate and democratic decision-making[11] that are needed.

The Uruguay Round of the General Agreement on Tariffs and Trade (GATT, now WTO) agreed on a continuation and reinforcement of the world market with its unhindered global shipping of biological species. This in itself – as every ecologist can tell you – is hostile to diversity, be it biological or cultural. GATT and its Trade Related Intellectual Property Rights (TRIPS) radically redefined the cultural, social and legal character of animals, plants and micro-organisms, and this happened without public discussion or democratic legitimation.

Similarly, the Earth Summit's action plan, Agenda 21, lends itself easily to being misread as a plan for the promotion of genetic engineering. The chapter on 'Sustainable Agriculture' is subtly misspelt by some as 'Sustaining Biotechnology in Agriculture'.[12] The chapter on 'Science for Sustainable Development' often gets interpreted as a call for the promotion of biotechnology in the arena of different scientific approaches competing for appreciation and funds. Chapter 16 of Agenda 21 does not need an implicit redefinition. It has the title 'Environmentally sound management of biotechnology'. The introduction states that: 'Biotechnology, an emerging knowledge-intensive field, is a set of enabling techniques for bringing about specific man-made changes in deoxyribonucleic acid (DNA) or genetic material, in plants, animals and microbial systems, leading to useful products and technologies.' So the chapter starts with the prophecy that this technology will prove 'environmentally sound' and 'enabling' and that its products will be 'useful'. The introduction goes on to name the aims of Agenda 21 in the field of biotechnology. Amongst these are: 'To engender public trust and confidence' and 'to promote the development of sustainable applications and to establish appropriate enabling mechanisms'.[13] It is quite frightening how quickly we are approaching the ballyhoo of technology acceptance and how fast the words of the debate on environment and development get worn and torn in the public relations of genetic engineering. More money is spent on the technology promotion and the production of public acceptance than on technology impact assessment and biosafety research. In an EU research proposal on 'Bioscience and -technology'[14] 10–16% of the total sum of 552 million ECU are reserved for 'prenormative research, biodiversity and social acceptance'. Biosafety issues are neither mentioned nor funded in this paper published in 1994. A UNIDO report submitted in preparation for the Meeting of the UN Commission on Sustainable Development in January 1995[15] even suggests that funds from the international community within the framework of the Commission on Sustainable Development should be made available for biotechnology promotion. The overall financial resource requirements for subsidizing and promoting biotechnology in developing countries given in the report are as follows:

1. Facilities and training in modern biotechnology in
   the fields of agriculture, health and environment   20 billion US$

| 2. Biosafety | 2 million US$ |
| 3. Endogenous biotechnology promotion | 5 million US$ |

The report stresses that biotechnology promotion is an attractive way for industrialized countries to comply with the United Nations target of 0.7% of the Gross National Product (GNP) for official development assistance (ODA).

This UNIDO paper is a regrettable demonstration of a twisted funding approach. The North requests funds of approximately 20 billion US$ for the export of its technological priorities to the South at a time when stock-market analysts of Wall Street pointed to losses of biotechnology companies of about the same amount. ODA again might prove a cynical tool by which to screen to the public of the North and promote to the public of the South already falsified investment strategies. The low figures given for biosafety requirements suggest that once again risk-externalization and risk-dumping are part of the promotion game. Here again we are reminded of Orwell's warnings.

Yet this is not a necessary development. A surprising move in the opposite direction took place at the Third Meeting of the Commission on Sustainable Development which met 11-28 April 1995, in New York. Chapter 16 was on the agenda of this meeting. It was one of the most controversial and hotly debated issues. The sensational outcome of the debate was the formation of a new pro-biosafety coalition between developing countries (G77 and China) and a group of OECD-countries which want to stop the rat-race for deregulation in the North (e.g. Norway, Denmark, Sweden, Austria and some Eastern European Countries.) Strong support and written background materials were provided by NGOs and critical scientists, both from South and from North.[16] The debate culminated in the decision not to follow the UNIDO suggestions and to issue a recommendation to the Conference of the Parties to the UN Convention on Biological Diversity for a Biosafety Protocol.

Not only Agenda 21 but also the Convention on Biological Diversity which was signed at UNCED in Rio enforces the international success of the Siamese twins 'biodiversity and biotechnology'.[17,18,19] If a difficult relationship wants to pose as an ideal partnership, it does not need realistic scientific research nor environmental impact assessment; it needs good public relations. 'Biodiversity and biotechnology' is such a difficult relationship. The fact that the Biodiversity Convention does not pertain to the irreplaceable and vitally important collections of the Consultative Group of International Agricultural Research Centers (CGIAR), is significant. Until recently, these collections were considered under the premisses of the UN Conference of Stockholm which took place in 1972. Animal, plant and microbial species were then regarded as 'the natural heritage of humankind to be safeguarded freely accessible for the present and for future generations.' Only twenty years later the fight for exclusive access and private property is in full swing. And it becomes evident that the factual legal status of whatever was collected before the year 1993 is dismally unclear and vehemently contested.

In June 1994 the World Bank attempted a takeover bid for the CGIAR collections. This was turned down, but the concept of Global Commons[20] has very real political weaknesses and will probably be threatened again. Commons can only be safeguarded within the rules of decency and the sanctions of their corresponding communities. The only globally functioning community, at the moment, is the world market, and its only rule of decency is the maximization of private profits. The global Commons are unlikely to thrive in this setting. Our form of economy has blatantly blundered in the task of using resources sustainably. Unfortunately, the technological fundamentalism of hypothetical technologies seems to go hand in hand with an economic fundamentalism that does not allow us to analyze and restructure our economies. This urgent task is left undone. Instead, an elaborate verbal haze is created. This haze is actively thickened with words taken from the environmentalists' vocabulary whose positive connotations are ridiculed, watered down or perverted. Again Orwell is brought to mind.

And again, this is not the only strand of activities and policies influencing reality. At the Second Meeting of the Conference of the Parties to the UN Convention on Biological Diversity, the South-North biosafety coalition which had established itself forcefully in New York in April, won the day again. In Jakarta, on the 16th of November 1995, a mandate to negotiate a Biosafety Protocol[21] was so decided. The draft protocol is to be prepared by an open-ended *ad hoc* working group in six sessions and is to be submitted in 1998. The precautionary approach, the legally binding character and the obligation for advance informed agreement have been firmly established. The first step will be the regulation of 'transboundary movement'. The scope and timing of the following steps is still contested. Additional hot spots of the debate in Jakarta were 'access to genetic resources'[22] which includes the issue of the CGIAR collections[23] and 'intellectual property rights'.[24] It was decided to initiate studies having a closer look at some of the implications of the GATT/TRIPS agreements for biodiversity, for local communities and for indigenous peoples.

A new and difficult round of intergovernmental negotiations on all these issues will take place at the Fourth International Technical Conference on Plant Genetic Resources in Leipzig, Germany, 17–23 June,

1996. Countries like the United States, Germany, United Kingdom and Japan, and new industrial NGOs like the 'Biotechnology Industry Organisation (BIO)' will have their opposing strategies ready in order to stop the 'New York-Jakarta Trend' of 1995. .

In the past, the following strategy proved to be very successful: Critics of genetic engineering are often themselves criticized as being hysterical, irrational and panic-driven. And here things really become difficult. Who decides what is rational? Modern science began with the rebellion of individual rationality and judgement against the reigning dogmatic definitions of 'reality' represented by the Holy Office. The former scientific rebels may – as many successful rebels do – copy the power mechanism of their former oppressors, and we may end in a sickening paradox. The promoters of genetic engineering may claim what one could almost call the 'inquisitorial privilege' of defining and administering the terms 'enlightened thinking, rationality and critical sovereignty'. Not only may they claim this privilege, but in fact they sometimes do.

Biodiversity has left the ecologists' Arcady and is revealing itself in political, technological and economic conflicts. In the turmoil of the political arena environmentalists face many new challenges. One important task will be to make sure that words rooted in civil opposition do not lose their 'Oldspeak' meaning. Another task is the search for suitable alliances. People engaged in nature conservation and species protection have so far not been strong enough. If they do not wish to be condemned to failure they must avoid being narrow-minded, orthodox or too fastidious in their search for allies. Careful evaluation is necessary, however. Genetic engineers are now offering to enter into alliances for the protection of biodiversity. What contributions can they make?

In this context the Merck–INBio deal[25] has become a nearly paradigmatic example. The two American giants in biodiversity research and promotion, Edward O. Wilson and Thomas E. Lovelock see it as a happy and fair co-operation between biotechnology and biodiversity. But do funds to create an infrastructure for the extraction of a resource really contribute to the safeguarding of this resource? This was certainly not the case with other resources in the past.

The role of experts deserves a closer look. Edward O. Wilson[26] sees the 'Louvre of biodiversity' burning. When I listen to long scientific controversies on whether there is a species extinction every fifteen minutes or every three minutes I can scarcely resist screaming. If not only the Louvre but also the Metropolitan Museum, the Hermitage and the Pinakothek are burning down simultaneously, this is certainly not the time to employ art experts to catalogue pictures; firemen are more important. And the search in all the museums for potential short-circuits and compulsive arsonists is also more important. A perfect scientific musical accompaniment to the funeral procession of lost species is not enough. In the past unique, vital, complex, endemic and co-evolving diversity thrived without scientific help – and it should be able to do so again. It is not enough to hospitalize it in zoos and botanical gardens, inventory it in herbaria and between book covers, document it in films and deep-freeze it in gene banks in order to resurrect it as a genetically engineered patchwork. The term 'conservation of biodiversity' allows many interpretations. A critical look at biodiversity policies will uncover the arenas of political conflict behind the verbal haze.[27]

To politicians, biodiversity is the title of a new political chapter. Its main theme is the drastic legal redefinition of living organisms as TRIPS and patentable 'inventions'. Public awareness of these trends takes a long time to grow. Linguistic astonishment might help: what is so intellectual about trade-related intellectual property rights? Is it an intellectual act to run a sequencing machine and to fill in the forms properly for patent applications, thus stopping living organisms from belonging to themselves and to the places and people where they have resided and have been used for centuries? We find another good reason for astonishment if we recapitulate the original function and purpose of patenting. Patents were meant as a protection for the financially and infrastructurally weak inventor, whose invention was thereby made accessible to the community while bringing just financial rewards to the inventor. Patents were devised as public tools against market concentration. But modern mega-technological progress takes place almost exclusively within the framework of institutions heavily funded by rich countries or by rich companies from the North. The function of the positive historical purpose of patents is being perverted into a legitimation of completely new structures. History is being rewritten in a such way that the protection of the weak is still being claimed, whilst the protection of the strong is what is actually taking place. Again, one thinks of Orwell.

Politicians inevitably focus on the promotion of their national economies. Will business adequately safeguard and promote biodiversity? Nature conservation is unlikely, in the long run, to win an uphill race against economic priorities. This was pointed out as early as 1932 by Nicolai Ivanovitch Vavilov, the famous Russian agronomist and geneticist:

the growing needs of civilized man and the development of industry make the introduction of new plants necessary. The vast resources of wild species, especially in the tropics, have been practically untouched by investigation.[28]

Vavilov made a very realistic assessment in assuming that the central decisions were likely to be taken in the economic domain of the 'development of industry and the growing needs of civilized man'. Many conservationists share his assessment and, even though this is rarely their own intrinsic motivation, they point to the potential market value of biodiversity as 'immense biological capital'.[29] They calculate the market value of birds and absorb nature into the economic calculus. This, however, has two sides to it. On the one hand, it may be the only way to get the attention of decision-makers who are aware only of monetary values. On the other hand, it completes the commercialization of our culture. Clearly economics has not yet proved itself a reliable guardian of long-term concerns which require unity of purpose between different countries and different generations.

Business and the economy certainly show an intrinsic interest in biodiversity, however. The tragedy of species loss, translated into economic terms, says: 'buy now and sell later'. Many years ago a private company, Campbell Soups, started to hoard tomato genes and is now in possession of a substantial fraction of the world's tomato biodiversity. The company followed a clear economic rationale which is probably an early precursor of things to come. The resource of biological diversity is getting scarcer every day. Why is that so? The demand for biodiversity is growing because diverse biological options become increasingly necessary as solutions to the man-made problems of climatic, agricultural, social and economic changes. Increase in scarcity and/or increase in demand: these are the normal economic preconditions for an increase in market value. The interest of the business world in biodiversity, therefore, does not mean that business has integrated environmental values and is applying the criteria of sustainablility. It simply means that the exclusive ownership of this resource promises to be good business.

But what do you do if you are not primarily interested in making a profit from imminent species loss, but rather want to halt it? It becomes increasingly difficult to make clear choices while our palates are being confused by the associated 'ketchup' of acceptance promotion which adorns every technological dish. Plans to protect biodiversity must be based on the existing historical knowledge of the conditions under which the continuous co-evolution and conservation of species thrived.

How did and does biodiversity come into existence? It certainly did not need global management or biotechnology to do so. On the contrary, globality and narrow selective aims are probably threats to the unfolding and stabilization of diversity.

The origin of diversity is a central question of biology. Since Darwin's time the 'survival of the fittest' has been linked to the scientific and public perception of biological evolution. Few reflect on the causal links between the two. Darwin carefully chose the term 'survival of the fittest', not 'survival of the best'. Fitness can only be defined in the context of a certain environment and a certain situation. Natural evolution is a highly complex and dynamic game, in the course of which changing players enter into competitive and cooperative interactions with each other. Fitness, strictly speaking, can only be defined retrospectively: 'Fit were the ancestors of those who are still around.' Essential evolutionary insights hide behind the simple waiving of a definition of present fitness. Genetic engineering is always linked to a very narrow selection of genes: hence, the temptation to define present fitness gains a new technological pungency.

Some basic facts are easily forgotten. Selection alone does not create diversity and complexity. Obviously, every act of selection reduces diversity. Selection is only part of the whole evolutionary dynamic.

Diversity is regenerated after every selective step by mutations, i.e. aberrations and errors that occur in the gene replication process. The 'survival of errors' and their recombination in every generation is critical for the evolutionary process. In one environment, these genetic errors may make an organism less fit (i.e. less well adapted to the environment) than another. But if the environment changes, these 'mistakes' may actually offer a survival advantage, thus increasing fitness. The 'survival of errors' and their recombination in every generation makes it possible for several of these errors to combine into a specialized fitness in part of the old environment, or even a fitness allowing life in a new environment. The mutation rate of organisms seems to be matched to the long-term success of co-evolving systems. The greater the rate of change in the environment, the more important variation becomes. As Ronald Fisher, one of the founding fathers of the mathematical theory of biological populations, formulated in 1930: 'The increase in fitness at a given time is proportional to the variance of fitness at that time.'[30] This means that to streamline evolution through the application of biotechnology is to hamper evolution. It also means that a galloping innovation rate combined with a perfectionist concept of monocultures is in principle unsustainable in evolutionary terms. And – in a sense – we all live under evolutionary terms.

The rise of 'fitness' from 'errors' is unpredictable and surprising. Who amongst us – if we had lived in the cretaceous period – would have bet on the evolutionary success of dwarfish dinosaurs with bones full of holes, fluffy scales and a strange tendency to flap their front extremities? More likely we would have bet on the success of ever-larger dinosaurs with thicker scales and more teeth. We would thus have dismissed the major evolutionary breakthrough of birds. If we plan to make future evolution dependent on our betting behaviour we need to know much more about evolution than is considered by departments of molecular biology or by multinational companies.

Barriers and limits create the free spaces which are a necessary precondition for the creative unfolding of diversity. The role of geographical, biochemical and behavioural barriers in differentiation, complexity, and co-operation and in the buffering of destabilizing rates of change[31,32] has been largely underestimated and neglected in the dominant scientific, political and economic debate. The present unprecedented rate of genetic erosion is probably largely due to the destruction of those barriers. 'Globally successful' products of genetic engineering will continue this trend. Unfortunately, the huge research and development costs of these products probably makes global successes economically necessary.

Genetic engineering overcomes the barriers between species. It should not be forgotten, however, that the active genetic separation of life-forms into species proved to be an overwhelming evolutionary success. Genetic engineering is proud of overcoming the species barrier: it is 'scrambling nature's algorithm'.[33] Is there nobody who ponders the evolutionary meaning of species barriers before celebrating their abolition? One function of the barrier, at least, seems to be evident. The ability of higher organisms to control their very fit and evolutionarily versatile pathogens seems to depend on species barriers. Even before the advent of gene technology, pathogens which jump species barriers were an extremely unpleasant prospect. This prospect may grow to be even more unpleasant if pathogens are offered genetically engineered trans-specific evolutionary highways.

The success of co-evolving contextual living systems depends on their ability to be error-prone and error-resilient at the same time. This allows them to make a highly creative and co-operative use of errors. For this combination I use the term 'error-friendliness' or 'errophilia.[34,35]' In Darwinian 'fitness' we have the history of past survival. In 'error-friendliness' we have the orientation towards the future. Fitness and error-friendliness could be called the two complementary legs of evolution. Their successful co-operation allows evolution to continue. Error-friendliness needs high genetic variance, a rate of change that is constantly kept below the 'critical speed of innovation',[36] and, last but not least, it needs a sufficient protection by barriers.

Let us sum up. Genetic engineering advertises its ability to increase the speed of innovation. It advertises its higher selective potential and precision. This focus makes easy access to 'clean', deep-frozen biological material highly desirable. The contextual regeneration of biodiversity in forest and field, on the other hand, is of no prime concern in the selective context. Banishment from ecosystems and being canned in deep-freezes as raw materials for biotechnology is the probable future for many species. Last, but not least, biotechnology prides itself on the removal of species barriers. If we compare the self-portrait of genetic engineering with a suitable framework for the further evolution of biodiversity we have to face the fact that the very successes of modern biotechnology might prove to be its most dangerous feature.

The conflicts about basic biological assumptions on evolution are conflicts about the historiography of nature. Orwell pointed out that he who has the power to write and rewrite history has totalitarian control. A reduction of evolution theory down to the level of flat Social Darwinism legitimizes and supports a shift in the social and political structures towards those areas in our society which are selection-orientated, not diversity-orientated.

A closer look at the new verbal Siamese twins of 'biodiversity' and 'biotechnology' has shown that biotechnology may well be a fox in charge of the chicken coop of biodiversity. Foxes undoubtedly love chickens. Foxes have certain types of expert knowledge about chickens. Foxes genuinely believe in the importance of monitoring and accessing chicken coops. Foxes may even have clever policies for the promotion of their public acceptance. Still, one should think again: all this does not predestine foxes to be good guardians for chickens.

References

1. Vandana Shiva analysed this historical shift and coined this expression.
2. E.g., the Research Proposal to the Council of the European Union entitled *Predictive Medicine: Analysis of the Human Genome*, Document of the Council No. 7929/88.
3. The Protestant Churches in Germany had established a Working Group on Genetic Engineering, whose report pays special attention to the analysis of the changes in the political and financial framework and in the organization of scientific structures. See: Kapitel II.1: Veränderungen in den Voraussetzungen und Rahmenbedingungen für Forschung, Technik und ihre öffentliche Kontrolle. In: *Einverständnis mit der Schöpfung. Ein Beitrag zur ethischen Urteilsbildung im Blick auf die Gentechnik*, Gütersloh, 1991, S. 29–39.

4. Schneidewind, U. (1994) York Lunau: Von Akzeptanzsicherung über Gefährdungsbegrenzung zu 'Globalregionalität für die Umwelt'. In: GAIA 3 No. 6, S. 311–314.

5. Eurich, C. (1995) Die Megamaschine. Darmstadt, Luchterhand, 1988. S 54 ff.

6. Philip J Regal: Critical issues in Biotechnology. In: *Third World Resurgence No. 53/54*, Penang, p. 33.

7. Taken from a collection of notes that I made on numerous panels on biotechnology.

8. Häfele, W. (1974) Hypotheticality and the New Challenges: the Pathfinder Role of Nuclear Energy. *Minerva, Vol. XII*, p. 401.

9. Ibid.

10. Wills, P.R. (1994) *The ecological hazards of transgenic varieties – Scrambling Nature's Algorithm*. Paper presented at the International Conference on Redefining the Life Sciences, Penang, Malaysia, 7–10 July. Forthcoming publication by Third World Network, Penang.

11. Burns, T.R. and Ueberhorst, R. (1988) *Creative Democracy. Systematic Conflict Resolution and Policymaking in a World of High Science and Technology*. New York, Greenwood Press.

12. Lesser, W.H. and Krattiger, A.F. (1994) Marketing 'Genetic Technologies' in South-North and South-South Exchanges: The Proposed Role of a Facilitating Mechanism. In: *Widening Perspectives on Biodiversity* (Krattiger *et al.* eds) IUCN & International Academy of the Environment. Geneva, 1994. The authors (representatives of the Agency for the Acquisition of Agri-Biotech Projects) were the core team of a series of round tables in Latin America, in Asia and in Africa organized by the Stockholm Environment Insitute in collaboration with the International Academy of the Environment which took place in 1994.

13. Report on Chapter 16 of Agenda 21: E/CN.17/1995/20.

14. Draft Proposal on a 'Special Programme for Biosciences and -technologies' submitted by the EU Commission to the President of the Council of the European Union on March 30, 1994. Document of the Council of the European Union No. 6277/94. Quoted on page 30 of Drucksache 431/94 of the Report of the German Government to the Bundesrat (Federal Council).

15. Report of the United Nations Industrial Development Organization (UNIDO) prepared for the Discussion on Chapter 16 of Agenda 21: Malee Suwana-adth and Virginia W. Campbell (Technology Promotion Section, Technology Service, Investment and Technology Promotion Division): *Financing Biotechnology for Sustainable Development*. January 1995, pp. 10–11.

16. E.g. Eghziabher, T. *et al.* (1995) The Need for Greater Regulation and Control of Genetic Engineering. A Statement of Scientists Concerned about Current Trends in the New Biotechnology. Penang, Malaysia: Third World Network, April.

17. von Weizsäcker, C (1992) *The Use and Abuse of Biodiversity*. A Feature from NGONET in Rio (Environment and Development Information for Non-Governmental Organisations), Montevideo 11000, Uruguay: NGONET.
18. von Weizsäcker, C. (1995) Gentechnik und Artenvielfalt. Eine schwierige Beziehung, die als ideale Partnerschaft gelten möchte. In: Jürgen Worters (ed.): Leben and Leben lassen. *Biodiversität – Ökonomie, Natur und Kulturschutz im Widerstreit*. focus: ökozid 10. Giessen: pp. 53–68.
19. von Weizsäcker, C. (1995) Biodiverse versus cognostic knowledge. In: *Research for Development. Sarec 20 Years*. Stockholm, pp. 91–103.
20. Daly, H.E. and Cobb, J.B. Jr (1989) *For the Common Good. Redirecting Economy toward Community, the Environment and a Sustainable Future*, Boston, Beacon Press.
21. Document UNEP/CBD/COP/2/CW/L.22
22. Document UNEP/CBD/COP/2/CW/L.24
23. Document UNEP/CBD/COP/2/CW/L.8/Rev.1
24. Document UNEP/CBD/COP/2/CW/L.25
25. See page 100 of this book
26. Wilson, E.O. (1992) *The Diversity of Life*. National Academy Press.
27. von Weizsäcker, C. (1993) Competing Notions of Biodiversity. In: Wolfgang Sachs (ed.): *Global Ecology. A New Arena of Political Conflict*. London: ZED Books, pp. 117–131.
28. Quoted from: M.S. Swaminathan, 'Genetic Conservation: Microbes to Man' at the 100th Anniversary of Academician N.I. Vavilov, Moscow, Nov. 1987, p. 1.
29. *The Global 2000 Report to the President – Entering the Twenty-first Century*, Harmondsworth, Penguin, 1980, p. 329.
30. Fisher, R. (1930) *The Genetical Theory of Natural Selection*, Oxford, p. 35.
31. Gould, S.J. (1980) Is a new and general theory of evolution emerging?' *Paleobiology 6*.
32. Biodiversity: There's a Reason for It. Short Report on the Ecotron-Experiments at the Imperial College, London, Centre for Population Biology, Project Leader: Shahid Naeem. In: *Science, Vol. 262*, 3 December 1993, p. 1511.
33. Wills, P.R. (1994) The ecological hazards of transgenic varieties – Scrambling Nature's Algorithm. *op. cit.*
34. von Weizsäcker, E. and von Weizsäcker, C. (1987) How to Live with Errors? On the Evolutionary Power of Errors. In: *World Futures: The Journal of General Evolution*/Ervin Laszlo (ed.), *Vol. 23/No. 3*, pp. 225–235. New York London Paris: Gordon and Breach.
35. von Weizsäcker, C. (1990) Error-friendliness and the Evolutionary Impact of Deliberate Releases of GMOs. In: Vandana Shiva and Ingunn Moser (eds.): *Biopolitics. A Feminist and Ecological Reader on Biotechnology*. London, Zed Books, 1995, pp. 112–120. Reprint of article

first publiched in: Leskien, Dan/Spangenberg, Joachim (eds.): European Workshop on Law and Genetic Engineering – Proceedings, S. 42–46. Bonn: BBU Verlag GmbH (Prinz-Albert-Str.43, 53 Bonn 1).

36. von Weizsäcker, C. (1993) Einführungsvortrag. In: *Bericht der parlamentarischen Enquête-Kommission betreffend 'Technikfolgenabschätzung am Beispiel der Gentechnologie' – Gutachten und Stellungnahmen, Band 3*, S.44, Wien: Österreichischer Nationalrat,.

3 THE POWER AND THE GLORY

3.1. The gene – that obscure object of desire

REGINE KOLLEK

What are genes?

Genetic engineering enables us to isolate and analyse the hereditary material from any living thing. Genes can be cut and pasted into the genetic material in the cells of any other organism which then expresses the new characteristics of the artificially transplanted genes. For instance, a gene from a flounder fish conferring resistance to cold has been transplanted into a tomato to make it frost-resistant. Cells, plants or animals modified in this way are termed *transgenic*.

This new-found ability to manipulate genetic material has great potential for commercial exploitation, since genes play a critical role in providing a blueprint for particular products or characteristics. The ability to patent individual genes is regarded as being vital to the exploitation of their commercial potential. But that is not as easy as it sounds, since the gene seems to be becoming an increasingly elusive and slippery entity to define.

Johannsen introduced the concept of the gene as the carrier of hereditary material, in 1909. In the early 1940s, Beadle and Tatum

postulated that each gene codes for one characteristic. Not long after, deoxyribonucleic acid (DNA) was identified as the complex molecule that acts as the vehicle for transmitting hereditary characteristics from one generation to the next. Genes were thought to consist of linear and continuous DNA segments coding for particular gene products. Genes were understood in two ways: in *structural* terms as DNA segments, and in *functional* terms in relation to the gene product, a protein, that they coded for.

This clear and simple model did not survive for long; over the last forty years the picture has become more complicated. It is now known that in addition to the structural genes identified initially, there are also regulatory genes which do not code for specific products but regulate and modify the action of structural genes. In addition, some genes, known as pseudogenes, are never actively translated into gene products, but are simply passed on passively to posterity. In the 1960s, repetitive sequences were recognized. The function of these short identical DNA sequences which recur frequently within the genome still remains a mystery. And in the 1970s it became apparent that even structural genes are not translated directly into products. Instead the active parts of the gene are separated by inactive chunks (introns) which are excised prior to translation.

Moreover, wandering DNA sequences known as transposons or 'jumping genes' have been found to have the ability to replicate themselves independently of the genome. If a transposon then 'jumps' to a different location in the genome, it can produce a different effect, such as changing the colour of maize.

The icing on the cake was the discovery that matching strands of the double helix making up the DNA molecule can code for different products. For example, one strand of a particular DNA molecule in the rat codes for a hormone produced in the brain, while the other strand codes for a chemical found in the heart.[1] It had previously been believed that the sole function of the second strand of DNA was to ensure that the gene is correctly duplicated during cell division.

Thus the gene is now very hard to define. It cannot be conceived as a separate structural entity, since sequence overlaps can occur both on the same DNA strand and on the opposite one. It is not a continuous sequence and does not necessarily have a constant location in the chromosome. Nor does it have a unique and discrete function, since it may depend on the activity of one or more regulatory genes. Moreover, genes with the same function do not necessarily share the same structure, and genes with an identical structure do not always have the same function.

The gene, therefore, is not an easily identifiable and tangible object. It is more a mental construct which has been shaped by history and a great deal of intellectual effort. It is virtually impossible to develop a clear, empirical definition of a gene. This is why the gene concept is burdened at every turn with the ballast of myriad unresolved problems, which are often lost in the attempt to establish a universal definition, or are swept under the carpet by superficial textbook formulations.

From genotype to phenotype

The genotype refers to the structure of an organism's genetic information. The phenotype is the outward manifestation of the genotype (such as eye colour or tail length).

Scientists generally regard a gene as a known quantity when its DNA sequence has been decoded and the function of the gene product has been described. It is generally assumed that when such a gene is transplanted into a different organism it will perform the same function as in its parent organism or will not be active at all. But there is growing evidence that the relationship is not as simple as that, as the following example illustrates.

Since many life forms share early parts of their evolutionary history, similar or identical DNA sequences are often found among a wide variety of organisms. Many of these perform identical or similar functions in a range of different cells and organisms. However, this is not always the case. For example, the gene for a particular protein, called isomerase, occurs in bacteria, yeasts, insects and mammals. In spite of their broadly similar structural and biochemical properties, the proteins perform completely different functions in the various species. In the fruit fly isomerase is involved in vision, while in mammals it regulates the maturation of immune cells.[2]

This example demonstrates that it is not just a gene's sequence which determines its properties, but that its location in its chromosomal, cellular, physiological and evolutionary context also plays a significant role. Position effects of this kind can influence the concentration of a gene product in the cell, or a gene's activation timeframe. It is know that structurally identical genes located on different chromosomes are capable of being triggered at different stages of embryo growth.[3] A particular gene's activity can also be determined by whether it is inherited through the mother or the father.[4]

According to Barbara McClintock, who first discovered jumping genes in maize, gene functioning is 'totally dependent on the environment in which they find themselves'[5]. The functioning of a gene is determined not only by the structure, but by the interplay of a large number of factors which need to maintain a specific relationship with each other. So it is only possible to make precise descriptions of the purpose of a specific DNA segment in a specific organism in relation to a specific constellation of biological and genetic factors.

Different concepts of the gene – different maxims for action

There is a trend in basic research and theoretical debate towards a partial dissolution of the traditional concept of the gene. However, this more fluid approach is not reflected by those concerned with the practical application of experimental findings. Here there are several different schools of thought which place varying emphases on different aspects of the relationship between genes and their environment. These varying perceptions can produce diverging responses to genetic engineering and the patenting of genes or transgenic organisms. The dominant viewpoints are:

(A) Genetic determinism
DNA is seen as carrying all the essential information that an organism needs to live fully. Less radical variants admit that the environment can play a part as well. But the fundamental starting point is that these environmental factors – like genes – can be considered in isolation and can have unambiguous and measurable effects. Because each contributing factor can be isolated and defined, manipulation of genes and organisms is seen as both logical and justifiable. From this standpoint, the organism is seen as a machine, and its physiology as little different from a series of industrial processes. Thus it follows that the patentability of genes and other genetic material is also both rational and acceptable.

One variation of this argument also accepts that hereditary material is the central component and control agency of the organism. However, a different value is attached to this fact than in the previous case. Since genes are the essence of life, it is seen as injurious to the integrity and dignity of the individual concerned to manipulate or patent its life source. While this and the previous view come to antagonistic conclusions about the legitimacy of genetic engineering and patenting, they both exaggerate the role of DNA in life processes, and sanctify it.

(B) The systems view
Genes are seen as an essential, but not the only, determining factor in the control of development processes. According to the developmental biologist H. F. Nihout, 'In a system in which every component and past history have come together at the right time and in the right

72

proportions, it is difficult to assign control to any one variable, even though one may have a disproportionate effect.'[6]

Nihout sees the control of development as being spread diffusely between gene products and structural elements of the surrounding tissues. Genes are passive material sources which a cell can call on when it has a need; they are not the control centre for the cell or organism. Nihout thus proposes a switch from a 'gene-centred' approach to an 'interacting components' model. Proponents of the systems approach see the development and maintenance of physiological functions as controlled by the whole organism, in an interconnected rather than hierarchical way.[7]

From the viewpoint of the systems approach, the deliberate and targeted manipulation of complex traits is extemely difficult, given that it is almost impossible to predict the synergistic effects which could be triggered between different components. Nevertheless, this position does not exclude the possibility that functions could be corrected by trial and error in certain straightforward cases.

Arguments against the use of genes in isolation (which is the basis of their commercial exploitation) or against gene patenting do not arise from this perspective. From the systems perspective, such arguments arise less from ethical posturing than from the pragmatics of such undertakings.

(C) Scientific constructivism

The constructivist view starts from the assumption that scientific activity (the development of hypotheses and theories coupled with experimentation) is fundamentally an act of construction. The intellectual and material products of science are the direct result of the assumptions and/or methods used to produce them. Any role which is assigned to hereditary material is seen as an artificial construct determined not only by the inherent properties of the object of investigation, but also by the premisses and conditions required to undertake such investigation.

This means that the manipulation of genetic material has nothing to do with the 'essence' of an organism, and is consequently not subject to any moral qualification. 'Genes' are seen as creations of the human mind and represent scientific 'inventions' against whose patenting there can be no objection, at least not within the logic of this line of argument.

Positions along these lines are added to the scientific debate by Donna Haraway, amongst others. Her 'Manifesto for Cyborgs' only half-jokingly calls on women, in particular, to contribute to the cultural and material construction of their own bodies and not to leave the process entirely to male scientists.[8]

Implications for the debate on gene patenting

All three attempts to explain the role of the gene are subject to ethical-moral and political pitfalls. Over-emphasizing the role of the gene creates the danger of genetic determinism, and some expressions of the radical rejection of genetic engineering are guilty of this. The systems approach inevitably raises the question of why genes should be treated differently from any other cell components. It suggests that genes should be given no more significance than any other substances isolated from plant or animal cells, and should therefore be freely available for patenting and manipulation. Adopting the constructivist approach makes the debate on whether genes have been 'found' or 'invented' unsustainable, since all phenomena emanating from scientific experimentation are perceived to be ultimately 'manufactured'.

What wisdom can we draw from this debate? Does the fact that the gene is so hard to pin down as a scientific object have any relevance for the patent debate? Is it not much more important to concentrate on the economic and social consequences that will flow from the extension of patent protection to genetic material and living organisms? While the last question is crucial to any political and ethical evaluation of regulatory regimes being drawn up for patents, the problem of defining the gene does raise some urgent and relevant questions. These relate primarily to the definition of the object or process which a patent is intended to protect.

The first step in the manufacture of transgenic cells or organisms is to select and isolate the DNA sequence whose coding information one intends to exploit and patent. The standard practice is not to use the structure as it exists in the organism, but to excise the introns and use only the area that codes for a particular protein. It is also general practice to use the gene of a single individual. However, not every gene is present in an identical form in different individuals. Gene sequences can vary somewhat without changing the characteristics of the derived gene product. These alternative forms of the same gene are known as *alleles* and occur at varying frequencies in different populations.

The so-called CTFR gene, whose mutation can lead to cystic fibrosis, for example, has more than 400 variants. Only very few are involved in causing the serious form of the illness. Alongside the variants that are found in those obviously suffering from the disease are others which do not have pathogenic effects. These are found in Northern, Central and Western Europe, and in varying frequencies in the USA.[9]

As a rule, only a single variant is used to create a transgenic cell in order to synthesize larger quantities of the gene or gene product; this is registered as a prototype under the patenting procedure. Consequently, patent protection can apply only to this specific variant and not to any 'gene', however it is defined.

Different alleles can vary not only in terms of their structure, but also their effect on the organism. Some CTFR alleles may be able transmit improved resistance to cholera.[10] Does a patent holder also inherit an automatic right to exploit such multiple properties of a gene or its alleles, even though the original patent application made no mention of them? Does the same scenario apply to other – as yet undiscovered – functions of the DNA sequence concerned, which might never come to light unless the sequence is implanted into a new host organism?

If every allele and every synthetic construction differs both structurally and functionally, then each patentable invention can only relate to a particular set of conditions within which a DNA sequence is made exploitable, and not to the DNA sequence itself. With this insight, the current trend towards awarding extremely broad patent protection for genes and their exploitation (see p. 89) is both dubious and absurd.

Until now, the debate within the scientific community over the patentability of genetically engineered products has paid scant attention to certain fundamental problems of definition. An explanation for this fact lies in the highly pragmatic nature of patent law procedures, which do not follow the logic of scientific argumentation but focus on the needs of the market and the commercial interests of inventors. Nevertheless, defining the object of the patent remains a problem which patent law will have great difficulty circumventing in the long term.

A framework of rules to resolve this issue will need to respect the interests not only of commercial users but also of scientists who fear that the patenting of genes will hinder their work. However, disputes over special interests must not take precedence over the principle that, however expressed, the new regime must not injure human dignity and must not denigrate other creatures as merely the servants of humankind's inventions.

References

1. Adelman, J.P., Bond, C.T. *et al.* (1987). 'Two mammalian genes transcribed from opposite strands of the same DNA locus', in: *Science* **235**, 1514–1517.
2. Fischer, G., Wittman-Liebold *et al.* (1989). 'Cyclophilin and peptidyl-prolyl cis-trans isomerase are probably identical proteins', in: *Nature* **337**, 476–478. Shieh, B.H., Stannes, M. *et al.* (1989) The ninA gene

required for visual transduction in drosophila encodes a homologue of cyclosporin A-binding protein', in: *Nature* **338**, 67–70. Takahashi, N., Hayano, T., Suzuki, M. (1989) 'Peptidyl-prolyl cis-trans isomerase is the cyclosporin A-binding protein cyclophilin', in: *Nature* 337, 473–475.

3. Bonnerot, C., Grimber, G. *et al.* (1990) 'Patterns of expression of position-dependent integrated transgenes in mouse embryos', in: *Proceedings of the National Academy of Sciences* **87**, 6331–6335.
4. Howlett, R. (1994) 'Taking stock in Stockholm', in: *Nature* 370, 178–179.
5. Quoted in Evelyn Fox Keller (1986). *Love, power and learning (Liebe, Macht und Erkenntis)*, Hanser: Munich, p 179.
6. Nihout, H.F. (1990). 'Metaphors and the role of genes in development', in: *BioEssays* **12** (9), 441–446.
7. See, for example, Strohman, R. (1994). 'Epigenesis: the missing beat in biotechnology', in *Bio/Technology* **12**, 156–164.
8. Haraway, D. (1985). 'A manifesto for Cyborgs: science, technology and socialist feminism in the 1980s'. In: *Socialist Review* **15** (2): 65–108.
9. Dörk, T., Schlösser, *et al.* (1991). 'Gene mutation analysis in German cystic fibrosis patients' (Mutationsamalyse bei deutschen CF-patienten) in: *Medizinische Genetik* Vol 3, 24–26.
10. Rodman, D.M., Yamudio, S. (1990). 'The cystic fibrosis heterozygote – advantage in surviving cholera?' in: *Medical Hypotheses* **36**, 253–258. Gabriel, S.E., Brigman, K.N. *et al.* (1994) 'Cystic fibrosis heterozygote resistance to cholera toxin in the cystic fibrosis mouse model', in: *Science* **266**, 107–109.

3.2. Patenting life – trends in the US and Europe

CHRISTINE NOIVILLE

It is very unusual for patent law to hit the news headlines. But that is exactly what has happened since intellectual property rights have been extended to the products of biotechnology and the patenting of life became a reality in Europe and the USA. Before discussing the implications of these developments, it is important to outline briefly what biotechnologies are, what patent law is and how these two subjects relate to biodiversity (Box 3.1).

A patent is a legal mechanism for offering a temporary monopoly of rights to any person presenting an invention that satisfies certain conditions. To qualify for protection, the invention must be:

- *novel* – original and not already known. In most countries (except the USA) the patent is awarded to the first person to apply, whether or not this person was the first to invent.

- *non-obvious* – not obvious to a person skilled in the technology, and requiring some degree of innovation to distinguish it from mere discovery.

- *useful* – it must have industrial application. Ideas and theories are not enough to warrant a patent.

The purpose of patents is to encourage technical innovation and progress by rewarding the inventor. A patent can be awarded for products *per se*, a specific use for a product, processes (rather than the product made by the process) and products made by a specific process.

From these principles, the connections between patents, biotechnology and biological diversity unfold. The building blocks of biological diversity are genes, which also represent the raw materials for biotechnology. When genes or cells are isolated from the natural environment or transformed by biotechnology, they can be considered as inventions and protected by patents.

Patents on life

Legal protection of biotechnological inventions has evolved in a climate of protest. Most of the objections to the patenting of life have questioned the 'utility' criterion required for a patent to be issued and the impact this could have on biological diversity. Many fear that ecosystems will come to be regarded merely as reservoirs of genetic resources protected by patents. Others have concerns about ethics, seeing the patenting of life-forms as appropriating the work of nature, envisioning abuse of the power to transform life as we know it, or simply as a desecration of life (see p 144).

Other objections are guided by ecological considerations. Patenting life could risk damaging biological diversity, not only because of the exploitation of the elements of this diversity, but also because it results in the creation of totally new organisms. Their release into the environment could provoke serious ecological disruptions, further endangering biodiversity. Finally, patenting leads to privatization of the elements of diversity, which could conflict with their sustainable use.

Patent law is seen by patent specialists as being neutral because it has no direct impact on biological diversity. Applying for a patent for

Box 3.1: Intellectual property rights – an introduction

'Intellectual property rights' refers to a bag of tools which can be used to protect an individual's knowledge. They are designed to promote and protect innovation, by allowing the 'owner' of the knowledge to have a monopoly of use over his or her invention for a specified period of time. It is only during the last 100 years that they have been applied to any great extent. Prior to that, there was considerable resistance to allowing such systems to develop, as common ownership of knowledge, products and materials was considered critical to sustaining society. Such systems were often seen as inappropriate and almost blasphemous. Today, this attitude is still sustained among many indigenous communities, but the general trend worldwide is towards privatizing knowledge through the IPR system. A brief chronology of the patent debate in the North is shown below.

A brief chronology of the patent debate in the North

7th century BC	Greeks permit a 1-year monopoly over cooking recipes
1474	First Patent Law established (Venice)
1623	Statute of Monopolies creates patent provisions for England
1790	First US Patent Act passed in compliance with American Constitution
1790–1850	Industrial patent laws established in many European states
1850–1873	Patent laws revoked or monopoly restricted in several European states
1873	Patent Congress at the Vienna World's Fair adopts compulsory licence compromise to overcome opposition to the industrial patent system
1883	A global patent system is established in the Paris Union
1900	Paris Union is amended and strengthened at Brussels meeting
1911	Paris Union is strengthened again at Washington meeting
1922	Germany accepts a process patent on a bacterium and a meeting of patent lawyers in London moots the possibility of protection for plant varieties
1925	Paris Union is amended and strengthened again in The Hague
1930	United States adopts the Plant Patent Act for fruits and ornamentals
1934	Paris Union is strengthened at its London meeting and definition of patentable material is extended to include flowers and flour
1961	Union for the Protection of New Varieties of Plants (UPOV) is established at Paris meeting
1969	Germany accepts process patents for the breeding of animals
1970	Patent Co-operation Treaty approved by 35 countries at Washington meeting
1972	UPOV Convention is modified and strengthened
1978	UPOV Convention strengthened again
1980	US Supreme Court accepts the patenting of micro-organisms
1987	US Patent Office expresses willingness to consider patents on animals
1991	UPOV Convention strengthened to, among other things, stop farmers from replanting protected varieties
1992	'Species' patent granted in the United States on genetically modified cotton

1993	US Government applies for patent rights over human cell lines of citizens of Panama, Papua New Guinea, and the Solomon Islands
1993	GATT agreement includes stipulation that all signatory states must have an IP system for plant varieties and for micro-organisms
1994	Second 'species' patent granted in Europe on the soybean crop – the first time a species patent is granted on a food crop
1995	European Parliament voted against the EC Directive on the legal Protection of Biotechnological Inventions which would have required all EC Member States to adopt the principle of patenting living organisms.

Source: *People, Plants and Patents*, IRDC, Ottawa, 1994

The trend began in the US and Europe in response to the development of the market economy. Over the last century, the combination of economic development and international trade brought new goods and ideas into a rapidly expanding network of exchange. The producers of these innovations sought instruments to realize the great economic gains that could be gleaned from them. Legal instruments were consequently drawn up that gave the owner a monopoly control over his or her invention preventing anyone else from copying, selling or applying the product without his or her authorization.

The trend towards intellectual property rights systems is driven by the belief in industrialized countries that IPRs drive innovation and technical progress. Many Southern countries dispute this. These fundamentally opposing views arise from the different positions countries find themselves in, primarily as exporters or importers of technology. IPRs favour more technologically advanced countries over those just embarking on technology development.

Developing countries, whether the US in the last century or Thailand today, have developed most quickly when they are able to tap human knowledge in an unrestricted manner. Their legal instruments have been designed to support this need. Historically, once these countries have established their own technology base, they often demand of less developed countries the restrictions that would have made their own progress impossible.

Patents do not themselves preclude access to innovations; rather, they permit the innovator to charge royalties to users of the innovation. This inevitably precludes access to those who cannot afford to pay. In practice, therefore, IPR systems tend to be scale-biased in favour of the large and powerful against the small and vulnerable. They control and therefore often stifle innovation and award power over technological development to the enterprises with the best funding and legal support.

IPRs consist of a bundle of mechanisms including patents, copyright, trade secrets and plant breeders' rights. These different forms of IPRs offer varying degrees of protection, and are often referred to as 'hard' and 'soft' forms accordingly. Patents offer the strongest protection and are increasingly favoured as the IPR of choice, particularly by industrialized countries.

a genetically modified plant does not guarantee exploitation of the plant by, for instance, cultivating it in a field or selling it on the market. It simply guarantees a monopoly of rights. It is up to the legislator to determine whether the exploitation of a plant is dangerous or unacceptable, and to prohibit or limit its use accordingly. Intellectual property rights experts have always considered patent law to be a technical law protecting and stimulating industrial development, and that it is not their responsibility to consider ethical or environmental questions. This is seen as the remit of other branches of law.

This is the context in which most of the patents affecting biological diversity have been issued. So long as the claims have been shown to fulfil the technical requirements for protection, they have been granted. To do this, it has often been necessary to modify the traditional criteria for patentability because they are poorly adapted to deal with living things.

Many of the patents on life granted so far are not inventive in the sense traditionally required by patent law, and could be considered to be discoveries. In both Europe and the US, this obstacle was overcome by considering the gene or micro-organism in question not to be an exact *replica* of that which exists in nature, but merely a *reflection* of it. It was deemed that the human intervention to isolate, purify and reveal its function takes the claim beyond mere discovery. It is this particular bias in interpretation that has opened up the patenting arena to living organisms.

The US vs Europe

Initially, legal traditions in the US and Europe challenged the patenting of living organisms, because of concern over the question of discovery or invention. Patents were created for inventions of inert products like sewing machines, and living systems did not easily fit the model. For a long time, the contribution of nature was considered more important than the human intervention leading to the discovery, identification, isolation and transformation of its components.

However, at the end of the 1970s a US judge granted a patent on a genetically modified micro-organism, reversing this position. In doing so, he abolished once and for all the boundary between the inert and the living, regarding the micro-organism more as a factory for chemicals than as a living being. Patenting micro-organisms leads fairly logically to patenting human cells, genes, whole animals and even higher beings. It is now possible to envisage a scenario in which everything that is useful to humanity could become the subject of a patent.

In Europe, the administration charged with issuing patents, the European Patent Office (EPO), lagged a few years behind the US in

Box 3.2: Intellectual property rights and the biodiversity debate

The question of ownership has become the thorniest and most politicized subject in the debate on the conservation of biodiversity. There are three main reasons for this. The first is simply the global explosion of technology with a high intellectual property (IP) content (things like books, chemicals and electronics) and the increasing importance given to technology by society. Biotechnology is only one of a number of technical fields producing such goods that is expanding and progressing rapidly. The second reason is the recent expansion of the GATT agreement to include intellectual property. And the third is the heated debate on IP issues in the Biodiversity Convention. These last two issues require more in-depth treatment.

GATT and biodiversity

IP became a trade issue with the launch of the Uruguay Round of GATT, which was charged with formulating minimum levels of protection for IP. This move came at the request of industrialized countries (which, as technology exporters, stand to gain from such regulation). It was argued that the absence of patent protection in some countries could set up non-tariff barriers to traded goods, hindering the free flow of trade espoused by the GATT. US negotiators at the talks maintained that patent and copyright piracy by developing countries results in a loss to US industry of somewhere between $43 and $60 billion.[1] However, they seemed to forget that losses from the developing countries are far greater. For instance, worldwide sales in pharmaceuticals in 1990 yielded $32 000 million, of which developing countries received only $551 million, despite the fact that they provided many of the raw materials and a substantial part of the knowledge[2].

Thus the latest GATT agreement contains 73 articles on Trade-Related Intellectual Property (TRIPS). Once ratified, signatory states are obliged to adopt a patent system for micro-organisms and to 'provide for the protection of plant varieties by patents or by an effective *sui generis* system' (Article 27:3b). In TRIPS, governments are left to choose whether or not to patent animals.

A *sui generis* approach could mean the adoption of other recognized IPR systems, such as Plant Breeders' Rights (p 168) or the UNESCO–WIPO Model Provisions on Folklore (p 170). But *theoretically* it could also offer a wider range of policy choices, including any arrangements that offer recognition to innovators – with or without monetary compensation or monopoly control. In practice, there is likely to be huge resistance to any such moves. This interpretation of what constitues an *effective sui generis* system provides the new legal framework within which future international battles on IPR will be fought.

Article 27:2 in the new GATT agreement allows countries to exclude from patentability any inventions whose applications are seen to cause 'serious prejudice to the environment'. To the extent that IPR on plants could adversely affect plant genetic diversity by accelerating genetic erosion, this clause may enable countries to restrict or avoid patent protection on plants. However, given the intricate and complex nature of this inter-relationship, it may be difficult to prove causation in court.

IPRs in the Biodiversity Convention

The Convention is very weak in dealing with the issues of ownership and rights, and takes up contradictory positions in different parts of the document. Article 16 (on access and transfer of technology) reflects an uneasy consensus in its final text, leaving the whole question open to interpretation:

> In the case of technology subject to patents and other intellectual property rights, such access and technology shall be provided on terms which recognize and are consistent with the adequate and effective protection of intellectual property rights

Like the potential loop hole in the GATT–TRIPS agreement, the Convention calls for '*effective* protection of IPRs'. The question is, who judges effectiveness? Southern signatories fear that they will be pushed into accepting a Northern-based IPR system, not necessarily in their national interests or even in the interest of biodiversity conservation. It is a fear not without grounds. The US and other Northern country signatories which are preparing interpretative statements conditional upon ratification interpret this clause as meaning a strong patent system for plants and animals. If this view is accepted, the Biodiversity Convention will become a 'fast-track GATT', taking the entrenchment of the IP system much further than GATT has.

This understanding of 'effective' protection applies only to the rights of companies, individuals and research institutions, as with the current system. If offers no effective protection for farmers, indigenous communities and many other groups.

However, at the same time the Convention does acknowledge the central contribution of indigenous and local communities to biodiversity conservation, and signatories have pledged to:

> respect, preserve and maintain knowledge, innovations, and practices of indigenous and local communities embodying traditional lifestyles relevant for the conservation and sustainable use of biological diversity and promote their wider application with the approval and involvement of the holders of such knowledge, innovations and practices and encourage the equitable sharing of the benefits arising from the utilization of such knowledge, innovations and practices.

This opens the door to farming communities claiming IPR, not only for the benefits they receive from biological resources, but for the part they play, or can play, in biodiversity conservation. However, it also gives governments priority in cases of conflict of interest between indigenous peoples' wants and conservation, which will depend on government's interpretation of conservation needs.

Given the deliberately vague and ambiguous language of the Convention, its practical translation will be moulded by future political and economic actions.

issuing patents on life. In this it has taken a new tack, quite distinct from the US approach. This move constitutes a fundamental change in the nature of patent law and the manner in which it could impact on the protection of biological diversity.

If adopted, the proposed EC Directive on the Legal Protection of Biotechnological Inventions will require all EC Member States to adopt the principle of patenting living organisms.* These would be considered patentable so long as they satisfy the traditional technical criteria for protection. This process is independent of any reflection on their utility or their ecological effects, from which patent law considers itself to be completely dissociated.

In the US, several years after granting patents on micro-organisms, patents were summarily extended to animals. The first claim was for a genetically engineered mouse used as a model for the study of cancer, the oncomouse. The patent was granted by extending the same principle of neutrality that had justified the patent on micro-organisms. The EPO, however, took a different stance. As this was the first claim for a patent on an animal, the EPO's ruling held implications for all future claims. The patent was granted, but protection was subject to certain new conditions. It is not enough for the animal to be novel, innovative and useful. It must also demonstrate some benefit to humanity, which must outweigh the harm inflicted on the animal and the environmental risks entailed.

In the case of the oncomouse, the animal obviously suffered, but the environmental risks were judged to be low because it was destined to live in a laboratory. The mouse's therapeutic potential was seen to outweigh other considerations. The ruling would probably have been different for an animal modified for some other purpose, such as a genetically engineered fish developed for more abstract scientific purposes. In this case, the fish might not suffer, but the benefits to society could be less than the ecological risks of releasing the fish into the environment.

---

* The Directive was rejected by the European Parliament on 1 March 1995, but the Directive simply aimed to harmonize the EU position – countries can still decide on an individual basis to patent living organisms.

This 'softening' of patent law by the EPO is significant. The new assessment technique, which emphasizes the utility of animals rather than just their physical attributes, seems to have been prompted by pressure from public opinion. Through this ruling, the EPO changed the traditional vision of patent law. Patent law must now judge technical progress more critically, since it reserves the right to veto a technology that presents risks to the environment. This is a major step forward because it forces the two branches of law concerned with biotechnology – patent law and environmental law – to work together. In this way, socio-political considerations can be drawn into a system that is largely economics-driven.

Limits of jurisprudence of the EPO

(A) Limiting the new conditions to claims on animals
Since one of the aims of the restrictions is to consider the risk that biotechnologies present to the environment, the conditions should be extended to plants and micro-organisms, since some of these present far greater risks to the environment than do animals.

(B) Assessing environmental risks
Environmental risk is extremely difficult to assess because of the wide range of potential impacts and possible knock-on effects (see Chapter 2.2). For example, if a salmon is given a rabbit gene, an evolutionary step is effected in the salmon species that cannot be achieved through sexual reproduction. Assessing the environmental risk of this release requires looking beyond the direct effect on the salmon species, to the complex interactions with the ecosystem into which it is released and the organisms with which it cohabits.

There is a further risk which has received little attention to date. If, as we hope, genetic manipulation leads to more rapid and effective gene selection, the existing difficulties in conserving biodiversity are likely to be exacerbated. The problems arising from the replacement of diverse races and varieties with more uniform ones is already painfully familiar, and this question should be addressed fully before taking the patenting of biotechnological innovations any further. However, this kind of risk assessment is too difficult and complex to be conducted by patent offices.

The impact of patents on the circulation and exchange of genetic resources

The most fundamental impact of extending the patent system to living organisms is that it transforms the modalities for exchange and

Table 3.1. Comparisons of main provisions of PBR under UPOV 1978 and 1991, and patent law

Provisions	UPOV 1978	UPOV 1991	Patent law
Protection coverage	Plant varieties of nationally defined species	Plant varieties of all genera and species	Inventions
Requirements	Distinctness Uniformity Stability	Novelty Distinctness Uniformity Stability	Novelty Inventiveness Nonobviousness
Protection term	Min. 15 years	Min. 20 years	17–20 years (OECD)
Protection scope	Commercial use of *reproductive material* of the variety	Commercial use of *all material* of the variety	Commercial use of protected matter
Breeders' exemption	Yes	Not for *essentially derived* varieties	No
Farmers' 'privilege'	Yes	No. Up to national laws	No
Prohibition of double protection	Any species eligible for PBR protection cannot be patented	—	—

Source: The Crucible Group: *People, Plants and Patents*, IRDC, Ottawa, 1994.

circulation of genetic material. In choosing to patent genetic material, we set out on a path of privatization, moving away from the common ownership of genetic resources. This could have huge implications for research in the formal and informal sectors, for global food security and for biodiversity conservation.

Once genetic material becomes the property of states, its collection is subject to the signing of bilateral deals between countries or between a country and a corporation. While this is certainly more equitable for the countries of origin of the resources than are the existing arrangements, it by no means guarantees access to those who need it. Conditions of access to both natural materials and protected innovations become strictly controlled.

The patent system does allow some sort of 'research exemption' which enables other innovators to use protected genetic resources for research purposes. However, unlike with Plant Breeders Rights (Table 3.1), the researcher cannot freely commercialize any invention he or she creates. For example, in order to commercialize a tomato variety created by crossing a high-yielding patented variety with a local disease-resistant variety, authorization must be gained from the holder of the patent for the high-yielding variety. There is no obligation on the patent holder to consent to this. Thus, access to genetic material is no longer absolutely guaranteed. This situation is already leading to problems and disfunctioning in research strategies.

Conclusion

I have described two opposing movements in the field of patents. On the one hand, in Europe there has been a positive effort to widen the patent brief and incorporate the considerations of environmental risk (including loss of biodiversity) into the appraisal process. On the other hand, the more general movement towards promoting bio-technologies via the patent mechanism tends to pull the process in the opposite direction.

References

1. Dullforce, W. (1990). 'EC Suggests Draft Text of Law on Intellectual Property. *Financial Times*, March 7.
2. UNDP (1994) *Conserving Indiginous Knowledge: Integrating Two Systems of Innovation*. UNDP, New York.

3.3. The changing face of patents

Most of the patents that have been granted on life forms have, at the very least, stretched the criteria required for protection, and in some cases there seem to have been outright violations of the basic criteria for awarding patents:

(a) *Patents challenging novelty* There are numerous examples of patents that have been issued to companies for products which have been used for centuries by communities in the South. The claim on the neem tree (see Box 3.3) is one clear example. Similarly, a patent granted to Lucky Biotech and the University of California for thaumatin, a natural sweetener from the berries, leaves and stalks of the Katemfe shrub, has caused dismay in West Africa, as this could lead to prohibiting some uses of the plants in the countries where they are endemic and in the communities in which they have been nurtured.[1]

Box 3.3: The neem claim

Seeds of a species of neem tree *(Azadirachta indica)* have been ground and scattered on fields by Indian farmers for centuries to protect their crops from insect pests. The tree has a multitude of other uses as well : it has therapeutic effects against malaria and intestinal worms; the leaves are used to protect grain from pests and clothes from moths; neem oil is used to make candles, soap and a contraceptive; the same oil can be used in diesel engines; and its stem is widely used as a toothbrush. Many of these discoveries were first made by members of Indian rural communities.

Two companies, W.R. Grace and Agrodyne, recently obtained patents in the US for derivatives of neem developed in their laboratories, even though the insecticidal, human non-toxic and biodegradable properties of neem in the claim are far from novel and non-obvious to millions of Indian farmers. No move has been made to limit the use of locally produced neem, but neither has there been any move to share any benefits with Indian farmers, who surely have more right to the intellectual property than the companies.

W.R. Grace is now producing neem pesticides with an Indian company in India. W.R. Grace estimates that the global market for their product may reach $50 million per annum by the year 2000.[2] Another patent has been granted in the US for an extract of neem bark effective against certain cancers. Agrodyne now has US government approval to sell neem-based bio-insecticides, and has applied for registration of its products in several European and Latin American countries.

(b) Patents challenging the inventive step   The neem and thaumatin claims are a clear challenge to the inventive step. The coloured cotton claim is another. Plant Breeders' Rights have been granted to a US breeder for strains of traditional Andean coloured cotton, which she modified through conventional plant breeding to lengthen the staple for commercial weaving. Critics maintain that the genius was not in lengthening the staple but in establishing the colour. The breeder has publicly acknowledged that Andean peoples bred the original cotton and the clothes made from it are even marketed as coming from 'the ancient peoples of the Andes'. Yet these 'ancient people', who are very much alive and living in the Andes today, will not be compensated for their contribution.

The important contribution of local peoples' knowledge to product development is not recognized in patent applications. WWF/Rautkari, Mauri)

(c) Patents challenging utility Current excitement over gene sequencing successes and competition for potential markets has led to a
spate of patent claims on genes and DNA fragments whose functions
(if any) have not yet been identified. By mid-1993 the US National
Institutes of Health (NIH) had laid claim to several thousand human
genes or DNA fragments related to the human brain. The claim challenged conventional interpretations of both the inventive step and
utility concepts. For this reason the US Patents and Trademarks Office
twice rejected the claim, but the case has caused great concern. The
NIH argued that since these fragments relate to the human brain, they
must be useful in some way. By extrapolation, a claimant could con-
tend that anything found in an ecosystem (plant, animal, microbe,
gene) must have utility and therefore be a valid subject for protection.

Under pressure from the scientific community, the new NIH administration announced that it would drop its attempt to claim intellectual
property rights over the brain. Nevertheless, lawyers who have stud-
ied the claim believe that it would be upheld. In April 1994, the US
company Incyte revealed that it had taken the NIH lead and applied
for a patent on 40 000 human genes and DNA fragments, and declared
that it would pursue its claims aggressively.[3]

If claims such as these are accepted in court, the implications for
agricultural research will be wide-reaching, as this path could lead
to monopoly control of the most important genes used in the
breeding of food crops. This 'driftnet patenting' could also impact
directly on bioprospecting since companies might be able to gather
up large quantities of flora and fauna and lay claims on them
simply because no one else has documented the existence of the
species.

(d) Driftnet patenting 'Driftnet patenting' is a catch-all, safety-net
approach to ensure that no opportunities for commercialization are
missed. Driftnet patent claims, like the NIH claim, are becoming more
and more common. Making patent claims as broad as possible leaves
options open for companies and offers more chances for economic
exploitation. There are two reasons for this – firstly that over the
course of time new applications may come to light; and secondly that
patent conditions may change.

Linda Bullard, who co-ordinates the Greens' position on genetic
engineering in the European Parliament, points out that 'the patent
system has been quietly trundling along for the last 100 years, gradually removing exclusion after exclusion without people taking too
much notice. Now it has reached the very last exclusion: that of
patents on life itself, which would make the system complete, applic-
able to everything under the sun.'

(e) Patenting human life   At present, human cells and genes removed from the body are patentable, but those attached to a living person are not. As Linda Bullard states, this is the last exclusion to remain limiting the scope of patent power. Proponents of patents argue that the existing legislation allowing the patenting of human cell lines and human genes is a totally separate issue from patenting human beings themselves, and that there is no question of this latter exclusion being removed. Opponents suggest that the dividing line between the two categories is woolly at best, and that patenting a cell line is the same as patenting an individual, because each cell contains the whole human genome. Even if there were no question of the exclusion being removed, for many people (particularly those with strong spiritual and religious beliefs or a different value system to the Western capitalist model), patenting of human genes in any form is unethical.

The issue of patenting life has become a major issue in the European Parliament. After a tortuous eight-year passage through the Parliament, the Directive on the Legal Protection of Biotechnological Inventions was voted down on 1 March 1995. The 'exclusion debate' was one of the thorniest issues to deal with, and this was probably the point that finally killed the directive. Had it been approved, the directive would have resulted in the harmonization of legislation on patenting of biotechnological inventions (including life forms) across the European Union. The directive has no direct influence on the European Patent Office, which can carry on giving patents on micro-organisms, plants, animals and human parts, just as before. But the decision may well affect the decisions made, since it reflects a shift in the climate of public opinion (see p. 185).

(f) Patents on species   In 1992 a patent was issued in the US for genetically engineered cotton. It was awarded to Agracetus, a wholly-owned subsidiary of one of the world's largest chemical companies, W.R. Grace. The sweeping claim, unless successfully challenged, gives the patent holder a monopoly over all forms of genetically engineered cotton, regardless of germplasm or technique. Agracetus could use the claim to prevent any other country from exporting genetically manipulated cotton (and maybe even finished cotton and clothing) to the US. The patent is also pending approval in Central America, China, Europe and other places.

In January 1994, a law firm in the US – representing an anonymous client – filed a request that the patent be re-examined. In June, the US Department of Agriculture, which itself conducts research on cotton, filed a similar request. Both argued that the critical inventive steps to transform cotton had already been published by other researchers before Agracetus made its patent application. In December 1994, the

'One day all this could be ours.' Agracetus' broad cotton patent would have allowed Agracetus to monopolize the world market.
(Sean Sprague/Panos Pictures)

US Patent and Trademark Office notified Agracetus that it intended to revoke both patents that the company had been awarded – a very rare step according to patent experts.[4] Agracetus was required to respond directly to the patent office, and if it was not convinced by the rebuttal, the company has recourse to appeal. Although such appeals rarely succeed, the outcome is not known at the time of writing.

The granting of this patent could profoundly influence the future of a $20 billion crop critical to the economies of many countries in the South. Some 69 developing countries produce cotton, and 250 million people are dependent on incomes from cotton production or processing. One major producer, India, took the unusual step in early 1994 of rescinding the Indian patent claim because it was seen to act against the interests of its people.

In March 1994 Agracetus received a similar species patent from the European Patent Office, this time on genetically engineered soybeans. This patent has been challenged by Rural Advancement Fund International, with the support of other NGOs around the world, on the grounds that it is neither novel or non-obvious, and because it represents a threat to world food security: monopolization of soybean technology will increase the price of seeds and hamper research into this important food crop, which is valued at $27 000 million annually, according to RAFI.

References

1. UNDP (1994). Conserving Indigenous Knowledge: Integrating Two Systems of Innovation. UNDP, New York.
2. (1993) *Ag Biotech News*, February, 4.
3. Fox, J. (1994). NIH Nixes Human DNA Patents: What Next? *Bio/Technology*, 12 (April), p348.
4. Mestel, R. (1994). Cotton Patent Left Hanging by Thread. *New Scientist* , December 17, p.4.

PART 2

The practice – bioprospecting or biopiracy?

4 GREEN GOLD

Bilateral deals drawn up between bioprospectors and the countries or communities of origin of genetic resources are becoming increasingly common as a mechanism for sharing the benefits of bioprospecting activities. The 1991 Merck–INBio agreement was the first such deal to be struck (see p. 100). It is now just one of a rapidly growing number of bioprospecting ventures. Japan has launched a major biodiversity research programme in Micronesia, the US National Institutes of Health is screening wild species for compounds active against HIV and cancer, and both Indonesia and Kenya are establishing inventory programmes similar to INBio's, and are exploring possible biodiversity prospecting activities.

Three main forces have prompted the emergence of such deals. Firstly, natural products are back in fashion for industry. Genetic and biochemical resources have long been important raw materials in agriculture and medicine, but recent technological advances in biotechology have opened up new frontiers for genetic resource use. The renewed interest in biological compounds has stimulated a search for sample material from almost the entire range of life forms, in every corner of the globe. Tropical corals are being screened for anti-inflammatory potential, soils for antibiotic activity, shark bile for anti-acne properties, and so on.

The second push has come from the growing acceptance that genetic resources are not a freely available global commodity and that equity and ethical issues must be addressed in bioprospecting activities. Over the last ten years several international agreements and treaties have forced attention to be paid to these issues. The extent to which these issues have been taken on board by policymakers is reflected in the fact that part of the Biodiversity Convention's remit is to establish a policy framework for bioprospecting activities addressing the issues of ethics and equity.

The third force is the growing recognition of the economic value of biodiversity, the threat of genetic erosion and the need for conservation globally.

The new bioprospecting deals are seen by their promoters as 'win-win-win' opportunities to address these three issues. Corporations and research institutions gain from the exploitation of biodiversity's green gold, while the countries and communities which provide the raw materials and knowledge supposedly share in the profits and are compensated for the loss of their genetic heritage. In addition, part of the compensation package is used to ensure biodiversity conservation in the host country.

There is a clear need for the regulation of bioprospecting activities given the surge in interest from the commercial sector (see Table 2.1, pp. 34–36), for environmental reasons as well as equity and ethics. In Kenya, nearly three tonnes of the widespread shrub *Maytenus buchanani*, source of the anticancer drug maytansine, was harvested as part of a screening programme undertaken by the US National Cancer Institute. When additional material was required four years after the initial harvesting, regeneration had been so poor that collectors had difficulty in obtaining it.

Bioprospecting initiatives such as the Merck–INBio deal are gaining popularity among policy makers, scientists and companies, particularly those in the North. But there is vigorous opposition from some NGOs and from indigenous communities. Their concerns range from practical conciderations about who should receive the benefits, to the ethics of commodifying life.

4.1. Equity issues in bioprospecting*

CHARLES ZERNER and KELLY KENNEDY

Biodiversity 'prospecting', under different guises and different names, has a long and complicated history linked to colonialism, the establishment of plantations and imperial botanical gardens, and the world trade in biological commodities. The term 'prospecting' itself contains the idea of a vantage point from which social, scientific, or botanical landscapes are viewed, or in anthropological discourse, are constructed. Every act of viewing or 'prospecting' in the developing world involves politics and power relations in which views of the

---

* This contribution is not intended as an exhaustive review or policy critique of the private-sector prospecting companies mentioned here. It is, rather, a brief look at some of the unanswered questions and varied institutional approaches to the issues of equity and return of benefits. All the usual disclaimers apply.

tropics, natural environments, and biodiversity, as well as of peoples and nations, are embedded. Prior to the post-World War II, post-colonial era, the flow of plant materials from gene-'rich' developing countries to gene-'poor' developed countries, especially if their commercial value was unknown or speculative, was not often the object of contentious discourse or protest. Plant materials were often treated as a free, open-access public resource, or as the property of colonial governments. Only within the past two decades has the search for wild and cultivated organisms, their genes and chemical products, and the ecological and pharmacological knowledge associated with them, been characterized as socially inequitable and, potentially, environmentally destructive.

The scene for bioprospecting in the tropics began to change dramatically during the post-colonial era as developments in screening technologies made a return to the tropics technically possible and potentially profitable. The institutional and contractual arrangements under which bioprospecting was conducted became subjects of intense contention. Debate concerning North-South inequities and uneven development, movements advocating recognition and respect for the rights of indigenous peoples and communities, and, since the 1970s, the debate on conservation and sustainable management, have all converged to highlight the controversy surrounding biodiversity prospecting. According to some critiques, it is not at all clear whether specific acts of bioprospecting, or bioprospecting in general, are acts of 'co-operation' or of 'co-optation'.

Contractual agreements are only one form of instrument, for articulating relationships between companies, nations, educational or scientific institutions, and local communities. Many recent policy pronouncements, at least by national and international environmental non-governmental groups, assume that capital- and technologically-rich, developed nations should equitably compensate the biologically-rich developing countries for access to their resources.

In this highly politicized arena, the description of several institutional and contractual arrangements offered below touches on many of the most contentious issues in the bioprospecting debate. On what legal theories and sources of law are claims to ownership or control of biological diversity justified? Will establishment of commodity values for biological organisms lead to conservation or sustainable management? What are the relationships and rights of indigenous peoples and local communities, nations, and the 'global public' to biodiversity, local territory, and local knowledge? Is making links between advocacy for local communities, conservation, and North-South equity, a practical and politically feasible objective?

Debates about biodiversity prospecting often centre on how the contractual arrangement is structured, whether it is responsive to the relevant communities, and whether it is equitable. Several key issues are embedded in discussion of how concerns for social, economic and environmental equity may be embodied in particular contractual arrangements:

○ What form should benefits take?

○ Which are the relevant communities?

○ Which institutions or actors are appropriate parties for negotiations with a 'prospector'?

○ What is the process by which benefits are determined?

Returning the benefits of the exploitation of local plants, remedies and peoples' knowledge to local communities is a vitally important but neglected step in product development. (Ron Gilling/Panos Pictures)

What form should the benefits take?

There are many forms of monetary and non-monetary options for providing immediate and longer-term benefits (see Table 4.1). The options for non-monetary benefits are numerous and can be targeted towards the needs and preferences of specific recipients, be they governmental or scientific bodies, specific communities or individuals. The most common non-monetary benefits offered are training, research exchanges, and contributions to scientific or institutional

Table 4.1. A matrix of options for return of benefits

	Immediate	Longer-term

Monetary	Supply payments
	  Per sample fee
	  Lump sum advance
	  payment
		Royalty payments
		  Based on net sales
		  Depend on contribution to
		  development of final
		  product

Non-monetary	Provision of health care Distribution of medicine Training in collection and specimen-identification techniques Contributions to institutional infrastructure	Technology transfer Research/academic exchanges Screening for tropical diseases Agreement to provide drugs at cost Agreement for supply of raw materials Sharing lab results

(Laird, 1993)

infrastructure. Innovative agreements may include unique technology and information exchanges, such as screening for host-country diseases.

Which are the appropriate parties for negotiation?

Agreements may be made at a national or regional level with governmental as well as with non-governmental organizations. Biodiversity prospecting agreements may also be concluded with national or regional federations representing local peoples, as well as with individual collectors, informants, or specific indigenous groups. A key political and social policy issue in all biodiversity prospecting endeavours is: which institutions, public or corporate, governmental or community-based, are ethically and legally entitled to negotiate terms for the exchange of biodiversity and local knowledge?

The specification of the appropriate community may be further complicated where particular genetic resources are dispersed throughout a region, a country or many countries, or ethnobiological knowledge is possessed, as is often the case, by more than one community.

How should the benefits be determined?

The use of terms such as 'benefits', 'compensation' and 'returns' reveals social and legal assumptions about the nature of the prospecting process. What is being extracted? What is being exchanged? Is there a legal 'injury', 'invasion' or 'taking'? If so, by which parties? What acts or injuries entail the offer of compensation? What are the processes, legal and institutional, by which decisions about the nature of the appropriate benefits are determined?

The purposes for which the benefits will be used are always policy decisions: what values and priorities underlie each contract? Are these policy decisions directly specified in the agreement or are they implied in the priorities and allocation principles employed by the biodiversity prospector, host country governmental agency, or indigenous people's organization?

Contractual agreements, because they are a form of 'private law', offer more flexibility than statutes in determining the goals, objectives, and means through which equity is achieved. It is as important to question the contractual priorities, how these decisions about priorities were reached, and the policy theory behind decisions, as it is to know the concrete terms of the agreement.

To investigate the issues posed above, we examine below aspects of policies and/or contractual arrangements made by three biodiversity 'prospectors: Merck, Shaman Pharmaceuticals, and Biotics. The discussion which follows should not be construed as an endorsement of any of these relationships, but rather as a lens through which some the equity issues posed above may be examined. It is hoped that concrete description of the details of these arrangements will stimulate further critical, comparative discussion of these and other arrangements.

Models of co-operation

The Merck–INBio deal

The Instituto Nacional de Biodiversidad (INBio) is a non-profit research institute established in 1989 by the Costa Rican government and a large number of biologists to meet the need for a unified biodiversity programme in Costa Rica. Although nominally independent, INBio is tightly linked to the national and private institutions that created it, including the Ministry of Natural Resources, Energy and Mines (MINREM). INBio has two aims: to conduct a comprehensive inventory of the biological species found in the protected areas of Costa Rica; and to exploit commercially the country's biodiversity in such a way that funds are generated for conservation efforts. INBio embodies a vision in which scientific research is a catalyst increasing knowledge of biodiversity, generating funds, and creating a stream of support for biodiversity conservation.

When negotiating commercial bioprospecting contracts, INBio insists on three kinds of benefits. First, direct payments in cash and in kind are required in exchange for the provision of samples and extracts. Second, direct contributions toward the cost of maintaining Costa Rica's National System of Conservation Areas (SINAC), or 10% of the initial project budget and 50% of royalties must be provided. Thirdly, royalty payments on net sales from the commercialization of biodiversity materials, must also form part of the agreement. In addition, INBio policies place priority on carrying out pharmaceutical research and development in Costa Rica, the source country; minimization of the period during which the prospector has exclusive rights to commercialization of the sample; a clear definition of sample and patent ownership; and chemical synthesis or cultivation in-country.

INBio's agreement with Merck   In exchange for a specified number of samples over a two-year period and the exclusive right to evaluate these samples for this time, the US pharmaceutical company Merck & Co provides INBio with research funding of $1 million and laboratory equipment and materials valued at $135 000. In addition, Merck will pay INBio a royalty of between 2% and 6% on any commercial product development as a reflection of INBio's contribution to product development. Merck owns any inventions created through this collaboration and has the right to file for patents. Merck also provides training for INBio staff in Merck facilities.

As part of the agreement, Merck receives the exclusive right to screen, develop, and patent new products derived from samples provided by INBio. The agreement also allows Merck access to all of the biological diversity located in Costa Rica's national parks, which constitute 25% of the country's total area. Due to the high level of government support for INBio, Merck also has access to a reliable supply of plant, insect and environmental samples which will be accurately labelled. Merck has generated and received considerable public relations benefits due to the high profile of the Merck-INBio agreement.

As a result of the Merck–INBio agreement, INBio gains funds and in-kind contributions for equipment, training, transfer of 'know-how', and support for the collection and inventory of biological resources. Costa Rica also gains increased support for conservation of biodiversity through more effective administration of its national parks.

Shaman Pharmaceuticals
In contrast to Merck, Shaman Pharmaceuticals (Shaman hereafter) exclusively uses ethnobotanical methods as a 'first screen' in the search for medically useful plant-derived compounds. Shaman seeks to extract, analyze, and scientifically build upon the knowledge and practices of local communities in developing natural product drug

leads. One of Shaman's most promising products is an antifungal agent derived from a species commonly used as a folk remedy for wound healing in Peru and parts of Mexico.

While the Merck–INBio agreement focuses on the allocation of benefits at a national level, Shaman concentrates on returning benefits to local communities. Shaman emphasizes a policy of 'immediate reciprocity', and company documents state that it has, or will, share benefits immediately with all communities with which it works directly. Benefits are said to be allocated via three mechanisms:

○ a common pool trust fund, administered by the Healing Forest Conservancy and supported by Shaman's profit stream, to distribute funds to all communities and countries in which Shaman works

○ support for sustainable natural product supply and extraction industries in local communities in host countries where Shaman operates

○ provision of immediate benefits in response to requests from local people.

With the exception of immediate benefits, Shaman's policies focus on contributions to a general fund for 'all' local communities or indigenous peoples, often through indigenous organizations living in areas where Shaman has operated, rather than creating streams of long-term benefits to those communities or individuals which directly contributed knowledge, practices or plant materials to commercial products.

In the words of one of its senior scientists, Dr. Stephen King, 'A ten-year waiting period for any potential benefits for any particular indigenous group is almost the same as never'. Immediate benefits, usually targeted at communities in whose areas Shaman is collecting specimens, have included the construction of an airstrip in a Quechua community and temporary co-ordination of a supply of methaloquine for Yanomami Indians to cure malaria. Decisions on the nature and scope of these benefits are determined by Shaman executives; principles determining priorities, amount of support, and the selection of beneficiaries have not yet been articulated.

The Healing Forest Conservancy (HFC) is a non-profit foundation funded through a capital donation from Shaman Pharmaceuticals. The theory of the HFC is that after Shaman commercializes a product, the HFC will channel a percentage of product profits to each community and country with which Shaman has worked. The allocation of benefits is determined by an independent board of directors. The Conservancy currently has four projects:

- *Medicine Women* provides education and training programme for indigenous women.

- *Terra Nova* provides support for an ethnobiomedical plant reserve in Belize.

- *Usko-Avar Amazonian School of Painting* sponsors exhibits and sale of paintings from a Peruvian art school which trains students to record myths and plant knowledge in painted form.

- *Richard Evans Schultes Award* presents an annual award to an individual or organization that has made an outstanding contribution to ethnobotany.

Biotics Limited
Biotics is a biotechnology consultancy and service company, founded in 1983, that specializes in natural product chemistry and sample procurement. Biotics is also a broker of plant materials to developed-country organizations and companies conducting high-throughput screening. Biotics embodies its agreements in a Letter of Intent which covers the first 100 samples provided to companies interested in commercial product development. If a company desires more samples, Biotics will negotiate an agreement for those samples that also retroactively applies to the first 100 samples. All agreements include a provision that Biotics' share of any royalties resulting from commercialized products will be shared equally with the collaborating institution in the source country.

Biotics does not articulate principles or priorities for the use of royalties derived from commercialized products, nor does it specify to in-country collaborating institutions the manner in which benefits must be dispersed. Biotics plans to establish a foundation or trust into which it will channel a part of its royalties, which will be allocated to 'source' countries or collaborating institutions.

Balancing the Benefits?

The characteristics of the three agreements are outlined in Table 4.2.

The INBio–Merck agreement: key issues
While initially heralded as a positive model for biodiversity agreements by many, the Merck–INBio deal raises many important questions. Did the money Merck paid represent the true value of Costa Rica's biodiversity, which has been estimated at millions of dollars, and should rights be sold at all for something for which the value is unknown?

Table 4.2. Comparison of approaches to return of benefits

	Form of benefit	Recipient of benefit	Use of monetary benefit — Priority	Use of monetary benefit — Basis of decision
Merck	$1 million advance payment Lab equipment ($135K value) 2–6% royalty on net sales of commercialized product Training Information sharing	INBio, a private non-profit organization authorized by the national government	National Inventory Conservation Infrastructure	INBio's charter as determined by national government Specified in contract between Merck and INBio
Shaman	Undisclosed % of profits to common pool trust fund administered by the Healing Forest Conservancy Projects requiring immediate assistance (co-ordination of donation of medicine, provision of health care) Agreement for supply of raw materials	All indigenous groups that Shaman works with	'Based on need' but not specifically defined	Decision made by HFC board of directors or Shaman executives on a case-by-case basis Not based on contribution
Biotics	50% of royalties received from the pharmaceutical companies it supplies	Collaborating institution in developing country	Not specified by Biotics There is usually a general agreement that it will go toward conservation, research, and development	Negotiated individually with collaborating institution

(Zerner and Kennedy)

104

National sovereignty over biological resources Did INBio, as a private, non-profit organization have the authority to grant access to control of Costa Rica's national genetic wealth? Whether or not INBio had the *de jure* authority to sign such a contract, is a quasi-governmental or non-governmental institution such as INBio an appropriate gatekeeper for expressly 'national' biological diversity? In the Costa Rican case, and other nations in which natural resources on public lands are considered a national patrimony, only governmental organizations with express authority to grant access for 'prospecting' purposes should possess the right to commercialize them. However, under the agreement with Merck, INBio possesses the right to determine how these national resources are marketed and how Merck funds are allocated. Has the Merck–INBio arrangement, in a *de facto* sense, privatized national resources? The refusal to disclose the royalty rate negotiated in the agreement is often cited as evidence to support the proposition that Costa Rica's biological diversity is being privatized and national sovereignty is being eroded. It was only under considerable public pressure that INBio revealed the range of the negotiated royalty rate, despite the fact that this is information relating to the sale of public goods obtained on public land.

National vs local community needs The agreement between Merck and INBio addresses equity and benefits at a national level, but it does not address the concerns or the rights of local communities, including recognition of potential land rights or intellectual property. Costa Rica is atypical of most developing countries in Latin America and many countries throughout the developing world, within whose borders live many diverse and demographically significant indigenous cultural communities. The applicablity of this model to other countries is limited.

Shaman Pharmaceutical's approach to return of benefits: key issues
Shaman's approach to the return of benefits to local communities also raises questions about compensation for indigenous knowledge, assumptions about the nature of local conceptions of property and its relation to ethnobotanical knowledge, and priorities and procedures for channeling trust funds to communities and countries. Because Shaman initally focuses on development of drug leads obtained by tapping into local practices and ethnopharmacological knowledge, it needs to articulate better the policy rationale for its common pool approach to benefits.

What problems, social or economic, does the common pool approach solve? While it obviates the necessity for calculating the 'worth' of individual contributions to the drug discovery process, it leaves unresolved several kinds of problems, including the question of individual contributions to the drug discovery process.

Local knowledge and the problem of authorship   If local knowledge is crucial, then which policies deal with compensation to local people who provide ethnobotanical leads? Or is the principle of 'authorship' of ethnobotanical knowledge, collective or individual, outweighed by the general needs of all indigenous communities? Shaman, like many other organizations concerned with rights to ethnobotanical knowledge, assume that such knowledge is a *collective* 'possession'. While such an assumption may be accurate in certain cases, it is certainly not justified as a generalization about tribal or peasant societies.

The cultural construction of ethnobotanical knowledge and property rights   Cultural and historic variations in how property rights are constructed, and deployed, are as nuanced as are the uses of ethnobotanical knowledge. To assume that ethnobotanical knowledge is a certain 'thing' which entails 'property rights' is to transpose a pre-existing cultural schema about property, knowledge, and rights on to peoples or individuals who may not share any of these assumptions or preoccupations. To assume further that such knowledge is a *collective* property is to assume that tribal or peasant peoples are somehow unable to create or value alternative notions of property, including individual property. What are the equities to be considered, moreover, when knowledge of a particular plant is dispersed among several communities?

Determining the proper community   How does Shaman determine the demographics and social composition of a particular community or of an 'indigenous people?' The social and topographic 'mapping' of ethnic communities is a problematic venture, subject to the vicissitudes of particular community histories, state policy, migration, and other factors. For example, are seasonal migrants or immigrants not considered 'members' of indigenous groups? Would they be disinherited from Shaman's benefit scheme?

There is another practical question about the trust fund approach: if Shaman's equity policy rests on providing a trust fund for communities in general, is it not possible that the amount of compensation potentially available to specific local communities may be negligible?

Meeting national needs   By focusing almost exclusively on meeting community needs as communicated by the local groups with whom it works, Shaman does not deal with the question of 'balancing the equities' between national and local needs. How are national needs and a public good larger than that of local communities to be met?

Biotics: key issues

Biotics' approach to the return of benefits raises critical questions about institutional responsibilities in the era of bioprospecting. Like the Merck–INBio arrangement, Biotics' *modus operandi* is to conclude an agreement with non-governmental institutions which do not possess legal responsibility for the management or conservation of national lands. Should a private company like Biotics be permitted to conduct operations with institutions that are not vested with formal responsibilities as 'national gatekeepers' to national resources?

Unlike Merck and Shaman, which have invested considerable resources, human and financial, prior to any 'pay-off', Biotics does not provide up-front benefits. Moreover, the relationships between Biotics' potential royalty payments to source country institutions and the purposes to which they are directed is relatively open and ambiguous. Biotics negotiates on an individual basis with collaborating institutions in developing countries: there are no assurances that collaborating institutions will allocate the benefits for social, economic or environmental equity.

Whether developed country institutions or companies should be empowered to shape the purposes of any trust fund or benefit plan for source country institutions, nations or communities – at any level – is a highly charged policy issue. It may be argued convincingly that the determination of allocation plans or principles by developed country institutions for developing countries or communities constitutes the imposition of another form of hegemony, whether 'green' or 'equitable'.

Conclusion

The comparisons and critiques offered in the above discussion need to be contextualized: whatever the imperfections, ambiguities or flaws noted in these private sector arrangements, they need to be recognized as exceptions to general practice. Preliminary results of an in-progress survey of pharmaceutical companies and research organizations being conducted by the Natural Resource and Rights Program of the Rainforest Alliance suggest that these companies are among a very small percentage of corporations that have actually developed concrete policies toward the return of benefits for natural product development or 'sourcing'.

These companies' attempts to address social equity and conservation policy within the context of commercial exploitation suggest a willingness to address problematic and highly politicized issues in areas where there are no simple solutions. While it is clear that colonial and neo-colonial assumptions about resource extraction and the institutional arrangements which underlie them are no longer acceptable, new arrangements inevitably bring to light a host of new challenges.

One of the fundamental lessons about designing equitable solutions in the era of bioprospecting is the recognition that there is no single appropriate model governing relationships among prospectors, source nations, non-governmental institutions, local communities and individuals. Generic contracts designed for generic developing countries may only obscure the needs of specific communities and countries. In an era where plants, peoples, ideas and molecules travel and combine in unexpected, and often unpredictable, ways we may be learning that locally-crafted solutions, engaging particular peoples, their needs and histories, may be far more appropriate and useful than generic principles or contracts.

In this era of intense mobility, social uprooting and rapidly migrating capital, moreover, where it is becoming increasingly difficult to specify, in simple social or topographic terms, the boundaries of particular social communities, the needs of immigrants, and pockets of poor and disenfranchised peoples living in cities and on their margins, need to be as much the object of global policies on equity and environment as are those groups we continue to imagine as locally rooted in the forest.

Sources

1. Brockway, L.H. (1988). Plant Science and Colonial Expansion: the Botanical Chessgame. In: Kloppenburg, J R (ed.): *Seeds and Sovereignty: The Use and Control of Plant Genetic Resources.* Durham, N C: Duke University Press.
2. Cox, P.A. and Elmqvist, T. (1993). Eco-colonialism and Indigenous Knowledge Systems: Village Controlled Rain Forest Preserves in Samoa. *Pacific Conservation*, 1: 11–25.
3. Cunningham, A.B. (1993). Conservation, Knowledge and New Natural Products Development: Partnership or Piracy? Draft paper prepared for 'IPRs and Indigenous Peoples' conference, Granlibakken, June 1993.
4. Findeisen, C. and Laird, S. (1991). Natural Products Research and the Pharmaceutical Industry in Tropical Forest Conservation. A report prepared by the Perwinkle Project of the Rainforest Alliance.
5. Gupta, A. and Ferguson, J. (1992). Beyond 'Culture': Space, Identity, and the Politics of Difference. *Cultural Anthropology*, **7** (1): 63–79.
6. King, S.R. (1994). Establishing Reciprocity: Biodiversity, Conservation and New Models for Co-operation between Forest-dwelling Peoples and the Pharmaceutical Industry. In: *Intellectual Property Rights for Indigenous Peoples: A Sourcebook*, 69–82. Society for Applied Anthropology, Oklahoma City, OK, USA.
7. King, S.R. and Tempesta, M.S. (1993). From Shaman to Clinical Trials: The Role of Industry in Ethnobotany, Conservation, and Common Reciprocity. A paper prepared for the Ciba Symposium.

8. King, S.R. and Carlson, T.J. (1993). Biological Diversity, Indigenous Knowledge, Drug Discovery and Intellectual Property Rights: Creating Reciprocity and Maintaining Relationships. A paper prepared for 'IPRs and Indigenous Peoples' conference, Granlibakken, June 1993.
9. Kloppenburg, J. and Gonzales, T. (1994). Between State and Capital: NGOs as Allies of Indigenous Peoples. In: *Intellectual Property Rights for Indigenous Peoples: A Sourcebook*, 163–178. Society for Applied Anthropology, Oklahoma City, OK, USA.
10. Kloppenburg, J. and Rodriguez, S. (1992). Conservationists or Corsairs? *Seedling* **9** (2–3), 12–17.
11. Laird, S.A. (1993). Contracts for Biodiversity Prospecting. *Biodiversity Prospecting*, pp 99–130. World Resources Institute.
12. Laird, S.A. (1994). Natural Products and the Commercialization of Traditional Knowledge. In: *Intellectual Property Rights for Indigenous Peoples: a Sourcebook*, 145–162. Society for Applied Anthropology, Oklahoma City, OK, USA.
13. Malkki, L. (1992). The Rooting of Peoples and the Territorialization of National Identity among Scholars and Refugees. *Cultural Anthropology*, 7 (1), 24–43.
14. McGowan, J. and Udeinya, I. (1994). Collecting Traditional Medicines in Nigeria: a Proposal for IPR Compensation. In: *Intellectual Property Rights for Indigenous Peoples: A Sourcebook*, 57–68. Society for Applied Anthropology, Oklahoma City, OK, USA.
15. Moran, K. (1994). Biocultural Diversity Conservation through the Healing Forest Conservancy. In: *Intellectual Property Rights for Indigenous Peoples: A Sourcebook*, 99–110. Society for Applied Anthropology, Oklahoma City, OK, USA.
16. Pistorius, R. and van Wijk, J. (1993). Biodiversity Prospecting: Commercializing Genetic Resources for Export. *Biotechnology and Development Monitor* **15**, 12–15.
17. Pratt, M.L. (1992). *Imperial Visions: Travel Writing and Transculturation*. London, Routledge.
18. Reid, W.V. *et al.* (1993). A New Lease on Life. In *Biodiversity Prospecting*, World Resources Institute.
19. Rubin, S.M. and Fish, S.C. (1993). Biodiversity Prospecting: Using Innovative Contractual Provisions to Foster Ethnobotanical Knowledge, Technology, and Conservation. *Colorado Journal of International Law and Policy* 5 (23), 23–58.
20. Simpson, R.D. and Sedjo, R.A. (1992). Contracts for Transferring Rights to Indigenous Genetic Resources. *Resources for the Future*, 1–6, 109.
21. Sittenfeld, A. and Gamez, R. (1993). Biodiversity Prospecting by INBio. *Biodiversity Prospecting*, 131–158. World Resources Institute.
22. Zerner, C. (1994). Native Daughters and Native Seeds: Nostalgia for Natural Origins in an Era of Hybridity. Paper presented at the Conference on Multiculturalism and Transnationalism, University of Massachusetts, Lowell, October 14–17, 1994.
23. Zerner, C. (forthcoming). Metaphor Wars and Native Seeds: Contested Visions of the Extraction of Biological Diversity in Tropical Developing

Countries. In: *The Poetics and Politics of Intellectual Property Rights in the Post-Colonial* Era (Jaszi, and Woodmansee, M, ed.). Duke University Press, Durham, NC, USA.

4.2. The Body Shop model of bioprospecting

MARK JOHNSTON

Introduction

There are two races running concurrently on planet Earth. The first, towards growth and development, will result in exhausting the planet of its resources before the end of the next century. The other is to find a more responsible manner for living on the planet.

Practical solutions are what we are looking for. There is no way we can wake up tomorrow morning and find that all the harmful elements of the marketplace have changed, and that we have a new set of rules. Neither can we continue waking up to the same dawn, one that gives us another day of non-stop environmental degradation. However, we can work to make the system more responsible. We can do this by understanding the production chain, by making sure environmental needs and human rights are addressed along the way. By following more responsible means of production we may extend life on the planet by a thousand years, and maybe give ourselves enough time to find a better future.

The first step towards more responsible production is sourcing and obtaining raw materials in a non-violent way. For this reason, the Body Shop is trading directly with several indigenous peoples. Groups like these are the custodians of much of the planet's biodiversity. Their knowledge is extensive, which is hardly surprising as their survival depends on it. Myth, religion, and lessons of the elders pass on that crucial knowledge, ensuring that in the future the experience of the past will keep the group in harmony with its environment.

One way to help the conservation of the biodiverse environments that indigenous people live in or near, is through providing them with the means to continue acting as custodians. This is one of the central tenets of The Body Shop's Fair Trade programme.

110

The erosion of cultural, as well as biological, diversity threatens the future of humanity. Many cultures are more endangered than the environments in which they live, and if they disappear their valuable knowledge of biodiversity disappears also. Recognizing and enshrining indigenous peoples' knowledge is crucial for the planet's future security.

Indigenous people* number some 300 million people around the world, according to the United Nations. However, the funds made available to this important constituency for the 1993 United Nations Year of Indigenous People was a paltry $500 000, reflecting governments' lack of interest in helping or recognizing their indigenous populations.

There is a Masai saying, 'Until the lions have their historians, tales of hunting will always glorify the hunter.' Likewise the historians of industrialized countries have already labelled this century an economic miracle. We trumpet the discoveries we have made, the drugs we've patented out of the jungle, the profits that have been gained. Yet the indigenous peoples who have seen their resources disappear have a different tale to tell. These groups are among the poorest inhabitants of the planet. One way of addressing this situation is through more equitable sharing of the wealth deriving from the biodiverse environments in which they live.

The moral and immoral economies

In the modern market economy, the moral dimension has been removed from the process of exchange, because producers and consumers rarely meet face to face. Care, responsibility and obligation, which mark the exchange process in traditional societies, have been replaced by interest, costs and profitability. The production trail is long and twisted, so it is easy to ignore or overlook the wrongs committed on people or the environment along the way.

In the moral economy, person-to-person relations are key to the trading process. The value of the product incorporates the value of the producer and seller. In traditional societies, buying and selling are fundamentally based upon the values of mutuality, trust, complementarity, and co-dependence. Direct relationships with primary producers and the better understanding of the path a product takes to the consumer could trigger the re-birth of the moral economy, helping consumers to make more ethical choices. The Body Shop's

---

* The United Nations uses the following definition of indigenous peoples: 'Indigenous peoples are the descendents of the original inhabitants of the lands where they live. They often share a common language and culture, and often live in a cultural environment which can operate independently of the majority cultures surrounding them'.

trading protocols are based on the principle that indigenous and traditional communities have a right to continue their traditional way of life and determine their own future.

Trading with the Mebengokre (Kayapo) Indians

Since 1991 The Body Shop has been trading with two Mebengokre communities of A-ukre and Pukanuv, for Brazil nut oil used in a hair conditioner product. These villages are two of sixteen Mebengokre communities which occupy an area the size of Holland in the Xingu River basin in the Brazilian state of Para. The Mebengokre number about three and a half thousand people, are fierce in defence of their culture and, until recently, were semi-nomadic hunter-gatherers.

The extraction technique and hand-operated pressing machinery for Brazil nut oil production were developed with ICI Brazil. The Body Shop agreed to fund the start up of the business in A-ukre with an interest-free loan of about $80 000. During the gathering season nearly everyone in the community is involved in the business. The Brazil nuts are collected from the ground, dehusked and then ground into a paste before being pressed to extract the virgin oil.

The Pukanuv business was started a year later, and the two communities are now each producing 2000 kilos of oil per year. This may be the upper limit that the community can produce without disturbing traditional life practices and without disrupting natural propogation of the trees. The price for the oil ($35 per kilo in 1993) reflects the long and difficult process to extract the oil. It is considerably higher than the market price of $15 per kilo for Brazil nut oil. This agreement was formalized in a legal contract between the company and the two villages.

As an interim step, a Brazilian indigenist was appointed as a liaison officer between the company and the communities to help keep the accounts, appoint officers, deal with export controls and so on. He will soon act merely as an adviser. Both the A-ukre and Pukanuv communities have formed trading companies, which are the first to be wholly-owned and operated by Indians in Brazil. The directors are elected by the company members from the communities.

One of the main challenges encountered by The Body Shop has been in helping the communities learn numeracy skills, handle money and accounts, and invest the profits for the benefit of the communities. Their direct involvement in product development and production has played a key role in this learning process.

In an attempt to make the trading relationship more equitable, The Body Shop has been developing some new initiatives, such as a health programme and working out a mechanism to protect the intellectual property of the Mebengokre.

This trading relationship has given the Kayapo the opportunity to earn income by carrying out an activity which does not take them away from their lands and which simultaneously allows them to carry on their traditional activities of celebrations, hunting, fishing and tending their gardens. The success of these initiatives has caused a further ten Kayapo communities to ask The Body Shop to help them set up similar projects.

Intellectual property rights

In line with the Declaration of Belem, which was adopted at the first International Congress of Ethnobiology in Brazil in 1988, The Body Shop is pursuing a policy of 'just compensation' to be made to indigenous peoples for the research information they provide to trading partners or research institutions. This means involving indigenous peoples in the planning and decision-making, recognizing them as contributors to all phases of the trade link, and considering their intellectual property to be equally important to that of the company. Mebengokre leader, Chief Paiakan has played a key role in educating villagers about the concepts of intellectual property rights.

It is unfair to suggest that only nation states should enjoy the riches reaped from their territories' biodiversity. But compensating indigenous communities is a senstive issue, and some advocate the involvement of local NGOs to disburse the rewards locally. This approach may work sometimes, but it is still patronizing to expect indigenous peoples to be dependent on intermediaries all the time. Trickle-down theory hardly ever works. And the expectation of some collectors that companies will sign third-party agreements with indigenous peoples, or that the collectors themselves will distribute some of the rewards to the primary producers, is slim at best.

The Body Shop is researching and developing a covenant which addresses intellectual property rights and other parts of its business relationship with the Mebengokre. This covenant embodies the spirit of the relationship between the company and the local people, and separate contracts are drawn up for each individual trading relationship using the covenant as a guide. The Nucleo Direitos Indigenas, the legal body which works for indigenous rights in Brazil, is overseeing the relationship between the parties.

The Xingu Health Project

Over the first two years of the trading relationship, The Body Shop initiated two health programmes for the A-ukre and Pukanuv communities, involving the training of Kayapo health officers and a dental programme. A wider and longer-term initiative, in partnership with

113

the Federal Indian Agency in Brazil (FUNAI) and the Brazilian Health Ministry is providing primary health care to all of the Kayapo villages as well as other ethnic groups living in the region. This is a long-term project, and the initial work in two villages has now been expanded to include many other indigenous groups in the Xingu region.

Business and sustainability

Up to now, a false taxonomy has been used in dictating who can act on issues concerning biodiversity and indigenous peoples, and business has not been considered a force to lead change. But categorizing and ghetto-izing actors according to their titles as business, NGOs or government will not effect change. We want to help break the mould that has dictated the form of economic development, by going straight to indigenous people to create models of responsible development.

This call to action is echoed by Mebengokre chief Pykatire Kayapo who called for more economic alternatives for indigenous peoples in threatened environments at the UN Working Group on Indigenous People in 1994. We believe that a new approach to resource utilization is crucial to the protection of these biodiverse environments, and the survival of their custodians: indigenous and traditional peoples throughout the world.

4.3. Indigenous peoples' responses to bioprospecting

MARCUS COLCHESTER

Indigenous peoples now face an intensifying challenge to the integrity of their societies. There is increasing pressure from outsiders to document, utilize and commercialize biodiversity and related indigenous knowledge. Some of this exploitation is being justified in the name of the conservation of indigenous culture. It is also being justified in the wider interests of humankind. The main threats that indigenous societies face from the wave of commercialization are:

o The expropriation of knowledge and resources

○ The debasement of knowledge through the violation of sacredness and loss of identity

○ The commodification of knowledge, biotechnologies and natural resources.

Indigenous peoples are now seeking new means of asserting their rights over knowledge and biotechnologies as part of a parcel of demands for the right to self-determination. The threats they see posed by the commercialization of their heritage are not confined to questions of intellectual property. The wider concern is to retain control of their territories, a struggle which has existed throughout history, but was intensified with devastating results with the expansion of colonial enterprises.

A historical perspective

It was immediately apparent to indigenous peoples that the invading societies held completely different views on their relationship to the land. Yet, encroaching Northern concepts of land ownership were hard to resist. Through a mixture of motives – some malign, some benign, but all largely misconceived – many indigenous peoples were accorded Northern-style titles to land. In many cases the results have been devastating: many communities discovered that the recognition of indigenous ownership rights to land was little more than a licence to parcel up, commodify and sell their lands and resources. The result was the fragmentation of indigenous territories and societies, and the wholesale alienation of land to outsiders. Outside forces were primarily responsible for this catastrophe, but internal division within indigenous societies were readily exploited. Individuals' shortsightedness, cash interest and personal gain all played a role in the break up of indigenous communities.

Many indigenous peoples concluded that indigenous and Northern concepts of land ownership were irreconcilable. A common statement among indigenous peoples up to the 1960s and 1970s was, 'We do not own the land, the land owns us'. However, in the ensuing years there was a more pragmatic acceptance that some kind of legal validation of indigenous land rights was necessary to secure their societies against the force of the market. In many countries, such as Colombia and Brazil, a conscious strategy was adopted to secure indigenous rights within the arena of the state.

Three concepts have been crucial to indigenous peoples in defining their relationship to land in Northern legal terms. The first is collective ownership as opposed to the individual titles favoured by the North. The second is the assertion of rights to 'territories' not to 'land', by which indigenous peoples assert their right to the whole ecosystem in which they live, including surface and subsurface resources, and not just the 'dirt' on which they dwell and plant crops. The third concept is 'inalienability' by which they mean not just that the land cannot be taken over by outsiders, but that indigenous peoples are one with the land and cannot be separated from their own territories. With these crucial modifications to Northern notions of land ownership, indigenous peoples feel better able to defend themselves against the pressures of the market in which they are increasingly involved.

However, even where these concepts are recognized in law and respected, indigenous peoples find that they are not automatically insured against exploitation. 'Inalienability' can be circumvented by a number of means. Imprecisions in the law about which collectivity owns land and resources may favour the interests of a few at the expense of the wider group. For instance, indigenous societies can

Box 4.1: What's wrong with the INBio–Merck deal?

A view from RAFI:

Bilateral bioprospecting agreements are not likely to provide adequate compensation either to indigenous peoples or to Southern governments unless they are made within the framework of broader intergovernmental arrangements. The Merck–INBio deal illustrates the point.

The deal requires Costa Rica to provide Merck with roughly 10 000 plant, animal or microbial samples in return for $1.3 million, or $130 per sample. Costa Rica is estimated to hold 5% of the world's biodiversity. If the Merck deal was replicated for the developing world as a whole, all the South's biodiversity would go for $26 million. Merck's sales in 1991 alone were $8600 million, while Costa Rica's entire Gross National Product that year was less than $5200 million. Merck's research budget in 1991 was roughly $1000 million. At present Merck has three drugs on the market with a sales volume in excess of $1000 million each. Since the company invests an average of $125 million on research for each new drug, the discovery charge for one single new drug arising from the Costa Rican agreement is barely loose change for Merck. The Costa Rica contract is cheap labour.

If, 10 or 20 years from now, Merck and Costa Rica dispute the origins of a plant-derived active ingredient, the country has comparatively little capacity to appeal to the international courts to resolve such a dispute compared with Merck's army of lawyers.

(*Source: Conserving Indigenous Knowledge : Integrating Two Systems of Innovation – UNDP, 1994*)

lease their lands to the state, which then leases them back to an élite intent on commercializing resources for their own benefit.

There are two main lessons in all this. The first is that the overhasty application of Northern legal concepts of ownership to indigenous commons systems can do more harm than good, which often leads to the process of commodification of resources and the breakup of society. The second is that resistance to outside pressures depends ultimately on the unity and coherence of the peoples themselves and is not something that can be provided through external laws. Where indigenous societies are internally divided, 'ownership' titles may hasten the process of alienation.

Strategies for securing indigenous control

Indigenous peoples have made a number of statements demanding control of their knowledge and biotechnologies. The *Charter of the Indigenous-Tribal Peoples of the Tropical Forests* set out in Malaysia in 1992, and the *Maatatua Declaration of Indigenous Peoples* articulated in 1993, demand the recognition of the rights of indigenous peoples as the exclusive owners of their traditional knowledge.

International law is in the process of responding to such demands. The 1993 draft of the proposed *UN Declaration on the Rights of Indigenous Peoples* states that indigenous peoples are entitled to the recognition of the full ownership, control and protection of their cultural and intellectual property. It also reaffirms that they have the right to special measures to control, develop and protect their sciences, technologies and other genetic resources, seeds, medicines, knowledge of the properties of fauna and flora, oral traditions, literature, designs and visual and performing arts.

However, in some areas, such as South and South-east Asia, many indigenous people have been much more cautious about asserting their demands in such terms. Echoing indigenous anxieties about the impositions of inappropriate forms of land ownership and as a result of their long experience with the loss of control of their seedstocks to multinational companies spurred by the Green Revolution, they have expressed concern that the assertion of legal ownership of traditional knowledge may hasten rather than delay the commodification of their knowledge and natural resources. Such groups view the whole notion of intellectual property rights as a sophisticated form of theft.

Divergent as these two strategies appear, they both aim to protect indigenous peoples from exploitation by commercial interests.

Some kind of legal protection of indigenous traditional knowledge seems warranted, but until the legal framework can incorporate the concepts of collective ownership, territory and inalienability, the fear is that overhasty prescriptions may backfire on indigenous peoples in the same way that individual land titling has. Legal measures, beyond those of standard Northern property rights regimes, that exist or that have been suggested for securing indigenous knowledge include the following (described further in Chapter 6.1):

○ *existing controls over indigenous knowledge:* e.g. confidentiality, secrecy

○ *direct control of natural resources:* e.g. territorial and land rights, exclusive rights to resources

○ *political control over access and use:* e.g. rights of control, management and self-government; 'discovery rights'

○ *new rights over indigenous knowledge:* e.g. Model Provisions on Folklore (UNESCO/WIPO); recognized and/or registered community ownership

○ *options to limit the power of commercial enterprises:* e.g. prohibition on the patenting of life forms; assertion and/or expansion of Farmers' Rights; codes of conduct and licensing of prospectors; model agreements between prospectors and the local people; licence of right to prohibit monopolization.

Outstanding dilemmas

The many dilemmas that indigenous peoples face in the assertion of their rights to maintain control over their traditional knowledge are discussed in Chapter 4.1. Some of the most thorny relate to the wide sharing of knowledge amongst these groups and to determining which indigenous institution should be the legal entity to hold and negotiate the use of the knowledge. It may be argued that in such circumstances indigenous peoples are better defended by the existing uncertainty than by the creation of new ambiguous legal mechanisms which would allow outsiders to sign contracts with false indigenous representatives.

In my view, none of the proposals put forward so far, by non-indigenous and indigenous people alike, offer convincing means of overcoming these problems. Some of the proposals may even create serious new problems. In particular, there is an uncomfortable feeling about proposals to compensate indigenous peoples for the use of their knowledge through trustee arrangements not under full indigenous control, such as those relying on the good offices of state institutions or mechanisms such as Farmers' Rights (see p. 165).

Most indigenous groups are demanding the vesting of rights of ownership and control with the indigenous peoples and communities themselves. The main concern here is that the provision of inappropriate rights to negotiate contracts may accelerate the process of commodification. The introduction of *sui generis* legislation results in a trade-off between protecting indigenous knowledge and biotechnology from being monopolised by commercial interests and facilitating the commodification of indigenous knowledge, albeit in a less exploitative manner.

One of the problems highlighted by indigenous peoples is the risk of uniform legal solutions being imposed on very diverse local social and political realities. The needs of peasant communities struggling to retain control of their seedstock may differ in important ways from indigenous communities trying to prevent the commercialization of sacred herb-lore, and will differ again from other groups trying to assert some kind of copyright over traditional designs produced for the tourist market. Uniform national legislation and, worse still, intergovernmentally imposed international laws (such as under GATT) may pose serious problems to indigenous communities.

It is in the nature of knowledge that it can be shared and transmitted between individuals and generations. It is thus replicable in a way that land and territory are not. A legal equivalent to 'inalienability' applied to knowledge may thus be a contradiction in terms. If this is so, the break up and commodification of indigenous knowledge may be an unavoidable consequence of indigenous peoples entering the global market, and legal defence may be able to achieve little more than mitigate some of the worst abuses. It seems obvious that no single legal option will deal with the huge range of problems thrown up by this meeting of worlds. The aim should be to ensure that proposed solutions are mutually reinforcing and not contradictory.

4.4. The losers' perspective

VANDANA SHIVA

Colonizing the seed

The biodiversity debate is at last receiving some of the attention it deserves. However, within this debate important issues are still being marginalized. One of these is the 'raw material' issue. Northern economic development could never have happened without colonialism, and thus access to the raw materials and markets of Africa, Asia and Latin America. Colonialism is a constant, necessary condition for capitalist growth: without colonies, capital accumulation would grind to a halt.

The industrial revolution required the Northern powers to have their feet firmly planted both in the sites from which they gained raw materials, and in the market. Both aspects had to be controlled, yet the raw material aspect, i.e. the impact of extraction practices on local communities and local economies, was ignored. In fact, destruction of local economies and structures was *required* to make these practices possible.

The second wave of colonization, the Green Revolution, has now been superseded by its 1990s counterpart, the biotechnology revolution. This third wave of colonization has shifted in focus, and is now overstressing the raw material angle. Everyone is talking about justice and compensation in their prospecting activities, but no one is questioning the technologies being used, the markets they create, or the impact they have on the societies which provided the raw materials in the first place.

The enclosure of life

Over the last few hundred years, capital has moved to wherever it could find sites for accumulation. And now that the world's land, forests and rivers have been exhausted and polluted, capital is looking for new 'colonies' to invade and exploit. The interior spaces of humans (particularly women), plants, animals and micro-organisms present the latest attractions. The technology enabling the colonization of new lands was the gun-boat. The enabling of the invasion and colonization of the life of organisms is genetic engineering, supported by the legal framework of intellectual property rights and patents.

The enclosure of living, self-renewing systems – by placing either legal or technological boundaries around free organisms – prevents free access to biodiversity and knowledge to the original custodians and innovators. Farmers, herbalists, and women – the sources of the biodiversity wealth on which our food and healthcare systems are based – are now being denied the gifts of knowledge and biodiversity.

The metaphor of piracy underlying the IPR debate reverses the roles of giver and receiver. Violence and plunder characterize this piracy, just as before. But now the exploited become the criminals and the exploiters gain protection. The North must be protected from the South in order to safeguard its continued exploitation of the South's resources. Farmers' exchanges of genetic material are treated by industry as theft, but protests by indigenous people over the theft of their genes by industry are not heeded.

Biodiversity: whose resource?

Common property biodiversity systems recognize the intrinsic worth of biodiversity, and indigenous social systems generally use biodiversity according to the principles of justice and sustainability. This involves a combination of rights and responsibility among users, a combination of utilization and conservation, a sense of co-production with nature and of gift-giving among members of the community. As John Todd, a visionary biologist, has stated, biodiversity carries the intelligence of three and a half billion years of experimentation by life-forms.

In contrast, regimes governed by IPRs see value as created through commercial exploitatation. IPR regimes are based on the denial of creativity of nature and the creativity emerging from the intellectual commons. Since IPRs are more a protection of capital investment than a recognition of creativity *per se*, there is a tendency for ownership of knowledge, and the products and processes emerging from it, to become concentrated in the hands of a few. Biodiversity knowledge and resources are alienated from the original custodians and donors and become the monopoly of the corporate sector. Local knowledge is devalued and local rights are displaced. This is being universalized through the TRIPS clause of GATT and certain interpretations of the Biodiversity Convention (see p. 81).

It is sometimes argued that monopolies exist in traditional communities. This is not the case in agriculture, where seeds and knowledge are exchanged freely. It is also not true of medicinal resources. It has been pointed out that in the Ayurveda classic, *Charaka Samhita*, healers learn about herbs and medicinal plants 'from cowherds, *tapasvis*, forest dwellers, hunters, [and] gardeners'. In traditional communities, folk knowledge and medical systems, such as Ayurveda, support each other, while in the Northern system peoples' knowledge is devalued and unrecognized as a resource. In addition, monopolies and profits do not guide the practitioners or suppliers of medicine in non-Northern medical systems. Indigenous medical practitioners may not always exchange their knowledge freely, but they gift the benefits of it freely, and do not use knowledge as a means of amassing wealth. They practise what is known in India as *gyan daan* or the gifting of knowledge.

If IPR regimes reflected the diversity of knowledge traditions in different societies, they would necessarily have to reflect a triple plurality – of intellectual modes, of property systems, and of systems of rights – leading to an amazing richness of permutations. However, those being promoted through GATT are a prescription for the mono-culture of knowledge. The TRIPs component of GATT is weighted in favour of transnational corporations, and against citizens in general,

121

and Southern peasants and forest dwellers in particular. And yet people everywhere innovate and create. In fact, the poorest people often have to be the most innovative, since they have to create survival while it is threatened daily.

Impact of GATT on farmers' right to seed

GATT-TRIPs is clearly not just about trade. It also calls into question the ethics of how we relate to other species and what we hold as moral and culturally valuable. It is a tragedy, therefore, that development directly related to the very fabric of society and our options for survival should be left in the hands of ministries of commerce.

IPRs imposed under GATT are highly restricted forms of rights. Firstly, they recognize only private as opposed to common rights. Secondly, they fail to recognize the value of innovation to meet social needs rather than to create profits. Thirdly, and most significantly, they must be 'trade-related', whereas the majority of innovation in the public domain is for domestic, local and public use. These restrictions will have a serious impact on farmers' livelihoods.

The requirement for countries to adopt 'patents or an effective *sui generis* system' to protect plant varieties (see p. 81) is the part of the GATT agreement that will most directly affect farmers' rights as innovators and plant breeders, and their community ownership of seed and plant material. While the phrase *sui generis* gives the impression that each country is free to set up its own IPR system, the inclusion of the word 'effective' makes the adoption of a global regime necessary. The use of the term 'effective' in all negotiations relating to IPRs and biodiversity is the result of pressure from the US to globalize IPR regimes to allow the patenting of all life-forms. The draft Plant Varieties Act that will soon be presented to the Indian parliament suggests that countries are under pressure to conform to industrialized country IPR laws as the universal standard.

Apart from patents, the only other IPR system which is considered 'effective' in international negotiations is UPOV's Plant Breeders' Rights (see p. 167). However, under the 1991 amendments to UPOV, farmers now have to pay royalties for saving seed on their own farms, so PBR is becoming as threatening to farmers as patents.

The farmers' movement in India has been protesting against the TRIPs component of GATT because of its far-reaching implications. In October 1992 the farmers of Karnataka State started the Seed Satyagaha movement at a five hundred thousand strong rally. In March 1993 farmers from across the country gathered in Delhi at the historic Red Fort to burn the Dunkel Draft of GATT. Indian farmers are not satisfied with government statements that India will negotiate to allow farmers the right to save and exchange seed non-commercially: for farmers, access to seed is a fundamental right, not a concession.

Plant breeders' rights, like patents, are aimed at weakening farmers as competitors of commercial plant breeders and making them more dependent on commercial suppliers of seed. 'Farmers' privilege' is a concession within this monopolizing system. But a privilege is not a right. Unlike 'Farmers' Rights', it is not a mechanism for recognizing the intellectual contribution of Southern farmers, the economic value of Southern diversity.

The very term 'privilege' implies that Southern farmers' knowledge and resources have made no contribution to the products being used. Seed varieties developed and conserved by farmers are declared to be 'land races' and 'primitive cultivars', whilst those developed by corporations are called 'advanced' or 'élite'. The tacit hierarchy of language becomes an explicit one in the process of conflict.

India already has experience of what happens when rights are replaced by privileges. During the reservation of forests by the British colonial regime, village communities which were losing their rights to their community forests started 'Forest Satyagraha' throughout the country in defence of these rights. However, these rights were reduced to privileges in the forest laws that were subsequently passed, and these privileges are now given at the whim and fancy of functionaries of the forest department. The original owners of the forests have thus been reduced to criminals and thieves. A similar process is now under way in the arena of biodiversity.

If the South is to retain political and economic control over its biological wealth, farmers' rights must not be reduced to farmers' privileges.

Diversity's choice – empowering local communities

It is often argued that patenting is a way of protecting indigenous knowledge and biodiversity. But is it? Protection of indigenous knowledge implies its continued availability to future generations in their everyday health care and agriculture. If we accept that the dominant economic system – i.e. capitalism – is at the root of the ecological crisis, because it has failed to address the ecological value of natural resources, expanding the same economic system cannot be an appropriate mechanism to protect indigenous knowledge or biodiversity.

What is needed is a transition to an alternative economic paradigm that does not reduce all value to market prices, and all human activity to commerce. Ecologically, this approach involves the recognition of the inherent and non-monetary value of all life-forms. At the social level, the values of biodiversity in different cultural contexts need to

123

Companies are looking to patent the pyrethrum plant, which has been used as a natural pesticide for centuries. (WWF/Elaine/Pierre Dubois)

be recognized. Sacred groves, sacred seeds and sacred species have been the cultural means for treating biodiversity as inviolable. Community rights to biodiversity must be honoured, as must communities' roles in protecting and nurturing biodiversity.

At the economic level, if biodiversity conservation is to be aimed at conserving life, rather than enhancing profits, then the incentives given to biodiversity destruction, and the penalties that have come to be associated with conservation, have to be removed. If a framework for protecting biodiversity guides economic thinking rather than the other way round, it becomes evident that intensive monoculture of crops and animals is an artificial construct. Productivity and efficiency need to be redefined, reflecting the multiple input/multiple output systems characterized by biodiversity.

In addition, the perverse logic of financing biodiversity conservation by using a small percentage of the profits generated by biodiversity destruction should be questioned. This logic encourages destruction, and reduces conservation to an exhibit, not the essence of living and producing.

Women as nurturers of biodiversity

Neither ecological sustainability nor livelihood sustainability can be achieved without a just resolution of the arguments about who controls biodiversity. Until recently it has been local communities, especially women, who have used, developed and conserved biological diversity. It is their control, their knowledge and their rights that need to be strengthened if the foundations of biodiversity conservation are to be strong and deep.

The marginalization of women and the destruction of biodiversity go hand in hand. Loss of diversity is the price paid in the patriarchal model of progress which pushes inexorably towards monoculture and uniformity. In contrast, women's work and knowledge is based on the principle of diversity, and is central to biodiversity conservation because women perform multiple tasks and work across the sectoral boundaries that characterize the patriarchal world-view (the boundaries between work and family, and between forest, livestock and crops).

In the production and preparation of plant foods, women need a wide range of skills and knowledge. To choose appropriate seeds they need to know about seed preparation, germination requirements and soil choice. To sow and strike seeds demands knowledge of seasons, climate, plant requirements, weather conditions, micro-climatic factors and soil enrichment. It also requires dexterity and strength. Nurturing plants calls for knowledge about the nature of

125

Women's knowledge of, and role in, nurturing biodiversity is often overlooked. (Cooper & Hammond/Panos Pictures)

plant diseases, pruning, staking, water supplies, predators, companion planting, growing seasons and soil maintenance. Harvesting requires judgements about weather, labour and grading; and knowledge of preserving, immediate use and propagation. It is because of this diversity of knowledge and an understanding of the interconnectedness of life that a woman farmer does not see rice simply as a food grain, but also as a source of cattle fodder and straw for thatch.

In most cultures women have been the custodians of biodiversity in agriculture. However, in common with other aspects of women's work and knowledge, this crucial role is often treated as non-work and non-knowledge, even though it is based on sophisticated cultural and scientific practices. Women's biodiversity conservation differs from the dominant patriarchal notion, where the conservation of diversity is seen as an arithmetical concept – 'the number and frequency of ecosystems, species and genes in a given assemblage'.

In contrast, biodiversity is seen by women as a web of relationships which ensures balance and sustainability. Each element acquires its characteristics and value through its relationships with other elements. Biodiversity is ecologically and culturally embedded. Biodiversity cannot be conserved in fragments, as scientists and industrialists would have us believe. Diversity is reproduced and conserved

126

through the reproduction and conservation of culture, in festivals and rituals which not only celebrate the renewal of life, but also provide a platform for subtle tests for seed selection and propagation. The dominant world-view does not regard these tests as scientific because they do not emerge from a laboratory or the experimental plot, and because they are carried out not by men in white coats, but by village women.

When women conserve seeds, they conserve diversity, and in doing so they conserve balance and harmony. *Navdanya* or 'nine seeds' are the symbol of this renewal of diversity and balance, not only of the plant world, but of the planet as a whole. The seed is sacred and is perceived as a microcosm of the macrocosmic world.

On the more earthly level, biodiversity implies co-existence and interdependence of trees, crops, people and livestock, maintaining the cycles of fertility through biomass flows. Mixtures of cereals and pulses create nutrient balance; crop mixtures maintain pest–predator balance; and diverse plant mixtures maintain the water cycle and conserve soil fertility. In the invisible spaces between all these flows and elements is women's work and knowledge.

Recovery of the biodiversity commons

Biodiversity prospecting is increasingly being promoted as a mechanism that will allow an equitable sharing of the benefits between a prospector and countries or communities where the biodiversity resides. Consequently, indigenous groups are being encouraged to enter into benefit-sharing agreements.

Biodiversity prospecting is the first step towards accepting the dominant system of monocultures and monopolies, and thus accepting the destruction of diversity. Taking knowledge from indigenous cultures through bioprospecting means developing an IPR-protected industrial system which must eventually market commodities that have used local knowledge as an input but are not based on the ethical, epistemological, or ecological organization of that knowledge system. This industrial system uses biodiversity fragments as 'raw material' to produce biological products protected by patents that displace the biodiversity and indigenous knowledge which it has exploited.

The issues of equity, fairness and compensation need to be assessed in a systemic way, both at the level of taking indigenous knowledge, as well as at the level of pushing it out through marketing of industrialized products. The key question to ask is: can the planet afford to have biodiversity and the 'alternative' lifestyles that conserve biodiversity swallowed up as raw material for a globally-organized corporate culture which produces only cultural and biological uniformity?

Recovering the biodiversity commons entails three levels of recovery and regeneration. It involves recognition of the creativity intrinsic in the diversity of life forms; it involves a recognition of common property regimes in the ownership and utilization of biodiversity; and it involves a recognition of intellectual commons – public domains in which knowledge of the utilization of biodiversity is not commoditized.

The first public demonstration in favour of the recovery of the biodiversity commons took place on India's Independence Day, 15 August 1993 when farmers declared that their knowledge and biodiversity is protected by a *Samuhik Gyan Sanad*. According to the farmers, any company using their local knowledge or local resources without the permission of local communities is engaging in intellectual piracy.

This concept has been developed further by the Third World Network. The positive assertion of 'collective intellectual property rights' (CIRs) creates an opportunity to define a *sui generis* system of IPRs centred on farmers' rights arising from their role in protecting and improving plant genetic resources. It requires the 'effective' clause in the TRIPS agreement (see p. 81) to be interpreted to mean effective in the specific context of different countries. IPR diversity that has room for a plurality of systems, including regimes based on CIRs, would reflect different styles of knowledge generation and dissemination in different contexts. *Sui generis* systems would develop a protection system for farmers' rights as plant breeders and for indigenous medical systems. Further, it would have to develop a relationship between Southern peoples' concerns and Northern IPR regimes which are unsympathetic to the style of inventiveness common in Southern societies. This relationship would need to be effective in preventing the exploitation of indigenous resources and knowledge, while maintaining their free exchange.

Sui generis systems that protect CIRs must necessarily be based on the assumption of biodemocracy – that all knowledge systems and production systems using biological organisms have equal validity – whereas TRIPs is based on the assumption of bioimperialism. If unchallenged, TRIPs will become an instrument for displacing and dispensing with the knowledge, the resources and the rights of Southern people, especially those who depend on biodiversity for their livelihoods, and who are the original owners and innovators in the utilization of biodiversity.

Understanding and education are prerequisites for empowerment. The debate on the labelling of genetically engineered foods illustrates how ignorance is cultivated and the public is disempowered. The corporations fear that if people know the truth, their monopolies will

128

be destroyed. So food goes unlabelled and consumers are denied access to information and the chance to make informed choices. Monopoly is first achieved in the mind, and then in the marketplace.

We can easily betray ourselves to the politics of uniformity. We can disempower ourselves by seeing the TRIPS route as the only way, and separating ourselves from other options. What we need is a politics of pluralism, in which we recognize our differences without dividing ourselves. We have to act together. Empowerment requires mobilizing local people in the South and consumers in the North. Acting together is not difficult: we have alternatives to build on and to share widely. But in examining our various solutions the key is to assess how many people can make use of the strategy and how many will be excluded from it.

Box 4.2: The Seed Keepers

Burn our land, burn our dreams, pour acid on our soil,
Cover with sawdust the blood of our massacred people
Muffle with your technology the screams of all that is free, wild and
indigenous.

Destroy, destroy our grass and soil
Raze to the ground every farm and every village our ancestors built –
Every tree, every home, every book, every law,
And all the equity and harmony.

Flatten with your bombs every valley
Erase with your edicts our past, our literature, our metaphor
Denude the forests and the earth till no insect, no bird, no word can find
a place to hide.

Do that and more
I do not fear your tyranny
I do not despair ever
For I guard one seed, a little life seed that I shall safeguard and plant
again.

Source: Indian woman farmer

The violence of the Green Revolution – the tragedy of Punjab

India's state of Punjab is the country's most prosperous region, with incomes 65% above the national average. Yet the region is seething with discontent and has suffered the largest number of killings in peacetime in independent India. The Punjab tragedy has commonly been represented as the outcome of conflict between two religious groups, but this view is misleading. Looking more deeply, the conflict also has political and economic roots, reflecting social breakdown and tensions between a disillusioned farming community and a centralizing state. At the heart of the conflict lies the Green Revolution.

The Green Revolution began in the early 1960s, gathered momentum rapidly and by 1968 nearly half the wheat planted in India came from Green Revolution seed. The key to the so-called 'miracle' varieties of wheat and rice that responded to intensive inputs of chemical fertilizers was the introduction of a dwarf gene. The taller traditional varieties tended to fall over with high applications of chemicals because they converted the nutrients into overall plant growth, causing lengthening of the stems. The shorter, stiffer stems of dwarf varieties allowed more efficient conversion of fertilizer into grain.

Worldwide, the revolution was promoted as a strategy that would create abundance in agricultural societies, thereby reducing the threat of communist insurgency and agrarian conflict in developing countries. Science and politics were welded together in order to change the agrarian relationships that had previously been politically troublesome. However, in Punjab, as in many other Green Revolution areas, the strategy failed. This in turn meant that, at the political level, it turned out to be conflict-producing instead of conflict-reducing. At the material level, production of high yields of commercial grain generated new scarcities in ecosystems and among rural people, which in turn generated new sources of conflict.

The Punjab crisis can be viewed as arising from a basic and unresolved conflict between diversity, decentralization and democracy on the one hand and uniformity, centralization and militarization on the other. The Green Revolution was based on the assumption that technology is a superior substitute for nature, and hence a means of producing growth unconstrained by nature's limits. Its proponents argued that nature is a source of scarcity and technology is a source of abundance. But at an ecological level, the Green Revolution produced scarcity, not abundance.

Two decades later Punjab has been left with diseased soils, pest-infested crops, waterlogging, and indebted and discontented farmers. Green Revolution technology required heavy investments in fertilizers, pesticides, seed, water and energy. This intensive agriculture generated severe ecological destruction, created new kinds of scarcity and vulnerability, and resulted in new levels of inefficiency in resource use. Instead of transcending the limits placed by the natural endowments of land and water, the Green Revolution introduced new constraints on agriculture by destroying land, water resources and crop diversity.

'Miracle' seeds and the destruction of diversity
The introduction of the Green Revolution 'miracle seeds' signaled the start of the privatization of agricultural genetic resources. After 10 000 years of producing and selecting their own seeds, peasants gave way to scientists as plant breeding specialists. Plant breeding strategies of nurturing genetic diversity and fostering the self-renewability of crops were substituted by new strategies centred on uniformity and non-renewability.

The bold claims made about the inherent superiority and productivity of the 'miracle seeds' belie reality. These claims are based on a reductionist analysis, in which the costs and impacts of using Green Revolution seed are externalized and misleading comparisons are made. The yield increases of the Green Revolution crops were at least partly counteracted by decreases in the yields of other crops in the farming system. In indigenous agriculture, cropping systems are based on a symbiotic relationship between soil, water, farm animals and plants. Green Revolution agriculture introduces a new element and eliminates some of the traditional inputs. In the reductionist analysis the interaction between the new seed/chemical package and soil, water, plants and animals is not taken into account in the assessment of yields.

Moreover, this analysis wrongly compares yields of single crops grown in a monoculture system with those of the same crop grown in a diverse, mixed farming system. Realistic assessments are not made of the yield of the diverse crop outputs in the mixed systems. And even where the yields of all the crops are included, it is difficult to convert a measure of pulses into an equivalent measure of wheat, because they have distinctive functions and values in the diet and in the ecosystem. The protein value of pulses and the energy value of cereals are both essential for a balanced diet, but one cannot replace the other. In Punjab, wheat has spread at the cost of pulses, barley, rape and mustard, which were usually sown as mixed crops with traditional wheat varieties. Rice spread at the cost of maize, pulses, groundnut, green fodder and cotton.

The term 'high-yielding' – often used to describe Green Revolution seeds – is a misnomer because it implies that the new seeds are inherently high-yielding. Palmer[1] has suggested that the term 'high-response varieties' is more accurate since, in the absence of additional inputs of fertilizer and irrigation, the new seeds can perform worse than indigenous varieties. The gain in output is insignificant once the increase in inputs is accounted for (see Table 4.3).

Genetic uniformity and the creation of new pests
The narrow genetic base of the Green Revolution varieties led to increased vulnerability to pests and diseases, whereas indigenous farming strategies are more resilient to pests and diseases because of

Table 4.3.   External input farming system

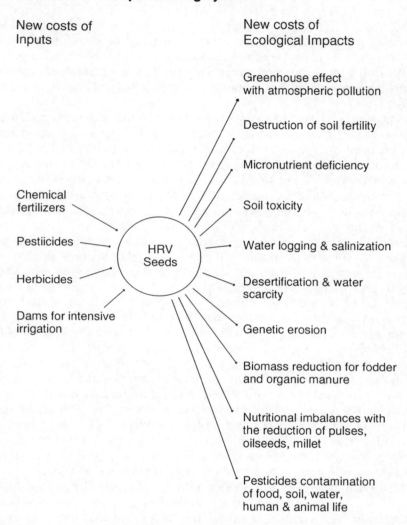

New costs of
Inputs

New costs of
Ecological Impacts

Greenhouse effect
with atmospheric pollution

Destruction of soil fertility

Micronutrient deficiency

Chemical
fertilizers

Soil toxicity

Pestiicides

HRV
Seeds

Water logging & salinization

Herbicides

Desertification & water
scarcity

Dams for intensive
irrigation

Genetic erosion

Biomass reduction for fodder
and organic manure

Nutritional imbalances with
the reduction of pulses,
oilseeds, millet

Pesticides contamination
of food, soil, water,
human & animal life

rotational cropping practices and the inherent resistance and diversity amongst the crops grown. Planting the same crop over large areas year after year encourages pest build-ups. Before 1965, rice was an insignificant crop in the Punjab, but the percentage of cropped area under rice increased from 5.5% in 1966–67 to 23.73% in 1985–86, when semi-dwarf varieties accounted for 95% of the rice produced.

New varieties had to be introduced in rapid succession because of their susceptibility to diseases and pests (Table 4.4). The first dwarf variety introduced in 1966, the Taichung Native I variety, was

Table 4.4. Outbreaks of rice insect pests and diseases in the Punjab

Year	Insect pests/ diseases appeared in outbreak form	Varieties	District affected by outbreaks
1967	Leaf-folder	Basmati 370, IR8	Kapurthala
1972	Root weevil	IR8, Jaya	Patiala
	Whitebacked plant hopper	Sabarmati, Ratna, Palman 579, RP5-3	Ludhiana
1973	Brown plant hopper	IR8, Jaya	Kapurthala, Patiala, Ludhiana, Ropar
1975	Brown plant hopper	IR 8, Jaya	Gurdaspur, Ferozepur,
	Whitebacked plant hopper	IR 8	Kapurthala
1975	Bacterial blight	IR8, Jaya, PR106	Gurdaspur, Amritsar
1978	Whitebacked plant hopper	PR558, PR559, PR562	Kapurthala
	Sheath blight	IR8, Jaya, PR106 PR103	Amritsar, Jalandhar, Kapurthala, Patiala
	Sheath rot	PR 106, IR8	All rice-growing areas
1980	Bacterial blight	PR106, IR8, Jaya, PR103, Basmati 370	All rice-growing areas
	Stem rot	PR106, IR8, Jaya	Amritsar, Gurdaspur Patiala, Kapurthala, Ferozepur
1981	Whitebacked plant hopper	PR107, PR 4141	Kapurthala, Patiala, Ferozepur
1982	Whitebacked plant hopper	PR107, PR 4141	Patiala, Ferozepur Kapurthala
	Thrips	HM95, PR103	Kapurthala, Gurdaspur
	Yellow stem borer	PR4141, PR106	Ferozepur
1983	Brown plant hopper, whitebacked plant hopper	PR 196, PR4141 Pusa-150, Pusa-169 PR4141, PR106	Patiala, Ferozepur Kapurthala
	Yellow stem borer	Basmati 370 Punjab Basmati 1	Ferozepur Kapurthala
	Thrips	PR106, Jaya, IR8 PR106, PR414, Punjab Basmati 1	Ludhiana, Kapurthala All rice-growing areas
	Hispa	PR 103, PR 106, PR 4141, IR8, Jaya, Basmati 370, Punjab Basmati 1	Kapurthala, Gurdaspur

Source: Shiva, V. (1991), *The Violence of the Green Revolution*, Zed Books.

susceptible to bacterial blight and whitebacked plant hopper. In 1968 it was replaced by IR-8 which was thought to be resistant to stem rot and brown spot, but proved to be susceptible to both. Later varieties were bred specifically for disease resistance, but few have held their own. PR 106, which currently accounts for 80% of the area under rice cultivation in Punjab, was selected for its resistance to whitebacked plant hopper and stem rot disease. Since its introduction in 1976, it has become susceptible tò both, and also to several other insect pests.

Poisoning the soil

Twenty years of Green Revolution agriculture have seriously damaged the fertility of Punjab soils, because it was mistakenly believed that chemicals could replace the natural fertility of soils. The nutrient cycle from soil to plant and back again has been replaced by a non-renewable flow of phosphorus and potash derived from geological deposits, and nitrogen from petroleum.

The erosion and degradation of land in the Punjab is a direct consequence of the rapid change in land-use patterns, irrigation practices and the use of chemical inputs resulting from the Green Revolution. Croplands are now kept constantly under soil-depleting crops like wheat and rice, rather than being rotated with soil-building crops like pulses. As Kang has cautioned, 'This process implies a downward spiralling of agricultural land use – from legume to wheat to rice to wasteland'.[2]

There are also micronutrient deficiencies and excesses. Organic manuring replaces trace elements such as zinc, iron, copper and manganese, but chemical fertilizers supply only nitrogen, phosphorus and potassium. More than half of 8000 soil samples taken exhibited zinc deficiency, which has reduced yields of rice, wheat and maize by up to 3.9, 1.98 and 3.4 tonnes per hectare respectively. Meanwhile, fluorine toxicity from irrigation has affected large areas and 26Mha of land is affected by aluminium poisoning. As a result of micronutrient problems, the increase in chemical fertilizer application has not produced a corresponding increase in the output of rice and wheat: productivity has been fluctuating or declining in most regions of the Punjab.[3]

Cultural costs

Perhaps the least recognized of all the Green Revolution's impacts are its cultural costs. The rapid and large-scale introduction of its technologies dislocated the social structure and political processes at two levels. It created growing disparities among classes, and it increased the commercialization of social relations. In Punjab, rather than sweeping away communal conflicts as expected, modernization and economic development hardened ethnic identities and intensified conflict.

The Punjab crisis resulted from three kinds of conflicts:

- Conflicts arising from the very nature of the Green Revolution, i.e. conflicts over river waters, the use of labour-displacing mechanization, the decline in the profitability of modern agriculture, etc., all of which led to a disaffected peasantry engaged in farmers' protests.

- Conflicts related to religious and cultural factors revolving around the Sikh identity. These were rooted in the cultural erosion of the Green Revolution which commercialized all relations and eroded traditional ethics. Religious revivalism, which emerged to correct the moral and social crisis, crystallized finally in the emergence of a separatist Sikh identity.

- Conflicts related to the sharing of economic and political power between the centre and state. The shift from local organization and internal inputs to centralized control and external, imported inputs undermined farmers' power and shifted power to the state.

To a large extent, the movements for regional, religious and ethnic revival are movements for the recovery of diversity. The ecological crisis of the Green Revolution is thus mirrored by a cultural crisis caused by the erosion of diversity, changing structures of governance and the emergence of centralized external control over the daily activities of food production.

Biotechnology – the third wave
In Punjab, the financial and ecological problems created by the Green Revolution necessitated new initiatives. Two options were available. The first involved moving away from capital- and resource-intensive agricultural technology to low-input and low-impact agriculture. The second was to move away from growing staple foods for domestic markets to producing luxury foods and non-food crops for export markets, with a new dependence on imports of high technology inputs like seeds and chemicals. This latter option was officially adopted as the strategy for the second agricultural revolution in Punjab.

The main elements of this second revolution are:

- substitution of wheat and rice with fruits and vegetables to be processed for export markets

- substitution of Green Revolution technologies, with bio-technologies more dependent on chemical inputs and designed for food processing

- total neglect of staple food production as a primary objective of public policy.

The first major project under this new policy, the Pepsico project, was justified on the grounds of diversification of agriculture, increases in agricultural income and employment, and the restoration of peace and stability in Punjab. However, like the Green Revolution before it, the project looks set to aggravate the existing crisis by introducing new vulnerability in agriculture.

The new plant biotechnologies being introduced in Punjab and elsewhere will follow the path of the earlier high-yielding varieties in making farmers ever more dependent on external technology. Biotechnology will probably increase the use of capital and external inputs, further marginalizing the poor and destroying the natural ecological rhythm. The use of chemical inputs will increase, since the dominant trend in research is not for fertilizer- and pest-free crops, but for pesticide- and herbicide-resistant varieties (see Chapter 2.2).

Biotechnology fundamentally changes the perceived value of biodiversity. By transforming the richness of the planet's genetic resources into a strategic material for the industrial production of food, pharmaceuticals, fibres and so on, biodiversity conservation becomes the conservation of the 'raw material' rather than conservation of a 'means of production'.

There is a belief that biotechnology development will automatically lead to biodiversity conservation. However, corporate strategies can lead to diversification of commodities, but they cannot enrich nature's diversity.

Similarly, the nature of seed is changed from being both a 'product' (the grain) and a 'means of production' to being just a 'raw material'. In the past, the penetration of capital into agriculture has been prevented by a simple biological obstacle: the nature of the seed is such that, given appropriate conditions, it can reproduce itself manifold. Therefore in order to be able to create a market for it, seed must be transformed materially.

Biotechnology renders seed inert without inputs, so that it cannot produce by itself. Modern plant breeding techniques also render it non-reproducible. In this way, biodiversity is transformed from a renewable to a non-renewable resource. The cycle of regeneration is replaced by a linear flow of free germplasm from farms and forests into corporate laboratories and research stations, and the flow of modified uniform products as commodities from corporations to farms and forests.

References

1. In Lappé, F.M. and Collins, J. (1982), *Food First*, London, Abacus.
2. Kang, D.S. (1982) 'Environmental problems of the Green Revolution, with a focus on Punjab, India,' in Richard Barrett (ed.) *International Dimensions of the Environmental Crisis*, Boulder, Westview Press, p. 204.
3. Punjab Agricultural University (1985). Department of Soils, mimeo.

5 HUMAN GENES – THE NEW RESOURCE

5.1. The human genome diversity project

The Human Genome Diversity Project (HGDP) is the brainchild of a group of scientists headed by Luca Cavalli-Sforza who proposed in 1991 to create a global map of human genetic variation. The aim of the project is to take blood, tissue and hair samples from some 700 ethnic groups in order to produce detailed information on the origins and migration histories of human populations and the genetic basis of their differing susceptibilities to certain diseases.

Who are we?

Where do we come from?

Where are we going?

The aim of the HGDP, contends anthropologist André Langanay, is to help answer the first two of the questions that humans have always asked themselves.[1] And so, it seems, genetic tinkering is going not only to cure world hunger and rid us of sickness and disease, but it is going to help us understand the meaning of life.

The cells of everybody alive today, regardless of where or how they live, contain the same 100 000 or so genes. Collectively known as the 'human genome', these genes contain all the information that distinguish us from other species. However, many human genes are described as 'polymorphic' because they exist in more than one form as different *alleles* (see p. 74). The physical differences (such as hair and eye colour) that help us to distinguish people are the results of genetic polymorphism. Each of us, apart from identical twins, is a unique individual, recognizably human but different from all other humans.

The genetic variation from one person to another reflects the evolution of our species, since it is the result, over many generations, of the survival or loss of different forms of genes or the natural introduction of new forms. The HGDP believes that 'studying this variation, which is the aim of the HGDP, can therefore provide a great deal of information about the development of our species which, integrated with findings from archaeology, linguistics, history and other disciplines, can lead to a much richer and more complete picture of our past than has previously been possible'.[2] It goes on to say that it will also provide the scientific data to confirm and support what is already clear from population studies – that, in biological terms, there is no such thing as a clearly defined race and thus it will 'undermine the popular belief that there are clearly defined races, to contribute to the elimination of racism and to make a major contribution to the understanding of the nature of differences between individuals and between human populations'. Biologically, there is only a continual graduation from one population to another.*

The third major contribution the HGDP is expected to make is to provide valuable information about the factors contributing to disease. The incidence of different diseases varies between populations and, while much of this variation can be explained by environmental factors such as diet, climate, the presence of parasites or pollutants, genetic factors are also known to have a predisposing effect in many cases. Scientists believe that studying the differences in the genetic composition of different communities will ultimately help to develop more effective ways of treating and preventing many diseases. Some of the areas on which the HGDP is expected to throw new light are the inheritance of disease, the development of cancer and the process of ageing.

The project was taken under the wing of the Human Genome Organization (HUGO) and the Human Genome Project (HGP), the European and US arms of the ambitious attempt to map the human genome using molecular genetic analysis. The HGDP can in some ways be seen as a natural extension of HUGO and the HGP, since it can complement the other two studies by helping to build up a more truly global picture of the genome. In Cavalli-Sforza's words, 'The "Book of Man" would be rather shallow if it were written without consideration of the well-known fact that everyone is different from everyone else.'[3]

The HGDP is expected to cost between $23 and $35 million over five years, funding for which is largely to come from the HGP. Although funds are still not completely assured, sample collections have already begun. Cavalli-Sforza was very concerned that the

---

* Until recently, studies of genetic variation relied on using the various proteins coded for by individual genes as 'markers' to determine genetic differences between individuals and populations. This is how blood groups are recognized. In the 1980s, researchers developed techniques to enable them to extend their repertoire of markers to include not only genes, but also stretches of human DNA that do not encode proteins. This led to the discovery of 'polymorphisms'. It is these advances that inspired Cavalli-Sforza's proposal for the HGDP.

project should get going as soon as possible because of the endangered nature of many of the indigenous groups.

Scope and strategy of the HGDP

More than 700 groups from all around the world were targeted for DNA sampling at the HGDP's Second Workshop meeting in 1992.[4] The group comprises 165 from Africa, 212 from Asia, 114 from South America, 101 from Oceania, 107 from North America and 23 from Europe. Among them are the Yukaghir of Siberia (with about 100 people remaining in the group), the Alcaluf of Southern Chile (less than 50 remaining), the Amazon's Akuriyo (50 survivors) and the Tench of Micronesia (about 80 remaining).

Biological samples of blood, hair, and/or cheek scrapings will be collected anonymously from each group, along with socio-demographic data, such as sex, age, place of birth, place of residence, and further parental information. Between 25 and 150 people will be sampled from each population, depending on the size of the group; researchers are clear on how many samples are needed to ensure that the material deposited in the central HGDP repositories is representative of the population being sampled. It is intended that most of the initial collecting and handling of samples will be done by local investigators; regional collection centres will need to be established for sample storage and analysis.

The HGDP Summary Document notes that 'not all regions of the world are experienced in the techniques of molecular biology and genetics and that some countries will not, in the foreseeable future, acquire the "cutting edge" technology that is needed for the mapping and sequencing of the HGDP. However, it is feasible for the more limited technological demands of the HGDP to be met by most countries, given training of staff and help with techniques'. The HGDP team see this as one of the 'most exciting aspects of the project', in that it 'offers all countries a unique opportunity to become involved in . . . the global genome initiative'.[2]

But according to critics of the project, there is a danger that the resources used for such capital-intensive initiatives could easily be diverted from more pressing public health projects in many countries. Some also question the justification of spending so much money on the HGDP, even if it isn't at the expense of other projects, when there are so many more immediate and pressing health needs for many communities. In defence of the HGDP, project organizer Ken Weiss points out, 'We are concerned about the well-being of these (indigenous) people. But a group of geneticists isn't going to save them. Stop clear cutting the Amazon rainforest. That will save them'.[5]

Many of the scientists behind the diversity project, he points out, have been instrumental in publicizing the plight of the Yanomami people in Brazil, whose population has plummeted in recent years as the result of unrestrained mining for gold and tin, and the concomitant destruction of their environment and the introduction of disease.

Once the samples are placed in the central repository, DNA will be extracted and stored 'for long-term use'. In order to provide a back-up source of the DNA, a number of blood samples will be immortalized as cell lines (all descended from a single cell). In principle, DNA can be made to last indefinitely through the application of a group of techniques known as polymerase chain reaction (PCR), which can even make copies of DNA from single cells.

Human bioprospecting Newspeak

At the outset the project organizers recognized that their planned activities could cause dismay among indigenous people and the wider public. According to the report of the second workshop on the project, 'the establishment of permanent cell lines needs to be explained in terms that are understandable, but that do not mislead subjects in any population. English terms such as "immortalization" of cell lines can be badly misunderstood . . .'[4] Many indigenous groups, however, feel that the careful avoidance of using such terms is a convenient way of not allowing them to become aware of the full implications.

The same document also points out that there is 'no fully acceptable way to refer to populations that are in danger of physical extinction or of disruption as integral units (gene pools); some existing terms such as "endangered" populations can have various connotations . . . in this report we refer to such groups as "Isolates of Historical Interest" (IHI) because they represent groups that should be sampled before they disappear as integral units so that their role in human history can be preserved'. The logic and rationale behind this Newspeak is one of the aspects of the project that indigenous groups have reacted against most strongly (see pp. 145–8). More recent public documents on the HGDP have dropped the use of this term.

The importance of promoting the good image of the HGDP is made clear in the Summary Document. 'Many people in the world have, at best, a limited understanding of human genetics. Some fear the consequences of human genetic research, in part because of the limits of their understanding. To scientists involved in the HGDP, such fears may not seem justified or even fully rational . . .' Nevertheless, it is seen as 'essential that a world-wide "public awareness" programme is included within the project to educate people about its aims, methods and results.'[2]

Box 5.1: Bioprospecting for human genes – the case of the Guaymi

The genes of the Guaymi Indians of Panama became the object of a bioprospecting initiative because of the tribe's innate resistance to leukaemia-causing viruses. An investigation was launched by the Centers for Disease Control of the US Department of Health and Human Services and the National Institutes of Health, in collaboration with Panamanian scientists into the rare human T-cell lymphotropic viruses (HTLV), one of which (type II) is known to be a causative agent of adult T-cell (a white blood cell) leukaemia and a neurological disease. For some unknown reason infection with HTLV type I is very common among the Guaymi and other Amerindian peoples in North and South America, who also donated samples as part of the project.

According to Isidro Acosta Galindo, President of the General Congress of the Ngobe-Bugle (Guaymi), 'the doctors came to the communities of Pandila in small groups and started to collect indigenous blood, pretending the indigenous people were suffering from a mortal disease and that this blood study was necessary to see what kind of malformation or what kind of disease they suffered. To compensate for loss of blood, they gave the people a small pill to strengthen up'.

One of three local women suffering from leukaemia was found to have an unusual capacity to resist the disease. A T-cell line infected with HTLV-II was developed in the US from blood donated in 1990, and a patent was filed by the US Department of Commerce later that year, first in the US and then worldwide. The patent was filed without notifying the woman or any of the other Guaymi people, the project's Panamanian collaborators or the Panamanian government.

Once discovered, the patent claim caused an international outcry. Galindo wrote to the US Secretary of Commerce demanding that the patent application be withdrawn, and to the Patents and Trademarks office to reject it. He also denounced the patent claim at meetings of the GATT Secretariat and the Biodiversity Convention, saying that making 'living cells. . . patented private property . . . is against all Guaymi traditions and laws'. Less than a month later, the patent application was withdrawn, allegedly because of the high cost of pursuing a patent claim. However, it seems very likely that the real reason was the international outcry.

Similar patent claims have been made on T-cell lines infected with HTLV-I viruses from indigenous groups in Papua New Guinea and the Solomon Islands. In the Papua New Guinea claim, the blood sample came from a member of the Hagahai, a group of 260 hunter-cultivators first contacted by government and missionary workers in 1984.

Box 5.2: Bioprospecting for human genes – the Aeta people

The Aeta people of the central Philippines are one of the indigenous groups to become the subject of bioprospecting activities. Researchers from Roche Molecular Systems (RMS), a subsidiary of Hoffman–la Roche, are eager to study their genes for possible diagnostic purposes and potential therapeutic applications against a variety of auto-immune disorders and infectious diseases, such as malaria, leprosy and cholera. These interests closely match the research focus of RMS. Hoffman–la Roche, meanwhile, is a market leader in antimalarial drugs.

According to Victoria Corpus of the Cordillera Peoples Alliance, 'The Aeta people are ancient people of the Philippines. They are small, frizzy haired and dark skinned, or "negroid pygmies" as anthropologists choose to call them, and were allegedly some of the first people to reach the territory of what we know as the Philippines via a land bridge. Being hunters and gatherers, they roamed the forests and up to now have kept to themselves, and are therefore "genetically pure". Their lack of contact with the outside world has been partly the result of discrimination against them because they looked and behaved differently – the government has never cared about the Aeta. They were driven out when the US built an airbase on their hunting grounds; disease, poverty, and finally the eruption of Mt Pinatubo in 1991 decimated the population.'

In 1993, researchers from Roche Molecular Systems first approached the Hawaii-based Aloha Medical Mission, which was involved in providing emergency medical care and support to victims of the Mt. Pinatubo volcanic eruption. On learning that the Mission would not be returning to the Aeta people in the near future, in May 1994 the researchers approached Dr Phillip Camara of the Makati Medical Centre in the Phillipines. In a letter to Camara, researcher Elizabeth Trachtenberg wrote that she understood that he came into regular contact with 'the endemic Aeta and other Pygmy Indian tribes' and wondered if he would be able to collaborate on the venture. She also added that 'it may be possible that we may also be able to contribute some monetary value to other projects in the region on behalf of your collaboration'.[8]

Dr Camara wrote a brief response declining the invitation, asking 'How will this technology be controlled? Who will benefit from this technology? To whom are the scientists accountable? What are the ethical implications of human genetic studies?' and 'What rights will minority people have over their DNA structure?'[9]

Trachtenberg's response reiterated that the research would hope to 'shed some light on the structure, evolution and function of man's immune system' and outlined the importance to such studies of isolated, indigenous groups whose genetic make-up has not been watered down by intermarriage. She insisted that 'because this is an NIH grant (see

Prior informed consent

Indigenous groups have strong ethical, religious and moral value systems, and it is critical that these are respected (see Chapter 5.2). HGDP
documents recognize that sampled populations must 'be provided a
full level of informed consent. Religious or other cultural concerns must
be protected'. However, this statement is qualified in that there is only
an expectation that the groups 'understand as fully *as practical* the
implications of the study, and its purposes'.[4] The vagueness of the
language leaves it open to wide interpretation. In a recent TV programme broadcast in the UK, which followed HGDP researchers on
their field work in Colombia, indigenous groups were given a very
limited view of the project. Its implications were not made clear to the
various communities and discussions of the wider objectives of the
project were overshadowed by the carrots offered to the communities,
such as opportunistic medical clinics set up to treat minor and immediate health concerns of the villagers and promises of the blood samples
being used to test for diabetes in the population.[6] By giving only half of
the picture, the HGDP is not being true to its own principles, nor to the
communities the researchers are dealing with.

Intellectual property rights

Earlier drafts of HGDP documents completely ignore the issue of
intellectual property rights, and later versions only touch on it, stating
that, 'Although very unlikely, it is nevertheless possible that the results
of the HGDP may lead to the production of commercially beneficial
pharmaceuticals or other products. Should a patent be granted on any
specific product, the project must work to ensure that the sampled
populations benefit from the financial return from sales'.[2]

Some critics argue that the HGDP is greatly understating the potential
economic returns from the project. According to RAFI, 'in the US, the
patenting of human genetic material is well underway. Blood samples
collected by the HGDP will be stored at the American Type Culture

143

Collection, near Washington D.C . . . In November, 1992, this respository held 1094 human cell line entries, more than one-third of which are the subject of patent applications'.[7] RAFI goes on to point out that backing for the HGDP's primary funder, the HGP, comes from the US Government's National Institutes of Health (NIH), which has already made patent applications on human genetic material. Bioprospecting for human genes is very much a reality already, and many indigenous groups are already very concerned about being treated as commodities.

The involvement of industry in the HGDP is ambiguous. While project organizers are keen to stress that the project has no commercial ambitions, industry seems to be closely involved in the project. Researchers from Roche Molecular Systems accompanied HGDP researchers on their field work in Colombia and Ecuador, and the company has been involved in several other cases of human gene prospecting. Researchers have, for example, already made several attempts to gain access to the Aeta people in the Philippines, who are on the HGDP's list of suggested sampling populations.

References

1. Oral presentation by André Langanay of the University of Geneva at the 'Patents, Genes and Butterflies' Conference in Bern, Switzerland, October 1994. Langanay recently resigned as a committee member on the HGDP.
2. The Human Genome Diversity (HGD) Project – Summary Document (1994).
3. From an article in *Genomics*, as reported in the *New Scientist*, 29 May 1993.
4. Report of the Second Human Genome Diversity Workshop. Penn State University, 29–31 October 1992.
5. Lewin, R. (1993) Genes from a Disappearing World. *New Scientist*, May 29.
6. The Gene Hunters, Channel 4 Productions, 1994.
7. RAFI (1993). Patents, Indigenous People, and Human Genetic Diversity. RAFI Communiqué, May 1993.
8. Letter to Phillip Camara c/o the Makati Medical Centre from Elizabeth Trachtenberg of Roche Molecular Systems, 1 March 1993.
9. Letter to Dr. Elizabeth Trachtenberg of Roche Molecular Systems from Philip Camara of SASFI, 11 June 1994.
10. Reply to Philip Camara from Elizabeth Trachtenberg, 26 July 1994.

5.2. Indigenous peoples' reactions to the HGDP

Indigenous peoples' network on biodiversity, ALEJANDRO ARGUMEDO

It is first important to understand that indigenous people are not minorities. We are significant peoples and we are nations. It has taken us 20 years of struggle at the UN to be recognized as such.

Indigenous people have a fundamentally different view of the world from the scientists that have dreamed up the HGDP. Three months ago I was in the mountains of the Sierra Nevada in Colombia where the Kogi live. The Kogi is a nation close to the Caribbean, and its people have a philosophy of life in which everything is sacred – the wind, every twig, every stone, every person . . . The Kogi see people outside their lands as doing 'wrong things'. They call themselves 'older brothers' and those outside 'younger brothers' because they see that the latter don't realize what they are doing. I once had the chance to meet a *mama*, a Kogi priest, who told me, 'If you see any younger brothers (by which he meant the scientists involved in the HGDP) tell them to stop, because nobody has the right to rape their own mother, and that is what they are doing to the earth'.

The HGDP is a manifestation of the commodification of the sacred, which I have to oppose. Because science has been used as a magic tool to control nature for so long, people have lost their sense of communion with the earth, their sense of belonging to nature. Science separates us from nature, thus separating us from the sacredness of life, from spirituality and the energy that flows through all things. This reductionist approach destroys the holistic view. By focusing on smaller and smaller things, like genes, you can't build up the full picture of life. You cannot explain life in terms of chemicals and genes, so you have to construct ethics to fill in the gaps. This reductionism is what causes the proponents of the HGDP to look at people in such a dehumanized way, seeing us as 'isolates of historical interest'.

The HGDP is business disguised as science. The real objectives are being hidden, and access to information is practically impossible for us to obtain. We are not against science when it is co-operative, participative, controlled and transparent. But the HGDP does not fit this mould, so we cannot support it. Democracy is being redefined as having access to markets, as having rights to compensation. We don't

The colonial era is far from over – it simply takes on different guises.
(Whitten Archive, Cambridge University Museum of Archaeology and Anthropology)

146

believe in that. Our basic principle is the sacredness of life, so we cannot accept this madness.

The questions that the HGDP tries to answer are those of the dispossessed. People that have lost their connection with nature and their respect for it lose respect for themselves. That is why they ask, 'Where do we come from?' and 'Where are we going?' Even with all this work on genetics, they are getting more confused – they don't even know what a gene is any more. Nevertheless, scientists keep pursuing this 'knowledge'. Stop. That's enough. Let's regain some respect for life. If we don't have any respect for ourselves, of course we are going to destroy what is out there in the name of science, of knowledge. Just look what is happening to the world out there.

This is why the HGDP is irrelevant to indigenous peoples. It focuses on issues that are unimportant to us. We know who we are. We know where we have come from and why we are here. Our concerns are about how we can protect our lands, how we can protect our lives and livelihoods in the colonialist states in which we live, and how to seek alternatives to the destruction we see around us. Around the world, people have lost their spiritual relationship with the world – reviving this link is what we should be striving for.

Cordillera Peoples' Alliance, the Philippines, VICTORIA CORPUS

Of the 722 indigenous groups targeted by the HGDP, 11 from the Philippines were included, including my own people, the Ifugao, from the Mountain Province. The Cordillera Peoples' Alliance has protested to the UN Commission for Sustainable Development about the project for the following reasons:

(A) Motivation for the project The HGDP starts from the premise that indigenous peoples are endangered. The main reason for this is because of the genocide and ethnocide that has been committed through colonialism. It is highly insulting to us that people claim to be concerned about our endangered position, yet they are more interested in collecting our genes than addressing the main causes of why we are endangered, such as poverty, militarization, and the fact that our rights to self-determination are not recognized. Why don't these researchers and corporations take action to help us? Why do they simply stand by as we die, and instead immortalize us in their gene banks. This type of research is immoral. It lowers our peoples to the status of living gene providers for the chemical industry.

(B) Collection Methods   Although prior informed consent (PIC) is a prerequisite for collection to take place, none of us trust this because of our past bitter experiences. In the Philippines, even contraception has been imposed on people without them knowing, and the simplicity of collecting blood and hair samples makes the acquisition of samples very easy without PIC.

(C) Fate of the materials   If our genes are found to have useful characteristics like disease-resistance, will they be commercialized? And if they are found to have susceptibility to particular diseases, we are potential targets for biowarfare. Many indigenous people are thorns in the side of governments and developers, because of their opposition to the building of dams, mines and so on. The easiest way to kill the protest is to release genetically engineered disease carriers into communities, just as smallpox virus was introduced into Indian communities in the Amazon.

We are told that the results are not for commercial ends, but we have little reason to trust the researchers. Patents have already been taken out on the cell lines of indigenous people without their consent (see p. 90), so our fears about the fate of our genes are not unfounded. The scientists may have valid intentions, but what happens when the information gets into the hands of industry? As part of a 'medical' mission a Hoffman–la Roche subsidiary is already collecting genetic material from the Aeta pygmies in the Philippines.

(D) Impact on ancestral rights   The project is to be used to study migration patterns. Does that mean that if Aborigines are shown to have come from Asia originally, this evidence can be used to deny their rights to their ancestral homes?

5.3. Glorification of the Genes – genetic determinism and racism in science

ALAN GOODMAN

Introduction

Most scientists know about the existence of the Human Genome Project (HGP)* and consider it to be biology's first 'big science project', patterned after the Manhattan Project and Los Alamos Atomic Bomb Projects. Biologists are quick to point out the advances made through the development of polymerase chain reaction technologies (used to replicate DNA in genetic engineering techniques) and that great strides are being made in working out the genetic code. They may also mention that genome research is well funded, and may realize that this takes away funding from other biomedical projects. Yet many scientists have not realized that something unusual is going on in biomedical research: something intense, fast-paced and potentially threatening. Only a few seem concerned with the ideological consequences of genomics or the economic and social implications of the commercialization of genetic information. These considerations are left to others.

Compare this lack of concern with views expressed in a recent popular book. The biotechnology revolution is said to be based on research that is 'thoughtless and frivolous'. The commercialization of molecular biology is described as 'the most stunning ethical event in the history of science'. Biotechnology is 'the greatest revolution in human history' . . . 'By the end of the decade [it] will have outdistanced atomic power and computers in its effect on our everyday life'. Finally, with the promise of private research funds and shares in biotechnology companies, 'Suddenly it seems as if everyone wanted to become rich'. Who sounds these warnings? It is Michael Crichton in the first two pages of *Jurassic Park*.[1]

This paper aims to explore some of the potential implications of genetic manipulation and examine the connections between hereditarianism, racialism and racism. Hereditarianism (or genetic determinism) is defined as the belief that patterns and differences in biology and behaviour are predominantly caused by patterns and variation in the genome.[2,3] It is the 'nature' in the 'nature–nurture' argument. Racialism

---

* The European branch of the Human Genome Project is managed by the Human Genome Organization (HUGO).

(or scientific racism) is the belief that humans are divisible into a finite number of types (races) and that individual biology and behaviour are explicable by race.[4] Racism is the belief in the superiority of certain races over others, combined with the power to act upon that belief.

Three issues will be discussed here:

o the problems of using race as a model of human variation

o trends toward hereditarianism and racialism in biomedical research

o the concurrent recent rise of genomics and hereditarianism in biological anthropology (as illustrated by the Human Genome Diversity Project) and how it gains legitimacy from the existing currents of racialism and racism.

Race in anthropology in the 1990s

The biological concept of race is often wrongly used as shorthand to refer to human biological variation. A racialist model of human variation suggests that humans are divisible into a finite number of nearly separate subspecies. However:

o Human variation is nonconcordant; that is, variation in one trait says little about variation in another. Height can predict weight but little else – not blood type or skin colour. So it is true to say that 'race is skin deep.'

o Variation is continuous, thus it is arbitrary where one group begins and another ends.

o Race explains only about 6% of human variability in a statistical sense,[5] and in a biological sense it explains even less. This is because what is generally assumed to be explained by race can just as well be explained by geographical proximity.

In short, human variation is real; race is an idea.

The forensic anthropologist tries to match skeletal remains with a previously living person. Forensic anthropologists justify their practice of racing skeletons by saying that 'race' is what law enforcement agencies want. But this is not true: agencies want to identify individuals and to know their 'official' race so that a form can be filled in. Forensic scientists continue to confuse official race with biological race and to reify race (i.e., to make it real or material) by complying with law enforcement needs without educating law enforcement agencies about the realities of human variation. Two listings from a recent catalogue of skulls universally used in the teaching of human biology and variation[6] give some insight into learning how *not* to

150

question the reality of race. The first listing is labelled 'negroid male'. The description of the skull states that it 'illustrates racial traits very well . . . this is wonderful cast!' The skull below is labelled 'caucasoid female'. It is described a similar fashion: 'illustrates racial traits very well . . . this is in excellent condition!'

What is the message here? Students do not learn about the discontinous and nonconcordant nature of human variation. Instead human variation is reduced to how well crania fit essentialized types and students learn a simplistic story about unchanging types of people. The presentation of these casts speaks volumes for the theory disseminated to those who work in the industry of forensics and physical anthropology.

But what does this have to do with genes? Firstly, race is all about 'essentializing' types of people – separating and dividing groups as if they were primordial types. It sees things in black and white. It does not allow for complexities of interactions or shadings. Hereditarianism shares similar essentialisms. Secondly, inflating the significance of race often follows from a prior inflation of the significance of genes.[7]

Glorification of the genes

Two fundamental problems arise repeatedly in assuming that differences in the expression of a complex trait are genetic and can be generalized to a racial propensity or predisposition. Firstly, the environment is seldom controlled or factored in. Secondly, the results – once assumed to be genetic – are reduced to equating genetic with pan-racial. Thus, we often are faced with the double leap of faith that a given disease is genetic in origin, and then that a genetic difference observed between two populations in one place will necessary apply to populations in other places. This assumes that the same variations in haemoglobin levels seen in black and white populations in the USA will be observed between blacks and whites in, say, Australia.

Research on race and anaemia provides an example of this double leap of faith. In the 1970s Garn reported that the adult black mean haemoglobin level was 1.0g/dl below the white mean.[8] Following this work the suggestion was made to institute separate cut-offs for anaemia for blacks and whites, in which blacks have a lower cut-off. Robert Jackson[9] re-examined these data and endeavoured to control for obvious environmental factors such as iron intake, and to eliminate from analysis low haemoglobin values that may be related to genetic anaemias. This reduced the mean haemoglobin difference by about 75% to around 0.20–0.30 g/dl.

Despite these data, separate cut-offs are still supported despite the fact that the purported 'race' difference in iron metabolism has no known genetic basis. There is certainly no evidence to suggest that blacks are uniformly more efficient than whites in their metabolism of iron, or that blacks somehow do just as well on less haemoglobin. Nor has it been proven that the difference is pan-racial. If the black cut-off is reduced by just half of the original proposed level, the prevalence of anaemia in nonpregnant, nonlactating black women would on paper be reduced from 20 to 10%.[10]

The health implications of this would be serious. The consequences of low haemoglobin values in ranges near anaemia cut-off values manifest in many ways in learning, work, immunological capacity and many other areas.[11] This is an example of how poor science thus becomes harmful public policy.

It's not all bad, however. A recent report from the US Centers for Disease Control makes clear that linking race with genetics is a serious constraint to public health. Among its conclusions are that 'race – as a biological concept – is not useful in public health surveillance.' Furthermore, emphasis on race in public health reinforces stereotyping and racism and diverts attention from underlying socio-economic factors.[12]

Race, hereditarianism, and anthropology

According to Daniel Koshland, the editor of *Science*, the nature–nurture debate has ended and nature has won: 'It is in the genes.'[13] The 'it' in question is anything from why black babies are smaller or black women are more anaemic, to sexual prowess, athletic ability, homosexuality, criminality, and even homelessness.

There are two major concerns in this hereditarian/biotechnology future. One is that the payoffs of genome research will be overstated. As one doctor stated in an article in *Time* magazine, soon all we will have to do to cure the myriad diseases facing society is 'simply treat patients by injecting a snippet of DNA and send them home cured'.[14] But this is far from the reality. These two examples illustrate how the oversold nature of genomic information and the sloppy process of naming genes by scientists and the media lead to misrepresentations of the scope and power of genomics.

Perhaps the greatest success of genome research to date in the location of the BRCA-2 gene. This gene is implicated in an estimated 2–4% of women who might develop breast cancer. How does locating the gene help us? Having the gene dramatically increases one's likelihood of getting cancer. However, it is not certain when, or even if, one ever will, but knowing one has the gene is likely to increase the probability of cancer developing. Knowing one doesn't have the gene is useless information. Worse, the information is something about which we can do little, since therapy lags way behind diagnosis.

Overselling is one concern; actual doing is the greater worry. One new application of biotechnology is the treatment of the medicalized condition of short stature. Genentech, one of the first biotechnology companies, markets a genetically engineered form of human growth hormone (HGH). Physicians are free to prescribe it to treat children who for any reason are short. A Genentech scientist recommends that HGH be considered for any child in the shortest 3% of the population.[2] Treatment of the lower 3% in the US alone would yield a $9 billion annual market!

Growth hormone is a powerful, wide-spectrum hormone with many systemic effects, some known and some yet to be determined. The only certainty is that HGH will do much more than promote an increase in linear growth. Secondly, the bottom 3% of a distribution is never lost. If those in the bottom 3% are moved up in the distribution then there will still be a low end 3%. What happens now? Do the new lower 3% get discriminated against because they are short? Do they then take growth hormone therapy?

What is happening here is exploitation for profit of an ideology favouring tallness in males.[2] This raises great ethical concerns, especially when only some can buy tallness. Where will this commodification stop? What would be wrong with a mammary gland growth hormone to increase 'attractiveness' in females? And in any case, what is so terrible about short stature? In richer countries, short stature is the result of complex interactions between genes, and between genes and environments. It is not, however, a health threat.

Among the poor, short stature is much more meaningful because it is caused by lack of access to food and other basic resources. Thus, short stature is a sign of other consequences of this lack of access, such as increased disease rates and learning difficulties.

The longest uninterrupted nutritional study has been going on in the town of Tezonteopan in highland Mexico since the late 1960s.[15] The mean difference in height between children receiving nutritional supplements and non-supplemented children at age 10 years was found to be 12.5cm. To treat short stature with HGH in Tezonteopan is to treat only the symptoms. In fact, growth hormone probably would not work if, as in this case, nutrients are not available to convert to human tissue. Access to nutrients is far more important for growth. The difference that good nutrition makes is very real and very powerful. Yet it does not make the headlines, and it does not make very many people rich.

The human genome diversity project

The Human Genome Project (HGP) embodies the rise in thinking that human nature is profoundly gene-based. It has enormous socio-political and economic implications. The HGP has already changed the course of biological research dramatically. It is not hard to see why legislative and financial support has been garnered with rhetoric from influential people like James Watson who stated that: 'We used to think our fate was in the stars, now we know, in large measure, it is in our genes.' As big as the project is, however, it is merely a symptom of deeper currents flowing within and between biomedicine and society.

The Human Genome Diversity Project (HGDP) is the anthropological arm of the Human Genome Project. As it was envisioned by population geneticist Luca L. Cavalli-Sforza, the founding father of the initiative, the HGDP will supposedly rectify an important limitation of the HGP, which was to look at a single genome, not the diversity among human genomes.[16] This project is regarded as the 'politically correct' Human Genome Project because it acknowledges variation and has a strong conservation biology rhetoric.

One of the organizers of the HGDP, Mary-Claire King, justifies this work because finally we have the know-how and because diversity is rapidly decreasing due to intermarriage and genocide.[17] Cavalli-Sforza is reported to have said that 'Anthropological fieldwork must catch up . . . with the rapidly disappearing data. Priceless evidence is slipping through our fingers as aboriginal populations lose their identity.'[16] Of course, this is neither the first time that scientists have bemoaned the disappearance of 'priceless evidence', nor the first time that one hears the argument that we must do research simply because we have the means.

Early on in HGDP planning, the big debate focused on sampling strategies, i.e. which groups and individuals would be selected and how many samples would be taken.[17] The late Allan Wilson favoured a uniform sampling strategy, in effect placing a grid over the world and selecting samples based on locations on the grid. But wider support was forthcoming for the more traditional method of selecting known 'anthropological' populations. This method clearly leads to a reification of population differences: the sampling methodology prejudices for finding differences between populations because transitional individuals and groups are eliminated. In this way, the HGDP could actually reinforce the belief in the biological basis of racism, rather than dispelling it, which is supposedly one of its aims.

The desire for acquiring data, and getting it as fast as possible, drives the project strategy. This is implicit in Cavalli-Sforza's answer to the questions about the scientific rationale for selecting 50 individuals per group: 'One person can bleed 50 people and get on the airplane in one day.'[17] Although issues of sampling are important ones, they may also deflect attention from the more fundamental questions of the

First they took the red paste in his hair for food colouring; now bioprospectors want this Colorado Indian's genes. (WWF/Parker, Edward)

scientific and humanitarian payoffs of the project. Will it be racialist science, and even lead to racism? Or will it increase our understanding of the invalidity of race, who we are, and our predispositions to disease? This much is certain: much of what the project becomes needs to result from thoughtful discussion, not just doing something because it is doable.

The HGDP, as it is envisioned, has the markings of violently reductionist science with a mechanistic and overly-deterministic approach to human biology. There is no built-in effort to examine interactions between genes, or between genes and the environment. In fact there is no discussion of gathering contextual information that would make this possible. Eventually sequencing strings of DNA can lead to the view that the person *is* the string.[18] Without contextual information, which would certainly slow down the project and make it more expensive, it is hard to envision how the project will do more than provide additional data on small and trivial polymorphic differences. It is repeatedly promised that the project will provide keys to understanding susceptibility to disease,[19] but this is not possible if all we have is genes without contexts.

Three slippery goals of the HGDP have been expressed by its proponents:

○ it will be a key to showing the invalidity of race

○ it will provide data to reconstruct human history

○ it will help to provide information on genetic patterns of disease susceptibility.

However, we already have the data to show that race has little explanatory value, and Cavalli-Sforza has himself stated that sufficient genetic data are already at hand to map lines of descent of populations of the world.[20] Furthermore, there is no reason to believe that the new data that may arise from the HGDP will lead to obvious or statistically less ambiguous ancestral trees. Finally, the methodology is not robust enough for studying disease causation. At best, the resulting data will provide preliminary associations between gene frequencies and disease. Thus, a real concern is that the project's intellectual payoffs will continue to be overstated and this will eventually turn public support away from science and anthropology. The pronouncement of King that the project will tell us 'who we are as a species and how we came to be'[16] is a slightly overblown claim.

Most concerning of all is the oversimplified idea of human variation that the project reifies. How will the mapping and comparing of thousands of DNA samples help us to appreciate the complexities of human biology and biocultural interactions?

156

Finally, behind the Newspeak of 'conservation biology' it is clear that the objects of conservation are genes, not peoples, nor cultures. It is no wonder that a number of indigenous groups, having finally learned about the project, have declared that they will not support it. Onendagah Council Chief Leon Shenendoah succinctly calls it a 'make work' project. Some may say that this work has nothing to do with race. But on a deep level I believe the discourse often invokes race. Genes are unthinkingly labelled as 'African' genes or 'Caucasian' genes, and scientific and popular articles discuss the evolution of races as if race were a reality.

Conclusions: genes, race and racism

Racism has recently thundered back into the discourse on genes and race. Three books published in 1994 on race and intelligence[21,22,23] all re-invent the following syllogism of Jensen[24] from a quarter of a century ago:

IQ = intelligence
IQ is inherited
Blacks have lower IQ than whites
Therefore black are inherently less intelligent than whites

I thought we had dealt with this already. I thought we had already shown that IQ was not an unbiased proxy for the complex trait called intelligence. I thought we had seen that much of the data on the heritability of IQ had been manufactured, literally so. I thought we had shown that blacks and whites are not groups. These ideas survive and resurface because they are keys to maintaining a power structure. This is, as Murray says, 'social science pornography'.[25]

Belief that human nature is driven by our genes is all around us. We find it in questions asked by doctors about family histories; in a newer form in the development of biotechnology companies; and the reporting of new genetic discoveries in our daily newspapers. The popular press tells us that there are genes dictating complex biological and behavioural traits – cancer genes, gay genes, violence genes.

But has nature/geneticization won, or is it just getting favourable press releases? Has nature been placed in the winner's enclosure simply because it is potentially profitable to do so? Stepping back from the media hype, what do the data suggest?

○ Race is a reified idea of paradigmatic magnitude. It is a worldview that is associated with a desire to separate *us* from *them* and to create power structures. The concept is dangerous, scientifically flawed, and should be abandoned.

157

o The denial of race is not a denial of human diversity. Rather it is a stance that suggests that human diversity is too complex to be explained by types. Similarly, human biology is more than strings of beads and mechanics. Humans are not composed of replaceable parts. A goal of biological anthropology should be to explain bio-cultural complexity.

o We have entered a historical phase of glorification of the gene. This is consistent with the search for simple biological solutions to complex problems, and it is also consistent with an upsurge in racialism. Genetic reductionism does not lead directly to racialism or racism. However, if one can use the past as a gauge then we see the extreme likelihood of such connections being made.

o Racism is more real than race. To deny race does not deny the study of racism. Race as biology and racism are often considered in human biological research, especially in studies of group differences in health and nutritional status. What is needed are more studies of the biological consequences of racism. The *status quo* is not OK. 'Nothing could keep race alive if we did not constantly re-invent and re-ritualize it. If race lives on today it is because we continue to create and re-create it'.[26]

o Genomics is popular because genetic information is patentable and perceived to be controllable; but control is a myth. The lesson of Jurassic Park, in the words of the chaos mathematician Malcolm, is that nature is not controllable. Properties emerge and are stochastic. Life is dynamic and dialectical. Life will get you.

References

1. Crichton, M. (1990). *Jurassic Park.* Ballantine Books, New York
2. Hubbard, R. and Wald, E. (1993). *Exploding the Gene Myth.* Beacon Press, Boston.
3. Lippman, A. (1992). Led (astray) by Genetic Maps: The Cartography of the Human Genome and Health Care. *Social Science and Medicine* **35**(12): pp.1469–76.
4. Todorov, T. (1993). *On Human Diversity.* Harvard University Press, Cambridge, MA.
5. Lewontin, R.C. (1972). The Apportionment of Human Diversity. *Evolutionary Biology* **6:** 381–398.
6. France Casting (1992). *Fall 1992 Catalogue.*
7. Goodman, A.H. and Armelagos, G.J. (1995) The Resurrection of Race: The Concept of Race in Physical Anthropology in the 1990s. In: LT Reynolds and L Liberman (eds) *Race and Other Miscalculations, Misconceptions and Mismeasures: Papers in Honor of Ashley Montagu,* General Hall Publishers, Dice Hill NY.

8a. Garn, S.M., Smith, N.J. and Clark, D.C. (1974). Race Differences in Haemoglobin Levels. *Ecology of Food and Nutrition* **3:** pp 299–301.

8b. Garn, S.M., Ryan, A.S. *et al.* (1975). Income Matched Black–White Differences in Hemoglobin Levels after Correction for Low Transferrin Saturations. *American Journal of Clinical Nutrition.* **28:** pp 563 -568.

8c. Garn, S. (1976). Problems in the Nutritional Assessment of Black Individuals. *American Journal of Public Health* **66:** 262–267.

9a. Jackson, R.T. (1990). Separate Hemoglobin Standards for Blacks and Whites: A Critical Review of the Case for Separate and Unequal Hemoglobin Standards. *Medical Hypotheses* **32:** pp 181–189.

9b. Jackson, R.T. (1992) Hemoglobin Comparisons between African American and European American Males with Hemoglobin Values in the Normal Range. *Journal of Human Biology* **4:** pp 313–318.

9c. Jackson, R.T. (1993) Hemoglobin Comparisons in a Sample of European and African American Children. *Ecology of Food and Nutrition* **29:** pp 139–146.

9d. Jackson, R.T. and Jackson, F.L.C. (1991). Reassessing Hereditary Interethnic Differences in Anemia Status. *Ethnicity and Disease* **1:** pp 27–41.

10. Pan, W.H. and Habicht, J.P. (1991) The Non-Iron Deficiency-Related Differences in Hemoglobin Concentration Distribution between Blacks and Whites and between Men and Women. *American Journal of Epidemiology* **134:** pp 1410–1416.

11. Scrimshaw, N. (1991). Iron Deficiency. *Scientific American.* October, pp 46–52.

12. Morbidity and Mortality Weekly Report (1993). Use of Race and Ethnicity in *Public Health Surveillance* **42** (No RR-10).

13. Koshland, D. (1987). Nature, Nurture and Behavior. *Science* **235:** 1445.

14. *Time,* 17 January 1994.

15. Chavez, A. and Martinez, C. (1979). *Growing Up in a Developing Community.* Mexican National Institute of Nutrition, Mexico City.

16. Roberts, L. (1991). A Genetic Survey of Vanishing People. *Science* **252:** pp 1614–1617.

17a. Roberts, L. (1992) Anthropologists Climb (Gingerly) on Board. *Science* **258:** pp 1300–1301.

17b. Roberts, L. (1992). How to Sample the World's Genetic Diversity. *Science* **257:** pp 1204–1205.

18. Lewontin, R.C. (1991). *Biology and Ideology: The Doctrine of DNA.* Harper Collins, New York.

19. Kidd, K.R., Kidd, K.H. and Weiss, K.M. (1993). Human Genome Diversity Initiative. *Human Biology* **65:** pp 1–6.

20. Cavalli-Sfoza, L.L. (1991). Genes, People and Languages. *Scientific American.* November, pp 104–110.

21. Herrnstein, R. and Murray, C. (1994). *The Bell Curve: Intelligence and Class Structure in American Life.* Free Press, New York.

22. Itzkoff, S.W. (1994). *The Decline of Intelligence in America.* Praeger,Westfield, Conn.

23. Rushton, J.P. (1994). *Race, Evolution and Behavior.* Transaction, New Brunswick.

24. Jensen, A.R. (1969). How Much Can We Boost IQ and Scholastic Achievement? *Harvard Educational Review* **39:** pp 1–123.
25. DeParle, J, (1994). Daring Research or 'Social Science Pornography?' *New York Times Magazine*, 9 October.
26. Fields, B.J. (1990). Slavery, Race and Ideology in the United States of America. *New Left Review* pp 95–118.

PART 3

Which way now?

6.1. Choices

Amidst all the confusion created by the stampede for the new booty of biodiversity and the North-South tug-of-war over access and ownership, it is difficult to see the way ahead for those opposed to the North's utilitarian model of biodiversity management. Bioprospecting is rapidly gathering momentum, and industry's eagerness to glean what it can before the rules and regulations are tightened up is placing great pressure on governments and local communities all over the world to respond to its demands.

Three main strategies stand out as options which could be adopted to deal with the weighty questions of equity, rights and access to the global genetic pool are being considered in all the major global agreements and action plans for the environment. This issue is taking greater and greater precedence in the Biodiversity Convention, Agenda 21, and the Commission on Sustainable Development. Indigenous groups are becoming highly vocal in this arena, and at the 1995 Biodiversity Convention meeting, a post was created in the secretariat specifically to address the concerns of indigenous people. A growing number of voices are pointing out the limitations of existing approaches to dealing with access, rights and equity. In the debates, three broad strategies for addressing these issues stand out:

○ *compensation or reward* – whereby compensation, in monetary or some other form, is given to a government, community or individual in recognition of its contribution to the development of a product

○ *intellectual property rights* – whereby communities or individuals gain legal rights to their resources and knowledge, and therefore have control over their use

○ *reclaiming the commons* – involving a rejection of existing mechanisms and advocating a much broader, stewardship-based approach to bioresource management.

The first two approaches require working with the system and adapting it to make it more equitable. The last requires a more radical reversal of the existing approach to biodiversity management. The pros and cons of each of these approaches will be discussed in turn.

Compensation
This approach can be beneficial if local people are interested in cash or other forms of compensation and they have a strong hand in the negotiations. For many indigenous peoples, however, this approach is sacrilegious since it entails commodifying the sacred. Many groups find them-

163

selves caught in a difficult situation where they do not approve of the compensation mechanism, yet fear that if they do not engage in a deal they will lose their resources and knowledge without gaining anything. As Darrell Posey points out, the compensation approach is largely being advocated by the North – it is not the preferred option for indigenous peoples, but they are often not aware that they may have alternative options.

Bilateral deals   Both monetary and non-monetary forms of compensation are being considered in bioprospecting deals. With monetary compensation, one of the greatest challenges of the compensation approach is assessing a fair price. Assessing the value of biodiversity is a far cry from assessing the value of tin or steel, partly because knowledge is implicit in the value of the 'commodity' and partly because the potential applications of a plant, chemical or gene are often unknown at the time of collection. The examples given in Chapter 4 demonstrate that corporations tend to regard compensation to local communities as a token gesture rather than treating them as equal partners in the deal.

Another problem lies in the fact that companies often consider that agreeing a price and writing a cheque is all they need worry about. They have little concern for ironing out a detailed agreement on who the beneficiaries are, in what form the benefits are given and how they are distributed (see Chapter 4.1).

A further problem is to establish intermediate forms of compensation and incentives that bridge the 10–15 year period sometimes required to develop a marketable drug. It is essential to ensure that false expectations of large immediate benefits do not develop in the source countries, but some form of short-term assistance could be provided. This could range from assistance in infrastructure development to support for social services, education and healthcare.

Christine Kabuye also notes that one of the difficulties in pursuing a compensation mechanism in bilateral deals, as advocated by the Biodiversity Convention, is that biodiversity is seen as being the property of sovereign states. If this is the case, governments will be the beneficiaries in any bilateral deals, and the communities which provided access to the resources and knowledge may not benefit at all.

According to GRAIN, in these kinds of deals the North calls the tune – it identifies the products it is interested in, largely determines the terms, and bases the assessment of a 'fair deal' on Northern ethical considerations. Consequently, these kinds of deals often tend to be paternalistic and over-simplistic in nature.

Conservation compensation   Owing to the shortcomings of bilateral deals, alternative mechanisms have been proposed. Farmers' Rights (Box 6.1) is one such initiative. The main attraction of the Farmers'

Box 6.1: Farmers' rights

Farmers' Rights offer a much broader view on the whole question of rights, extending the scope of protection to elements not considered by most other rights systems. Adopted by the UN's Food and Agriculture Organization (FAO) in 1989, they were designed to overcome the shortcomings of other IPR systems which fail to address the inventive process of informal systems or, for technical or economic reasons, are inaccessible to rural innovators. They offer a conceptual base for the development of mechanisms that could promote equitable sharing of benefits between the users and donors of germplasm.

Farmers' Rights are those rights 'arising from the past, present and future contributions of farmers in conserving, improving and making available plant genetic resources, particularly those in the centres of origin/diversity. These rights are vested in the International Community, as trustee for present and future generations of farmers, for the purpose of ensuring full benefits to farmers, and supporting the continuation of their contributions, as well as the attainment of the overall purposes of the International Undertaking'. (FAO International Undertaking on Plant Genetic Resources, 1989.)

The Crucible Group, in which representatives across the spectrum from industry to grass-roots movements come together to discuss IPRs in relation to biodiversity, has proposed a strengthening of the Farmers' Rights concept, which would be based on the so-called GIFTS system:[2]

Germplasm – control of their own resources and access to as wide a gene pool as possible

Information – control of their own knowledge of genetic resources and access to information available elsewhere

Funds – funding to develop their resources

Technology – the ability to develop their own, and use and adapt other technologies

Systems – freedom to control and develop their farming systems, including rights to land and markets

These GIFTS are ensured through a consistent international funding mechanism, which is a key feature further distinguishing Farmers' Rights from other forms of IPR. Most other forms of IPR espouse bilateral arrangements. With this system, funds are used not to compensate individual farmers or indigenous people, but to reward meritorious work that encourages conservation and use of genetic resources. The empowerment of local communities is a central focus of the initiative.

Farmers' Rights are being considered as part of a possible protocol by the Biodiversity Convention.

Rights approach is the elimination of a legal mechanism for intellectual property protection. Indigenous communities could be compensated on the basis of development needs and opportunity, without reference to law courts, patent offices or legal departments.

According to Jack Kloppenburg[1] a multilateral system of compensation is particulary important for agricultural crops, for a number of reasons:

○ Unlike the bioactive agents sought by pharmaceutical companies, which are easily definable, the genetic material of value for agricultural development is not static and cannot be isolated. Even if a specific gene sequence can be linked to a certain characteristic, such as disease resistance, it must be embedded in many different varieties adapted to local or regional agronomic conditions in order to be effective.

○ Only a multilateral framework can provide equitably for compensation for materials for which there is no unique ethnic or geographic provenance.

○ Bilateral deals cannot be achieved for the majority of the genes collected in the world's communal genebanks, which are recognized as common heritage.

It might not look like a gene bank, but Andean farmers grow up to 60 varieties of potato in their fields

However, according to some critics a multilateral approach is open to abuse because the central fund is used not to compensate individual farmers or indigenous people, but to reward meritorious work that encourages conservation and sustainable use (see Chapter 4.3). There is no guarantee that farmers in a particular country will actually bene-fit from the compensation, because their government is the recipient of the reward.

Intellectual property right mechanisms
The advantage of IPRs is that they provide a certain amount of security and a defence against piracy. The drawbacks of IPRs are discussed more fully in Chapter 3, but can be summarized by two main points. Firstly, IPR provides for a monopolistic appropriation which may foreclose ben-efits to others. And secondly, Northern IPR law – the dominant model – does not, and cannot, recognize informal community innovation (Box 6.2). Again, as with compensation, IPR would not be the mechanism of choice for indigenous peoples and farmers, but given the momentum given to this model by GATT and the Biodiversity Convention, many groups are considering ways of adapting and improving the IPR system.

Modifying the patent system Several mechanisms have been sug-gested to ensure greater equity in the existing IPR system. One sug-gestion, advocated by RAFI, is to adopt new deposit rules for gene bank accessions, requiring the attachment of detailed information about the source of the material, including names of individuals or communities where appropriate. This information would remain at-tached to all patent applications. Other ideas include the protection of all gene bank materials from patenting; introducing IPR ombudsmen to investigate patent claims on behalf of indigenous communities; and the establishment of a fund to cover IPR costs, such as maintaining gene bank deposits, and funding patent tribunals and legal representation for indigenous communities.

None of these suggestions would impose an unacceptable burden on the system and could be factored in to the existing fee structures used by patent offices.

Plant breeders' rights In the 1960s, there was controversy in Europe over whether monopoly rights should be granted for food, chemicals, plants and animals by drawing them into the patent regime. It was eventually decided that plants and animals should stay out of the patent regime and a new system was drawn up for the protection of plants. The Union for the Protection of New Varieties of Plants (UPOV) was formed in 1961 and its convention was signed by a number of states – mainly from Europe and the US.

Box 6.2: Why IPRS are inappropriate for indigenous people

○ **The nature of monopolies**
Controlling something and keeping others from having it is alien to indigenous people. In these communities, the sharing, not the keeping, of a resource brings power. Wealth comes from giving, not from taking and keeping. In many communities the leaders are often the 'poorest' in our eyes, because they give everything away.

○ **Individuality vs community**
Individuals are the beneficiaries of IPRs in our society. In indigenous communities, knowledge is communally owned. Individuals do have specialized knowledge, but this knowledge is not owned by them, it is merely expressed by the person. Knowledge is the people's inheritance, and can consist of the right to grow a certain crop, raise a particular animal, sing a certain type of song or wear a particular kind of feather. Knowledge is held in trust by individuals for the benefit of the community and for future generations.

○ **The sacred vs the profane**
Some objects cannot be possessed, such as things that belong to the ancestors or things that are sacred. For example, things that belong to the ancestors are also seen as belonging to future generations. In this context the concept of property is completely inappropriate. You may hold land in trust, for example, but you do not possess it. The lack of respect for the sacred is what makes the industrialized, materially-orientated world insensitive to, and disrespectful of, native cultures.

○ **Holism vs particularism**
Indigenous communities do not make a distinction between scientific IP and cultural IP, because their system is holistic. A seed may function to feed someone, but it is also sacred. A forest may be a place to gather food, but it is also a temple. The indigenous world is multidimensional and goes beyond the visible, biological world that the North recognizes. The invisible energies and spirits of plants, ancestors and gods have to be consulted. They are the ones that balance nature and society.

○ **Accumulated knowledge vs the unique act of discovery**
Patents cannot protect information that does not result from a specific historic act of discovery. Indigenous knowledge is transgenerational and communally shared.

○ **Time frames**
The decision-making process is quite different in companies and in indigenous communities. Companies make decisions rapidly using a hierarchical, unilateral process, whereas indigenous communities use a consensus-building process; making a decision may take a year and you cannot put a time limit on it.

Source: Darrell Posey, Centre for Traditional Resource Rights

UPOV, however, has never really been effective internationally. Evidence began to appear showing that because of PBR, multinational companies were starting to take control of the breeding sector. It was also argued that the PBR system promoted a further impoverishment of genetic diversity because of its requirements for uniformity. To date there are only 18 signatories, and the gathering momentum of acceptance of the patent system as the preferred method of protection for life forms means that UPOV may well fade further into the background. This is somewhat ironic given that patents are a much more serious threat to the concerns which originally held back the adoption of PBR.

The major difference between patents and PBR lies in the scope of the protection granted (see p. 85). While patents can protect the entire genetic make-up of an organism, PBR does not provide ownership over the germplasm of the seed, it gives only a monopoly right for the marketing of a specific variety. Like patents, and for similar reasons, the PBR system has been undergoing change. There has been a progressive strengthening of the protection offered, which appears to favour commercial breeders and undermine the interests of farmers.

Sui generis *systems*   Given that both the Biodiversity Convention and GATT allow the adoption of *sui generis* systems of IPR as an alternative to patents (see p. 81), there is scope for countries to introduce alternatives. However, who judges the acceptability of *sui generis* systems has yet to be clarified.

Many indigenous communities and governments are not aware that IPR systems include a number of options that do not imply exclusive monopoly control over inventions. Among these options are Community Intellectual Property Rights (see Box 6.3), the Model Law on Folklore (see Box 6.4) and Inventors' Certificates. The latter provides the option of discarding financial compensation altogether in favour of non-monetary awards and non-exclusive licensing arrangements. Governments can adjust the terms of compensation to promote local innovations in domestic or export markets, or to attract a foreign invention where access to the invention is deemed to be in the national interest.

Intellectual integrity   RAFI has proposed the development of a framework that would allow indigenous communities to ensure the intellectual integrity of their ongoing innovations rather than to obtain intellectual property rights. This would ensure recognition of peoples' innovations, ensure access to them and protect them from piracy, without having to assign ownership to an individual or group. This could include some aspects of the various proposals described above, along with a few others. Indigenous communities would not need to

169

endorse IPR systems in order to have their intellectual integrity protected. UN and other agencies would do this for them. Implicit in such a framework would be a strong focus on information exchange and information, so that indigenous groups can contribute more meaningfully to policy formulation and their views can be understood more deeply by people with a Northern value system and world view.

Traditional resource rights Traditional Resource Rights build on the concept of IPR and refer to a bundle of rights that can be used for

Box 6.3: Community Intellectual Rights

In a backlash against the Green Revolution, a militant movement has arisen among the farmers of India who want to protect their way of life (see Chapter 6.2). India does not allow patents on seeds at present, but is being pressured through TRIPS to introduce some form of IPR. According to Vandana Shiva, TRIPS have 'failed to recognize the more informal, communal system of innovation through which Third World farmers produce, select, improve and breed a plethora of diverse crop varieties'.

Community Intellectual Rights (CIRs) have been proposed as a form of *sui generis* IPR, whose fundamental principles are incompatible with the patent system. Rather than rewarding an individual, whole communities will be awarded ownership of an invention. Instead of one-step innovation, recognition will be given to the incremental and dynamic nature of innovation, without ignoring past, present and future 'owners' of the knowledge. The notion of utility is also rejected, and protection would be extended to innovations of domestic, common and social value.

CIRs insist on the protection of local peoples' knowledge *systems*. This means that their creativity in the form and manner in which the communities understand this term, must be accorded formal recognition. Doing so may be crucial to the preservation of biodiversity itself, as recognizing and protecting the knowlege of communities requires doing the same to the cultural and social traditions of these communities which embody practices supportive of biodiversity.

The farmers' movement in India is using CIRs to assert their rights to seed, claiming that any corporation using local knowledge or resources without the permission of local communities is engaging in intellectual piracy. The neem controversy is a case in point (see p. 87).

CIRs bear some resemblance to Farmers' Rights, but operate on a bilateral compensation mechanism, rather than as a multilateral fund. Communities are rewarded for stewardship and free exchange of resources is recognized, except where commercialization is involved. In this case a fixed percentage is paid by the user of the knowledge, whether or not it is demanded by the community. In some instances an intermediary, such as an NGO or the state, may act as trustee for the community.

Seed fairs are regaining popularity as farmers recognize the importance of conserving and sharing traditional varieties. (ITZ/Margaret Waller)

Box 6.4: Model law on folklore

Although not designed with biological systems in mind, the Model Law on Folklore, adopted in 1985 by UNESCO and WIPO, offers three elements which are particularly appropriate for the protection of biodiversity. Firstly, communities can be the legally registered innovators; secondly, community innovations are not necessarily fixed, but can evolve and still retain protection. Thirdly, communities retain exclusive monopoly control over the innovations for as long as they continue to innovate.

Although scientific inventions are not included in the law, it could easily be adapted to do so. The Model Law still has to be formalized into a legally binding agreement, but a number of African countries, including Nigeria, have enacted legislation based, at least in part, on the Model Law.

protection, compensation and conservation.[3] The term 'property' is omitted, since property for indigenous peoples frequently has intangible, spiritual attributes, and, though worthy of protection, can belong to no human being. The term encompasses a wide range of international agreements already in existence, and TRR could be used as the basis of a *sui generis* system of protection. IPRs are only one of these bundles of rights, and the term also encompasses human rights, re-

171

ligious rights and religious freedom, environmental integrity, cultural heritage rights, neighbouring rights, and customary law and practice, among others.

US lawyer Dinah Shelton suggests that international human rights law may provide the best framework for protection for communities and local environments in the future. Human rights bodies increasingly call for environmental protection because of the connection between human rights violations and environmental degradation. Invoking these rights could introduce more justice into the process of determining access to, and control over, biological diversity and local peoples' knowledge.[4] TRR is a favoured mechanism amongst indigenous people because it is rights-driven, not economically motivated. It goes beyond other *sui generis* models, in that it seeks to protect not only knowledge but also asserts the right to self-determination and to safeguard culture in its broadest sense.[5]

Reclaiming the commons

Both the IPR and compensation mechanisms described above see biodiversity very simplistically and are concerned primarily with the products of biodiversity rather than its more holistic counterpart, which defines it more broadly in terms of systems and relationships (see Chapter 4.4). The dominant world-view cannot accommodate this definition of biodiversity. Addressing the question of biodiversity conservation and management in this context requires more than just tinkering with the current system. A radical shift is required not only to change practices but also to alter the underlying philosophy and value system (Chapter 6.2).

The process of reclaiming the commons involves community empowerment that is explicitly linked with local ecological and economic regeneration. In relation to biodiversity, this means empowering communities, enabling all people to secure their rights and needs. It is through these processes that people are empowered to care for the environment and democratize control over the end uses of knowledge and biological resources.

References

1. Kloppenberg, J. (1994). *W(h)ither Farmers' Rights?* Paper written for a seminar held by GRAIN in Montezillon, Switzerland.
2. The Crucible Group (1994), *People, Plants and Patents*, IDRC, Ottawa.
3. Posey, D.A., Dutfield, G. *et al.* (1994). *Beyond Intellectual Property Rights – Protection, Compensation and Community Empowerment.* Report for WWF-International.

4. Shelton, D. (1995). *Fair Play, Fair Pay – Strengthening Local Livelihood Systems through Compensation for Access to and Use of Traditional Knowledge and Biological Resources.* Report for WWF-International.
5. Posey, D. (1995). *Indigenous People and Traditional Resource Rights: A basis for Equitable Relationships?* Green College, Oxford, UK.

6.2. Reversals for diversity – a new paradigm

ROBERT CHAMBERS

In all of history there has probably never been a period as dramatic as the late 1980s and the 1990s for the scale and scope of unexpected and divergent changes in the human condition. In some regions wealth increases and concentrates and consumerism flourishes to excess; in others war, famine and civil disorder bring destitution and death. The communications revolution is touching people's lives and transforming their awareness and aspirations, not only in the centres of prosperity in the North but also in the poor, rural and indigenous communities in the South. Almost everywhere, in different ways and in different directions, change seems to be the norm, and universally the pace of change is accelerating.

While this occurs, a new paradigm has been coalescing. The word 'paradigm' is used here to mean a mutually-reinforcing pattern of concepts, values, beliefs, methods and behaviours. The prevalent or normal paradigm tends towards global homogenization through the interlocking effects of the market, communications, technology and professionalism. The emerging paradigm of 'reversals' turns this normality on its head. It seeks and supports diversity in many dimensions. And it does this as a means to sustainable livelihoods and a good quality of life for all.

The normal

To appreciate reversals, we must first understand what is meant by the 'normal' paradigm and its dominant concepts, values, beliefs, methods and behaviour. Appreciating reversals means learning to be open to the realities as seen by the majority (but seldom heard) population, rather than the dominant minority. In the normal paradigm, which continues to dominate our world, four dimensions stand out as common and powerful:

○ Bureaucracy – tends to centralize, standardize and control.

○ Professionalism – creates and works in controlled environments with precise measurements, using reductionist methods which tend to generate standard and simple packages and solutions.

○ Capitalism and markets – tend to homogenize all aspects of life, appropriating diverse resources and exploiting them in uniform, capital-intensive ways, and seeking a unified global market.

○ Development/conservation – rely on blueprint planning and top-down control-orientated implementation, with targets and regimented actions at the local level. They distrust people and participation and result in the ring-fencing of projects, national parks etc.

These four dimensions have been mutually reinforcing. They have combined in many ways through centralization, standardization, control, reductionism and the appropriation of resources by the wealthy and powerful. Centralization, standardization and uniformity have always been inherent in the structure and dynamics of large bureaucracies and of the state: in the classical Fordist mass-production line; and in the practical universality of Newtonian science, with its applications in engineering, medicine and other fields which deal with physical things in predictable environments. In agriculture, this generated the Green Revolution packages in which environments could be controlled to fit standard, high-yielding genotypes. Henry Ford is reputed to have said that Americans could have their mass-produced Model T Ford car in any colour they liked as long as it was black. Transfer of technology packages and large-scale cultivation of uniform monocultures are biological analogues of the Model T.

These tendencies link in and resonate with patterns of North–South dominance. North and South are used here in their literal sense and also as metaphors. Many relationships can be seen as North–South, as magnets generating their own mutually reinforcing fields (Fig. 6.1). The Norths, or Uppers, dominate the Souths, or Lowers. Each magnet, or person, reinforces the field through dominance and instruction, North to South, or submission and compliance, South to North. It is then difficult for any one magnet to flip round against the force of the pervasive magnetic field.

Chain reactions of dominance pass downwards. Let us assume that a World Bank staff member puts pressure on an official in a country in the

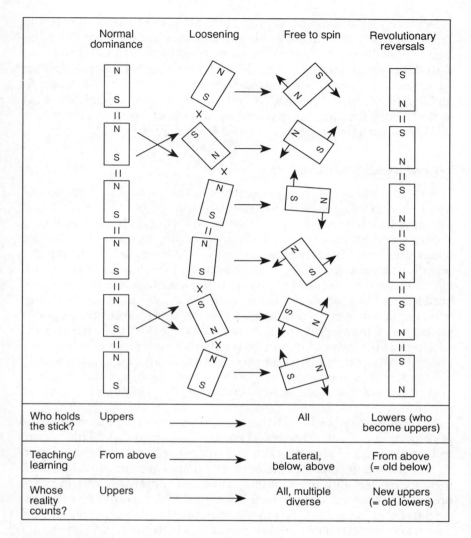

	Normal dominance	Loosening	Free to spin	Revolutionary reversals
Who holds the stick?	Uppers	→	All	Lowers (who become uppers)
Teaching/ learning	From above	→	Lateral, below, above	From above (= old below)
Whose reality counts?	Uppers	→	All, multiple diverse	New uppers (= old lowers)

Figure 6.1   Dominance, reversals and freedom

South, who then pressurizes a subordinate, who does the same to another lower official, who turns on a field worker, who goes home in the evening and takes it out on his wife, who shouts at the children, who go out and throw stones at the dog which, conceivably, chases a cat . . .

Bureaucracies, professions and markets can be thought of as mutually reinforcing. Their normal North–South dominance standardizes and simplifies, generating and transferring monocultures and Model Ts. The challenge is to weaken the magnetic field which sustains these; to offset and neutralize the patterns of dominance. It is not to cause complete flips from South to North, for these repeat the paradigm, reproducing the old patterns with different actors on top – as with Robespierre after Louis XVI, Lenin after Tsar Nicholas, Mao after the Chinese emperors, or Mengistu after Haile Selassie. It is rather to replace the old paradigm with a new one; to loosen the relationships so that people are free to spin and relate laterally as well as upwards and downwards in an egalitarian and open manner.

Whose reality counts?

The reality which those who are central and powerful seek to construct is universal, simplified, standardized, stable, controlled and measurable. The concept of poverty is an example: in the usual economist's definition, poverty is reduced to the measurable, a single dimension which is either low income or low consumption. But deprivation as experienced by poor people is multi-dimensional, including vulnerability, isolation, physical weakness, powerlessness and humiliation. But what has been measured – as income-poverty or consumption-poverty – masquerades as the much larger reality. Poor people have many other criteria of well-being (Fig. 6.2). But normal economists define poverty not by the many dimensions of the experience of the poor, but by their own reductionism to a single measurable scale. It is then not the needs of the poor, but the needs of powerful professionals, which construct the dominant reality of poverty.

The contrasting reality of the livelihoods and farming systems of poor people is local, complex, diverse, dynamic and difficult to control or measure. Although normal professionals often fail to understand this, many poor people seek to complicate and diversify their livelihoods and farming systems. They add enterprises to increase production and reduce risk. Farming systems, like natural ecosystems, tend to be more resilient the more complex they become. So farmers create and protect micro-environments in which they cultivate greater biological diversity. They add to their enterprises, multiplying linkages on- and off-farm, for example through aquaculture, composting, agroforestry, adding to livestock species, and so on. By complicating and diversifying their farming systems and livelihoods they buffer themselves against bad times and shocks. Their motto, as coined by Porter *et al.*[2] is 'More diversity for more certainty'. A recent estimate[3] is that there are almost as many people in the world who depend for their food on these complex, diverse and risk-prone (CDR) farming systems as on the simpler, more standardized and more controlled Green Revolution farming.

Farmers and villagers in two villages in Rajasthan in India were asked to determine their own categories and criteria of changing economic status; they named 38 criteria. Comparing data from fieldwork in the 1960s and 1980s, Jodha[1] found that the 36 households which were more than 5% worse off in per capita real incomes were on average better off according to 37 of their own 38 criteria. (The one exception was milk consumption, as more was being sold outside the village). The improvements included quality of housing, wearing shoes regularly, less dependence in the lean season, and not having to migrate for work. Several of the criteria reflected greater independence:

Indicator of well-being	% of households	
	1960s	1980s
One or more members working as attached or semi-attached labour	37	7
Residing on patron's land or yard	31	0
Taking seed loans from patrons	34	9
Taking loans from others besides patrons	13	47
Marketing farm produce only through patrons	86	23
Family members seasonally out-migrating for work	34	11
Selling >80% of their produce in post-harvest period	100	46
Making cash purchases during slack-season festivals	6	51
Adults skipping third daily meal during scarcity period	86	20
Women and children wear shoes regularly	0	34
Houses with only impermanent traditional structure	91	34
Houses with separate provision for humans and animals	6	52

(Source : Jodha, 1988)

The reality of these income-poorer villages contrasts sharply with a normal economist's reality. The economist sees them as poorer, but in their own terms they were on average much better off.

Figure 6.2   For richer or poorer – whose reality?

Resilient and adaptable small CDR farmers have often found themselves at odds with the normal paradigm. They have been encouraged to adopt technologies developed for the standardized and controlled conditions which they do not have. What they want is not a Model T package of practices, certified by bureaucrats and scientists, for transfer to controlled and uniform conditions, but a basket of choices from which they can mix and match the combinations to enhance adaptability, reduce risk and increase returns for their particular needs and environments.

The normal and new paradigms can be contrasted (Fig. 6.3). The *normal* focuses on things, blueprints and planning; the *new* serves people through process and participation. Linked with these are contrasts between modes of intervention and interaction – between dominating and facilitating, 'motivating' and enabling, controlling and empowering. The normal is more the paradigm of the powerful, dominant and wealthy; the new reflects more the conditions and needs of the weak, subordinate and poor.

177

	NORMAL	NEW
Analytical assumptions and methods	Reductionist Universally applicable	Systems Locally chosen, adapted or invented
Working environment	Controlled Predictable	Uncontrollable Unpredictable
Technology	Standard package 'Model T'	Basket of choices 'Toyota'
Interactions with local people	Dominating 'Motivating' Controlling	Facilitating Enabling Empowering
Dominant orientation	Things Blueprints Planning	People Processes Performance
Diversity	General	Cultural

Figure 6.3   Two paradigms contrasted

	NORMAL TENDENCIES	NEEDED REVERSALS
PROFESSIONALISM	Things first Men before women Professional set priorities Technology transfer – packages Simplify	People first Women before men Poor people set priorities Technology choice – baskets Complicate
BUREAUCRACY	Centralize Standardize Control	Decentralize Diversify Enable
CAREERS/BEHAVIOUR	Tying down (family) Inwards (urban) Upwards (hierarchy)	Also releasing Also outwards Also downwards
MODES OF LEARNING	From 'above' Rural development tourism Questionnaire surveys Measurement and statistics Extractive	From 'below' Rapid, relaxed and participatory appraisal Ranking, scoring, judgement Empowering
ANALYSIS BY	Us	Them

Figure 6.4   Reversals for diversity and realism

The challenge is to move from the normal to the new; for the powerful to ask themselves how normal professionals and centrally-placed bureaucrats construct their reality and how this contrasts with the reality of those who are local and poor. The questions then are 'Whose reality counts?', 'Whose reality *should* count?' and 'How can the reality of those who are local and poor count more?'

Reversals

The paradigm of reversals answers these questions by turning the normal on its head, and reversing imbalances and power (Fig. 6.4). It puts people first, seeks to redress gender balance by putting women before men, and seeks to enable poor people to set their own priorities and to make their own choices. Sustainable livelihoods are an equalizing focus of reversals.[4] For the rich, sustainable livelihoods mean much lower consumption. For the poor, sustainable livelihoods require choices, adaptability, versatility, participation, enhancing capabilities, and supporting cultural, biological and ecological diversity.

In this paradigm, diversity is not a static quality to be preserved through capture and protection, but a function of the permanence of change. Diversity is sustained and enhanced through versatile opportunism, adaptability, and the creation and exploitation of physical and economic niches. There are resonances between the strategies of poor CDR farmers and the precepts of avant-garde, post-modern business management. For example, Tom Peters' *Thriving on Chaos,* which was written as advice for business in the US, stresses diversity, 'becoming obsessed with listening', finding and exploiting transient opportunities, inventiveness and learning from mistakes.[5]

The three 'D's' of decentralization, democracy and diversity underpin the paradigm of reversals. They interlink with and support the capabilities of poor people and their dynamism in relation to the market (Figure 6.6). The challenges to achieve the empowerment of poor people are for bureaucracy to decentralize, for political systems to become more democratic, and for professionals to embrace and contribute to diversity and choices. Together, these can enable poor people in communities to cope better with, and make use of, the market without being dominated by it.

For this local empowerment, four elements stand out:

o *rights, security and territory* to empower local people to resist the drives of capitalist organizations to appropriate territory and resources, to standardize agroecologies, to diminish the biodiversity on which local livelihoods depend, to reduce the security of people, and to infringe their rights

179

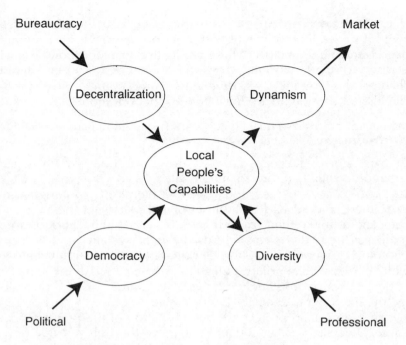

Figure 6.5   Reversing imbalances and power

○ *information* to enable people to defend and manage their resources better, and to operate in and gain from the market

○ *organization and political action* to countervail centrally-based
dominance and exploitation

○ *analysis by local people themselves* to enhance their effective com-
mand over resources and management of their lives. Local people's
analytical capability has been vastly underrated in the past, partly
because of the top-down approaches that have been used to 'help'
people. New techniques and methods, such as Participatory Rural
Appraisal (Boxes 6.5 and 6.6) are building on and complementing
earlier approaches to empowerment through participatory appraisal, analysis, planning and action.

Reversals are gaining ground. Increasingly professionals in agriculture
and forestry are providing diversity of choice rather than standard
packages. Democratic decentralization is a widely-stated political objective in many countries. Many movements seeking to reverse centralizing standardization are achieving success. The challenge now is
to establish firm alliances, networks, mutual support and exchange
of insights to liberate the magnets from North-South dominance,

Box 6.5: Participatory rural appraisal

Participatory rural appraisal (PRA) is a collective term for a growing family of approaches and methods which enable local people to present and analyse their knowledge, to plan and to act. Appropriate behaviour and attitudes allow outsiders to establish rapport, convene, catalyse, facilitate, watch, listen, learn and respect. Local people's empowerment grows as *they* map, model, interview, quantify, rank and score, inform and explain, discuss and analyse, plan, present and share their knowledge and experience.

In the past, outsiders have been slow to recognize the diversity and complexity of local knowledge, partly for lack of methods for its expression. Now participatory mapping, sequencing, estimating, listing and sorting, and comparing and diagramming, enable local people to present visually an often unexpectedly wide range of detail. Methods such as social mapping, matrix-scoring, seasonal calendars, trend and change analysis, well-being ranking and linkage diagramming enable local people to express relative values, judgements and connections with a wealth of nuance and differentiation. Their past supposed ignorance and inability to analyse have proven to be largely artefacts of the ignorance of outsiders.

It is now common for matrix-scoring of 20 or more trees to be completed by women and men for 10 or 20, or even more, criteria. A group of herders in Somaliland matrix-scored 25 water supplies, before and after improvement, against their own 45 criteria of assessment. Trend and change analysis reveals repeatedly how the environment has changed – in numbers of birds, wild animals, fish, and trees; in water supplies; in cultivated land, numbers of livestock, human population and so on.

Farmers map their farms and then diagram and estimate nutrient flows within their farming systems. In doing this, it is their reality, not a mirror of that of outsiders, which is expressed and shared. Environmental analyses like these have been conducted by local people in countries as diverse as Bangladesh, Bulgaria,[6] Cambodia,[7] India,[8] Kenya, Vietnam and Zimbabwe.

In South India, a local NGO, Myrada, conducted a PRA study with farmers in 1989. The farmers brought up the problem of their having lost in the drought of 1974 a variety of sorghum which was highly valued for its fodder. One farmer described the impact this had on farming practices:

> Our local sorghum variety was wiped out during the earhead stage. Because we couldn't get seed the next year, we were forced to switch to hybrids. Hybrids do not give us as much straw as our local varieties did. Therefore we were forced to extend our cultivated areas to include grazing lands. Because the grazing land was reduced we were forced to graze our cattle in the forests.

The International Crops Research Institute for the Semi-Arid Tropics (ICRISAT) was approached, but could not trace the particular variety, so the NGO arranged a bus for a farmers' expedition to the neighbouring state of Maharashtra, where they found the sorghum variety and brought it back.

Box 6.6: PRA – how it is done

o The learning process is reversed; learning with and from rural people, directly, on site, and face-to-face, gaining from local physical, technical and social knowledge.

o A learning process is employed that is progressive and flexible, allowing for the unexpected and for improvisation, rather than following a pre-set blueprint.

o Biases, especially those of rural development tourism, are offset by being relaxed and not pushy, listening not lecturing, being unimposing instead of domineering, probing keenly and seeking out the poorer people and women to learning of their concerns.

o Trade-offs are optimized, relating the costs of learning to the value of the information. This includes the principles of optimal ignorance (knowing what appears to be *not* worth knowing), and of appropriate imprecision (not measuring more than is really needed – this often involves comparing, estimating or scoring rather than measuring).

o Diversity is sought out. This means seeking variability rather than averages, sampling a range, deliberately looking for, noticing and investigating exceptions, contradictions, anomalies and differences.

o Triangulation is used; that is, applying and learning from a range of methods, types of information, analysts, social groups, locations, and/ or disciplinary viewpoints to capture and express diversity and complexity, to cross-check and converge on valid insight, and to enhance credibility.

o Facilitation is the key – local people learn to investigate and analyse, so that they present and own the outcomes, and also learn. This often entails an outsider convening, catalyzing and initiating a process and then sitting back or even walking away; not interrupting, but listening, observing, assessing and quietly supporting the process of analysis, expression and presentation of their reality.

o Being self-critically aware, sensitive and responsible, and ever trying to do better is paramount. This means embracing error as an opportunity to learn and improve, and using one's own best judgement at all times. It means accepting personal responsibility rather than vesting it in a manual or a rigid set of rules.

o Information and ideas are shared: among rural people and between them and the facilitators. The sharing of field camps, training and experiences between different organizations is encouraged; as is the sharing of information and insights, without seeking ownership or acknowledgement.

The participatory learning of PRA is more than a collection of innovative techniques. It is a way of being, and of relating to others. For outsider facilitators it involves self-critical awareness of their own attitudes and behaviour, and for local people it entails engagement in an on-going participatory process.

allowing and enabling them to spin freely, offsetting the normal with reversals.

Primacy of the personal

The ultimate reversal is personal, yet this crucial dimension has been curiously neglected. 'Uppers' need to step down and to become allies, convenors, consultants and facilitators of 'Lowers'. This entails reversals and transfers of power, rights, claims and responsibilities, from centre to periphery and from strong to weak. It also entails some personal disempowerment for almost all peoples, since almost all are 'Uppers' in some of their relationships.

To induce these reversals, two approaches are needed:

○ *Confrontation, negotiation and persuasion.* Quite often some conflict and tension is inevitable where change is implicated, which threatens, or is seen as threatening, to the powerful. This can apply to bureaucrats, business people, politicians and professionals.

○ *The satisfaction and rewards of disempowerment, mutuality, and altruism.* These tend to be neglected. It can, however, be hugely satisfying for an individual to devolve power to others. Part of the challenge is to find new ways of enabling the powerful to save face, so that it is easier for them to 'hand over the stick', and to experience those satisfactions.

Faced with normal market capitalism, bureaucracy, politics, law and professionalism, the individual appears powerless: the forces seem too universal, too strong, too overwhelming to be affected by personal action. But the 'magnetic' fields of these forces are no more than the product of the habits and actions of individuals. If individuals change, so too do the fields. So an important step is to recognize the primacy of the personal, that every individual has an effect, that analysis and action can start with the individual. This is the final reversal – to put the personal at the centre and on top. It is to recognize that individual action can make a difference; that we are not just the helpless victims of blind forces, but are collectively their creators; and that change comes about through accumulations of personal decisions to change and be different.

References

1. Jodha, N.S. (1988). Poverty Debate in India: A Minority View. *Economic and Political Weekly*, special number, November, pp. 2421–28.

183

2. Porter, D., Bryant, A. and Thompson, G. (1991). *More Diversity for More Certainty. Development in Practice: Paved with Good Intentions*, Routledge. London and New York.
3. Pretty, J. (1995). *Regenerating Agriculture*. Earthscan. London.
4. Chambers, R. and Conway, G. (1992). Sustainable Rural Livelihoods: Practical Concepts for the 21st Century. *Discussion Paper* **296**, Institute of Development Studies, University of Sussex, Brighton, UK.
5. Peters, T. (1989). *Thriving on Chaos: Handbook for a Management Revolution*. Pan Books. London.
6. Bulgarian Society for the Conservation of the Rhodopi Mountains and WWF-International (1995). *Planning for conservation: Participatory Rural Appraisal for Community-Based Initiatives*. Report of the Participatory Rural Appraisal (PRA) Training Workshop held in Ostritza, Bulgaria, 14–22 June 1993. Gland, Switzerland.
7. Neefjes, K. *et al.* (1993). *Participatory Environmental Assessment and Planning for Development*. Report of a workshop held in Cambodia in Nov/Dec 1992. Oxfam, Oxford, UK.

6.3 SEEDS OF HOPE

A Vote for conscience over capital

On 1 March 1995, eight years of bitter squabbling and noisy protest finally came to an end when the European Parliament voted against a controversial directive on biotechnology patents. After heavy lobbying from groups opposed to the patenting of animals, plants and human genes, it resolved by 244 votes to 188 to abandon the directive. The directive's ousting was claimed as a major moral victory by those who had fought it, and was a big blow to industry.

The directive would have ironed out differences between national patent rules, so that a patent awarded in one member country would be accepted in the others. A setback for industry perhaps, but some representatives were relieved at the decision because the directive was a mess, reflecting the confusion among parliamentarians about the implications of the directive. Nick Scott-Ram of the BioIndustry Association is reported to have said that the final draft of the directive contained ambiguities that left some points of ethics open to more than one interpretation. This could have left patents vulnerable to challenge, thus holding up commercial development. The woolliest compromise, according to Scott-Ram, was the attempt to draw a moral distinction between human genes in the body – which were deemed unpatentable – and synthetic versions of those genes produced in the laboratory – which the directive suggested could be patented. In industry's eyes, there is no question that they should *all* be patentable.

Throwing out the directive will have little *direct* impact on the awarding of patents, since this still remains under the jurisdiction of the European Patent Office, but it may have quite an impact indirectly, as it may indicate a change in the climate of opinion among parliamentarians. The following is the response of one NGO representative to the European Parliament's vote:

It was agony sitting in the semicircle of the European Parliament. MEPs spent two and a half hours voicing their final concerns about the directive, before passing to the resolve of action. The body was clearly divided, and the arguments were clearly split. Some said the directive meant 'white', while others insisted it meant 'black'. The power of science beckoning humanity's absolution through the directive was evident. The meaning of the law was confusing, while deciphering the ethical implications was the real challenge. And the Parliament's sense of fear grew.

The vote against the directive was historic and moving because it was an act of social responsibility not typical (unfortunately) of democratic institutions these days. The feelings were palpable as I cast my eyes across the room : these people, just for a moment, pushed all the talk of money away and acted as human beings. The interests of capital were momentarily cast aside and the primacy of conscience was allowed to guide and rule. For that alone, we have to salute the European Parliamentarians. They were fearful, but they were even more brave. The importance of this has to be recognized and honoured. In that final moment, what was scaring people most was the idea that this piece of legislation would not only:

○ strengthen and harmonize intellectual property rights law in the European Union

○ have a powerful normative function on the future of biotechnology R&D in Europe and elsewhere

○ bear huge ethical implications, which are recognized by patent law but not embraced by it

but it would allow the patenting of human genetic material and bestow some form of legitimacy on to the permanent genetic alteration of humankind by humankind.

The directive would have provided financial returns to investors, on top of the numerous subsidies that public and private biotechnology researchers already receive from taxpayers. In addition, by seeking to determine what is patentable and what is not, the directive would have determined the parameters of what is economically-sanctioned research in the field of life sciences, keeping it in line with the needs of intellectual monopolies. What's more, this included human beings. But the Parliament said 'No thanks'.

We must salute that body for its courage. Money is intimidating. How could we powerless NGO folk forget the day back in 1991 when two of us walked into a Dutch MEP's office to talk to him about the issues raised by the patenting directive. He handed us a small card, 'Here is my lawyer'. Or, in other words, 'Pay up if you want to talk to me'. His ears – and his voting hand – were for hire, not for public duty. The Parliamentarians could easily have backed off from their moral disconcertedness and said, 'Okay, this legislation will promote research, which is good for industry and public health'. But they didn't. Dignity was the key word on people's lips. It was not to be sold off so easily.

186

The business press scoffed that the EP forgot the law of dollars and cents (= sense) and bowed to emotion instead. Why should we be intimidated? Why can people not ask questions and take brave decisions? What is politics if we are punished for being human? Why talk about democracy if all human rights are to be swept under the rug with derision?

For us NGO people who have been involved in the battle from the start – trying to raise awareness, trying to promote broad public debate on the issue despite its seemingly abstract and technical nature – the vote was a strong political statement to the world. It said, 'There are ethical problems with the way that biotechnology is being used in society and there is something very wrong with the idea of patenting life forms, especially human genes. We need to set rules for science and technology that are socially responsible'. For five seconds, industry's stronghold over politics was tempered by the politicians' attention to social values.

This is a unique awakening. In the 1980s we started 'greening' the world economy. The EP decision could be a signal that in the 1990s we are starting to 'moralize' it. Of course people are scared; this is new; this is urgently needed. NGOs are only new clothing for what people have always done: fighting for liberation and justice.

On March 1, conscience, values, ethics, morality and dignity overrode the seduction of capital's greed and power. The fear was there at the final hour of the directive's fate. Let us not denigrate that fear: we should embrace it and help it metamorphose into understanding, strength and appropriate action this time – such as a total renegotiation of what innovation is, how we promote it and how we can protect people's rights in relation to it.

Source: Renée Vellvé, GRAIN

Europe's moratorium on BGH

Since 1986 farmers, consumers, animal welfare and environment organizations in the European Union have been demanding a ban on bovine growth hormone or rBGH (see p. 38) and products derived from its use. At the end of 1993 The European Commission recommended a ban on rBGH until the end of March 2000. The European

Parliament voted for an unlimited ban on BGH. Nevertheless, the European Council of Agriculture Ministers decided to extend the existing moratorium for only one more year, until 31 December 1994.

It seemed that the Ministers wanted to keep their options open until they saw how BGH was received in the US, it having just been approved there. A year later the Council of Ministers agreed to extend the ban on rBGH for another 5 years, to the relief of the 300 groups that had campaigned against its introduction.

Monsanto, the manufacturer of rBGH, and US trade officials had previously warned the EU that a ban on US rBGH-derived milk, dairy and beef products might constitute, under new GATT regulations, an illegal 'restraint of trade'. But in a bluntly-worded letter sent to David Kessler, US FDA commissioner, Friedrich-Wilhelm Graefe zu Baringdorf, vice-president of the EU Agriculture Committee, stated: 'Consumers in the European Union and their representatives in the European Parliament are apparently much more concerned about the unresolved human health issues related to rBGH than your agency was when it authorized the product.'

Graefe zu Baringdorf further warned the FDA that the only way to avoid a wholesale ban of US dairy exports to Europe would be to label genetically engineered meat and dairy products – a move that the Clinton administration and the biotechnology industry oppose. Polls indicate that if genetically engineered foods are labelled as such, consumers will not buy them.

The fate of rBGH in the US will be critical in determining whether rBGH is embraced or rejected altogether in Europe. NGOs are confident that as long as parliamentarians have access to reliable information, rather than industry propaganda, there is no likelihood of rBGH being approved. As Linda Bullard of the Greens in the European Parliament points out, 'There is clear resistance from both producers and consumers in the US. Where, for example, are the signposts showing that it is being enthusiastically welcomed? There are no reports of voluntary labels stating "brought to you with pride from cows treated with rBGH".'

A gene bank working with farmers

Ethiopia is one of the world's richest centres of crop genetic diversity. It is the original home of major world crops like sorghum and many millets, as well as coffee. All the coffee grown in Latin America can ultimately be traced back to a single cutting from a coffee bush in the Ethiopian Highlands. But Ethiopia is being hit hard by the plague of genetic erosion. Among the various factors contributing to the decline of its genetic heritage are the replacement of indigenous landraces (traditional varieties) by new, genetically uniform crop varieties, changes in agriculture and land use, the destruction of habitats and drought.

As new crops like corn, oats and imported varieties of wheat spread, old crops like teff, barley, and even sorghum have gone into decline. By the end of the 1970s, 37% of the wheat land was sown to 'improved' or 'high response' cultivars. The Ethiopian famine of the mid-1980s had many causes – overgrazing, water management problems, politics, and, of course, the drought itself. But unnoticed among those problems was the pressure imposed by outside 'experts' for Ethiopia to abandon its drought-tolerant crops in favour of Green Revolution varieties. The seeds may have been low yielding, but they would germinate even after long periods of drought, and there would always be *something* to harvest at the end of the season.

Throughout the famine, staff from the Plant Genetic Resource Centre (PGRC/E) were being dispatched in jeeps and on donkeys almost every day to search the fields, bins and hills for the traditional seeds that might otherwise have become extinct. The circumstances of the famine had made them realize more acutely than ever that Ethiopia's food security may depend on the survival of the old landraces.

The PGRC/E was set up in 1976 with the aim of conserving Ethiopia's biological resources. By 1992, the centre's gene bank held more than 50 000 samples of some 100 crop species comprising indigenous landraces recovered from all over the country. It is a genebank with a difference. In addition to the standard refrigerators, computers and white coats, the genebank uses another great asset: farmers who have nurtured Ethiopia's genetic heritage and have made it the important and rich resource it still is, despite heavy losses. Throughout the country, farmers have established networks to facilitate seed supply, including the exchange of seed through local markets. This provides them with an assortment of crop types with a wide range of adaptability to cope with unpredictable conditions.

The on-farm conservation and enhancement of landraces has been an aspect of the PGRC/E's work since 1988, involving farmers,

scientists and extension workers. Farmers are not only the beneficiaries of technical assistance in improving their crops, but they act as
an important source of knowledge for the PGRC/E in the identification of useful plant material. In addition, their fields act as dynamic
field gene banks. For example, in order to improve crop security,
local varieties of coffee are planted by farmers along the edges of the
fields that they sow with the more uniform lines distributed by the
Government Coffee Improvement Project. These living gene banks
are a tremendous boost to the Centre's efforts to maintain genetic
resources in the field, especially as it is difficult to store coffee seed
safely on a long-term basis. Farmers also participate in the collecting
missions undertaken by the Centre, more than 115 of which were
made in its first 14 years of existence.

Sources: Growing Diversity, *IT Publications, London, 1992;* The
Threatened Gene, *Lutterworth, 1990*

The MASIPAG experience

The MASIPAG programme was born out of Filipino farmers' bitter-
sweet experiences with the Green Revolution. Throughout the 1960s
and 1970s, the Philippine government heavily promoted the adoption
of high-yielding varieties (HYVs) and high-input agricultural production systems. The CGIAR's International Rice Research Institute (IRRI)
played a key role in researching and marketing the new rice varieties.
By 1970, 78% of the country's ricelands were planted with HYVs and
the initial results were encouraging as crop production soared. Problems began to emerge with the global oil crisis in 1974 when prices of
imports exploded. The government continued to import the agricultural inputs on which it depended so heavily to sustain its food
production campaigns. At the same time, it pursued foreign loans to
build the massive irrigation systems needed to support the Green
Revolution seed, and funded expensive promotional campaigns for
the 'miracle' rice. While debt increased, forest reserves decreased and
farmers began to lose faith in the miracle.

By the late 1970s many farmers were seriously disenchanted with
the Green Revolution. The problems they faced included the rising
cost of seed and fertilizers; the increasing concentrations of chemicals

required to keep production up; deterioration of the seed; and increasing pest problems and environmental degradation. Over the next five years, a farmers' strategy emerged from various formal and informal consultations. The strategy proposed, amongst other things, the launch of an initiative to develop a national agricultural programme independent of foreign support; an agrarian reform programme to address the problems posed by large plantations of bananas, coconut and sugar cane; a review of the government/IRRI programme with options of nationalizing its management or stopping its operation; and building a truly Filipino institution to research rice.

When their proposals were ignored by government, the farmers took the initiatives forward themselves, which resulted in the formation of MASIPAG, or the Farmer–Scientist Partnership for Development as it is known in English, in 1986. MASIPAG's activities centre on organic farming, the research and propagation of traditional rice varieties, alternative pest management and diversified farming systems integrating the production of rice, vegetables, livestock and aquaculture.

MASIPAG gives first priority to the needs, problems and aspirations of farmers since they know best what is good for them. Training focuses first on what farmers want to learn, and second, on what they need to know as perceived by MASIPAG's scientists and NGOs. By 1993 MASIPAG had the support of about 10 000 individual partners, spread among a variety of national and local NGOs and farmers' organizations. Between 1987 and 1993, MASIPAG trial farms were established in 28 locations in 16 provinces across the country.

Although seed collection was not seriously pursued, by 1993 MASIPAG had accumulated about 350 rice cultivars, which is about one tenth the number held by its big brother, IRRI. MASIPAG's seed collection contains traditional and improved varieties grown mostly on lowland irrigated and upland rain-fed areas. They exhibit diverse characters, productiveness and eating qualities, and offer a wide range of choice for farmers' use for commercial growing, home consumption and for varietal improvement work or breeding.

MASIPAG's breeding programme has demystified science for many farmers, who participate in practical programmes on the farm and at various centres. A thriving seed distribution network has also been set up. Monitoring and evaluation work demonstrated that between 1989 and 1992 traditional improved varieties and farmers' selections from MASIPAG farmers' fields outyielded IRRI's varieties, using lower levels of chemical fertilizer and biocides, in 22 regions. Farmers also reported a general decrease in quality of life during the 'IRRI years', followed by a sharp increase in the MASIPAG era. The quality of life in the MASIPAG years far exceeded that not only in the IRRI era, but in the pre-IRRI period.

Source: The MASIPAG programme: an Integrated Approach to Genetic Conservation and Use, Perfecto R. Vicente, MASIPAG, Philippines. In: Growing Diversity in Farmers' Fields, Proceedings of a Regional Seminar for Nordic Development Co-operation Agencies, *Lidingo, Sweden, 1993.*

The butterfly rises

PAT MOONEY

It is appropriate that the title of the symposium referred to butterflies. The butterfly is the symbol of chaos theory, and chaos is exactly what we need to create in this world in its march towards uniformity.

Having spent the two days of the symposium talking about how terrible things are and how much worse they are going to get, it might seem difficult to be optimistic; but I am optimistic. The optimism comes from having been fighting this issue for so long, and seeing every year so many more people involved, with such a diversity of activities going on at the local level, the national level, and the international level. More and more people are fighting patents, saving seeds, struggling for indigenous rights and working together. There has been a tremendous change in the last few years and it gives me hope.

First of all, we must beware of the misleading language that is used in this arena, and see things as they really are. We've been talking about a 'genetic supply' industry. I think we should rename it the 'life' industry, because the same companies that are involved in pharmaceuticals are into pesticides, and those same companies are leading the biotechnology field – it is a life industry and its corporations are turning into dinosaurs.

We also need to get the IP debate right. The world does not need IP: it needs a kind of intellectual integrity. We need to get back to celebrating innovation by communities, innovation as a collective social act, innovation where human beings work together towards a

192

common goal, for the benefit of society, not for the purpose of profit. We need to re-evaluate the relationship between innovation and society and determine whether the social contract that was drawn up in Vienna when the IP system began almost 125 years ago needs to be rewritten. Because it is crazy; it is out of control. It is no longer IP, it is a kleptomonopoly. The rules of the game, once so clear and so strict, that were designed for dealing with microphones and sewing machines, are now grappling with the products, the processes, and even the formulae of life; and that cannot be allowed.

We need to get some of the broad international agreements set straight; it might seem impossible, but it is not. GATT is a multilateral agreement that wants to homogenize the world to adopt one common morality, one world view: a multilateral agreement to impose a unilateral ethic on all of us. When it is reviewed in a couple of years time, *we* need to be the ones to review it.

We need to get rid of this idea of 'bioprospecting'; there is no such thing. In the absence of a convincing global ethic, and in the absence of clear rules and systems of understanding between the poor of the world and the rich of the world, there is no bioprospecting; there is only biopiracy. There has to be a moratorium on collecting anything, unless the people themselves agree to it. We should be arguing for this until the rules are straight.

We need to look at the Biodiversity Convention. It is merely a multilateral umbrella imposing bilateral contracts between very large companies and very small countries and communities; this cannot be fair. As it was signed in 1992, it is a protocol for piracy, not the conservation of biodiversity. But it can be changed because it is a very hollow document. We can do it by talking to our governments and to our local communities. It is possible to restructure it to move towards a fairer global ethic.

We can work in a number of ways:

We can co-operate. We need co-operation, like butterflies do, to move between the local level and the global level – between the stratosphere and the biosphere of the realities. That means not just that those of us who travel internationally come down to earth occasionally, but that indigenous communities and farmers also work at the global level. We need to work laterally with each other – we have our differences but we also have commonalities: a common enemy and a common opportunity. We must also achieve a harmony between the citizens and the scientists. We need somehow to bring the two systems of innovation together – formal and informal.

William Blake said that anyone who talks about the common good is a fool. Art and science can only be conducted in minutely organized particulars and that is at the level of the community. Ultimately the strategies of science and politics must be to strengthen the community – indigenous communities, rural communities, urban communities – to give us all more independence and to bring the force of innovation back to the people.

We simply need to say 'no' to the patenting of life-forms; just plain 'no'; it is not acceptable; it can't be allowed; it is just immoral; life is not for sale. This is our most important task of all.

But, meanwhile, we can do some other things:

We can adapt the intellectual property system. In my view this should be in the form of the Michaelangelo computer virus of a few years ago that we can insert into what I see as a corrupt system. We need to say that there should be no IPR system unless it is open to everyone, and force the system to open up to incorporate indigenous rights, farmers' rights and so on. I don't think it will work, but the system will probably self-destruct in the process of trying to be honest and fair.

We can also suggest that intellectual property should be moved from civil law to criminal law, so that if someone steals the coloured cotton from the people of the Americas and takes it to the US, they can simply have the pirates thrown into jail. We should also create in our patent offices a post rather like an ombudsman, a 'plantsbudsman' who can represent the rights of those people who can't be there. We should also be looking at alternative systems of rights, such as traditional resource rights which stretch way beyond the boundaries set by intellectual property.

A few years ago, those of us who were campaigning on these issues could have met together in a telephone box. If all of us here now go away and apply ourselves to these issues at every level at which we live, we can be optimistic that in a few years time we will need to meet together in a conference hall much bigger than this, and there will be real hope of changing the way of the world.

After all, butterflies are what survive as the rest of the world collapses. When the volcano erupts, the butterflies stay around. We can keep on moving back and forth and we are very hard to catch. And we can survive. I like the concept of 'iron butterflies', the tough ones, the ones with muscles. NGOS are much more efficient than anyone else. We can beat our wings together and rise above the mire of patents and intellectual property rights. We can flap our wings and . . . oops! there goes Cibasaurus Rex . . . there goes GATT . . . .

About the Authors

Janet Bell is a pharmacologist, writer and researcher based in the USA. She writes mainly on food security issues related to biodiversity.

Robert Chambers is a Fellow of the Institute of Development Studies at the University of Sussex. His books include *Rural Development: Putting the Last First* (1983) and *Challenging the Professions* (1993). He works on concepts of poverty and participatory approaches in development.

Marcus Colchester is Director of the World Rainforest Movement and is the author of numerous books and reports on indigenous people and biodiversity.

Alan Goodman is Associate Professor of Biological Anthropy and Dean of the School of Natural Science, Hampshire College, Amherst, Massachusetts. He teaches and writes on the interaction between biology, ideology and political economy.

Mark Johnston is International Projects Co-ordinator for The Body Shop International and co-ordinates all anthropological materials and fieldwork for the company. He previously worked for the Canadian Broadcasting Corporation and helped produce the television series *Millennium: Tribal Wisdom and the Modern World,* a ten-hour documentary series.

Kelly Kennedy is a graduate student of the Harvard Business School and was a 1994 Summer Program Associate for the NRRP.

Jack Kloppenburg is an Associate Professor of Rural Sociology at the University of Wisconsin-Madison. His current research focuses on the emergent social impacts of biotechnology and on the distinction between 'scientific' and 'local' knowledge. He is author of *First the Seed: The Political Economy of Plant Biotechnology, 1492–2000* (Cambridge University Press, 1988) and editor of *Seeds and Sovereignty: Use and Control of Plant Genetic Resources* (Duke University Press, 1988).

Regine Kollek is a molecular biologist at the Institute of Social Sciences, Hamburg, and co-author of *Die ungeklarten Gefahrenpotential der Gentechnologie* (1996) and *Wissenschaft als Kontext – Kontexte der Wessenschaft* (1993).

Pat Mooney is an NGO activist who has worked on international environment and development issues related to sustainable agriculture and biodiversity for more than 25 years. He has been the recipient of The Right Livelihood Award and the US' 'Giraffe Award' given to people 'who stick their necks out'.

Christine Noiville is a lecturer in law at the University of Paris. Her doctoral thesis was on the legal protection of marine genetic resources.

Michel Pimbert was formerly Director of WWF-International's biodiversity programme and is currently Director of WWF-Switzerland. He is an agricultural ecologist with extensive experience of participatory approaches to the conservation and sustainable use of biodiversity.

Vandana Shiva is a physicist, philosopher and feminist, and is Director of the Research Foundation for Science, Technology and Natural Resource Policy in Dehra Dun, India. She is also the Science and Environmental advisor to the Third World Network.

Christine von Weiszäcker is a writer and biologist living in Bonn, Germany, where she also presides over a large family. She writes on the implications of technology and economics, and is particularly concerned about the marginalization of the domestic sphere in industrial society and the invasion of life's 'commons' by genetic engineering.

Charles Zerner is Director of the Natural Resources and Rights Program (NRRP) of the Rainforest Alliance in New York. He is a South-east Asia specialist and lawyer with extensive experience in the analysis of community environment relationships to law, culture and conservation.

Acronyms

BGH	Bovine Growth Hormone
BST	Bovine Somatotropin
CDR	Complex, Diverse and Risk-prone (farming systems)
CGIAR	Consultative Group on International Agricultural Research (US)
CIMMYT	Centro Internacional para Mejoramiento de Maiz y Trigo (Mexico, CGIAR)
CIR	community intellectual rights
DNA	deoxyribonucleic acid
EP	European Parliament
EPO	European Patent Office
EU	European Union
FAO	Food and Agriculture Organization of the United Nations
FDA	Food and Drug Administration (US)
GATT	General Agreement on Tariffs and Trade
GEF	Global Environment Facility
GIFTS	Germplasm, Information, Funds, Technologies and Systems
GMO	genetically manipulated organism
GRAIN	Genetic Resources Action International
GNP	gross national product
HFC	Healing Forest Conservancy
HGDP	Human Genome Diversity Project
HGP	Human Genome Project (US)
HGH	human growth hormone
HTLV	human T-lymphotropic virus
HUGO	Human Genome Organization (Europe)
IARC	International Agricultural Research Centre
ICRISAT	International Crops Research Institute for the Semi-Arid Tropics (India, CGIAR)
INBio	Instituto Nacional de Biodiversidad (Costa Rica)
IP	intellectual property
IPRs	intellectual property rights
IRRI	International Rice Research Institute (Philippines, CGIAR)
MASIPAG	Magsasaka at Syentipiko para sa Pagpapa untad ng Agham Pang-Agnkultura (Farmer–Scientist Partnership for Development)
MEP	Member of the European Parliament
NAFTA	North American Free Trade Agreement

NCI	National Cancer Institute
NGO	non-governmental organization
NIH	National Institutes of Health (US)
OECD	Organization for Economic Co-operation and Development
PBR	Plant Breeders' Rights
PCR	polymerase chain reaction
PRA	participatory rural appraisal
RAFI	Rural Advancement Fund International
R&D	research and development
TRIPS	Trade-Related Aspects of Intellectual Property Rights (negotiating group of GATT)
UN	United Nations
UNCED	United Nations Conference on Environment and Development (or 'Earth Summit')
UNDP	United Nations Development Programme (New York)
UNEP	United Nations Environment Programme (Nairobi)
UNESCO	United Nations Educational, Scientific, and Cultural Organization (Paris)
UPOV	International Union for the Protection of New Varieties of Plants (Geneva)
USDA	United States Department of Agriculture
WHO	World Health Organization
WIPO	World Intellectual Property Organization
WWF	World Wide Fund for Nature

Glossary

Accession: a sample of seeds or plants collected for storage in a gene bank.

Allele: alternative versions of a gene. A gene for eye colour may have several alleles, coding for green, brown, grey or blue eyes.

Agenda 21: the plan of action drawn up at the Earth Summit in Rio de Janeiro in 1992. It is a comprehensive set of programmes of action to promote sustainable development into the 21st century. Although non-binding, Agenda 21 is an important document representing a consensus of the world's governments.

Biodiversity: the diversity of life. The term refers to the millions of life-forms found on earth, the genetic variation between them and their complex ecological interactions. Biodiversity can also be thought of as a web of relationships between organisms and the environment which ensure balance and sustainability.

Biome: a major portion of the living environment of a particular region, such as fir forest or grassland, characterized by its distinctive vegetation and maintained by local climatic conditions.

Bioprospecting: the exploration of commercially valuable genetic and biochemical resources.

Biotechnology: any technique that uses living organisms to make or modify a product, to improve plants and animals, or to develop micro-organisms for specific uses. Often (wrongly) used synonymously with 'genetic engineering', but the term 'biotechnology' covers a much wider spectrum of techniques and processes.

Bovine Growth Hormone (BGH): a naturally occurring growth hormone found in cattle that, amongst other things, increases milk production. It can be produced synthetically using recombinant DNA techniques, inserting the gene into bacteria which act as mini-factories for BGH. The hormone is then harvested, purified and injected into cattle.

Bovine Somatotropin (BST): the scientifically correct term for bovine growth hormone.

Bt toxin: a generic term for a group of toxins produced by the bacterium *Bacillus Thuringiensis* which are active against a wide range of crop pests. The toxins are sometimes sprayed externally on to plants, but more interest is now going into transplanting the genes' coding for the toxins into the crops themselves.

Chromosome: a long, thread-like chain of genetic material found in cells of most organisms. Chromosomes consist of DNA and protein wound together to form a double helical structure.

Community Intellectual Rights: a suggested form of *sui generis* intellectual property rights in which communities, rather than individuals, are rewarded for innovation.

Conservation: the management of human use of the biosphere so that it may yield the greatest sustainable benefit to present generations while maintaining its potential to meet the needs and aspirations of future generations. Thus conservation is positive, embracing preservation, maintenance, sustainable use, restoration, and enhancement of the natural environment.

Consultative Group on International Agricultural Research (CGIAR): an informal coalition of donors (largely from the North) that funds and promotes R&D into international agricultural research via its organs, the International Agricultural Research Centres (IARCs).

Convention on Biological Diversity: a legally-binding agreement for the conservation and sustainable use of biodiversity. Adopted in Nairobi in May 1992, the Convention was opened for signature and signed during the Earth Summit by over 150 countries. By October 1995, it had been ratified by 128 countries and the EU.

Cultivar: a cultivated variety of plant, used interchangeably with 'variety'.

Deoxyribonucleic acid (DNA): the molecule found in chromosomes that is the repository of genetic information in almost all organisms. The information coded by DNA determines the structure and function of an organism.

Dwarf genes: the genetic powerhouse of the Green Revolution. These genes produce varieties of crops such as wheat, rice and maize with shorter, stiffer stems, so that the plants can put more energy into the production of grain at the expense of peripheral parts such as stems, leaves, etc.

Ecosystem: a dynamic complex of plant, animal, fungal, and microorganism communities and their associated non-living environment interacting as an ecological unit.

Endemic: restricted to a specific region or locality.

Ex-situ *conservation:* 'off site' conservation. Keeping components of diversity alive outside of their original habitat or natural environment.

Extension (worker): extension is the process by which insitutional scientific results are brought and transmitted to the farmer. An extension worker is responsible for doing this. They are often government employees, but may work for NGOs or other organizations.

Fauna: all of the animals found in a given area.

Flora: all of the plants found in a given area.

Farmers' Rights: a broad interpretation of intellectual property rights, designed to overcome the shortcomings of other IPR systems which fail to address the inventive process of informal systems.

Gene: the functional unit of heredity usually carried on the chromosome and made up of DNA. A gene codes for a particular protein molecule. A single gene sometimes codes directly for a particular characteristic, but more often a particular trait is the result of the interaction between several genes and the environment.

Gene bank: a facility established for the *ex situ* conservation of seeds, tissues or reproductive cells of plants or animals.

Gene flow: exchange of genes between different, usually related, populations. Genes commonly flow back and forth amongst plants via transfers of pollen.

Gene pool: the sum total of genes in a population (not an individual) at any one time.

Gene therapy: transplanting genes into individuals for therapeutic purposes. The only medical application of this therapy at present is for cystic fibrosis sufferers.

Genetic determinism: the belief that patterns and differences in an organism's biology and behaviour are largely determined by their genes. Also called 'hereditarianism'.

Genetic diversity: the variation in the genetic composition of individuals within or among species; the hereditable genetic variation within and among populations.

Genetic engineering: modifying the genetic make-up of living organisms using molecular biology techniques that can transfer genes between widely dissimilar organisms.

Genetic resources: strictly speaking, the physical hereditary material (germplasm) which carries the genetic characteristics of life forms. In the broader sense, genetic resources are the germplasm plus information, funds, technologies and social and environmental systems (GIFTS) through which germplasm becomes a socio-economic resource.

Genome: the entire collection of an organisms's hereditary material contained in its genes.

Genomics: the study of the genes and genetics

Genotype: the genetic make-up of an organism.

Germplasm: the genetic material that comprises the physical basis of the inherited qualities of an organism.

Green Revolution: The changes in world agricultural practices which occurred in the 1950s, 1960s and 1970s as the result of the introduction of the so-called 'high-yielding' varieties.

Herbicide: a chemical weed-killer.

Hereditarianism: see 'genetic determinism'.

High-yielding variety: a variety that has been bred to produce a high yield of a particular crop. This was achieved with Green Revolution crops largely by the introduction of 'dwarf' genes (see above). Some critics think that 'high-response' variety is a more accurate term, since in the absence of fertilizers and irrigation, they perform worse than traditional varieties.

Intellectual Property Rights (IPR): a bag of tools designed to protect people's knowledge. They are designed to promote and protect innovation by allowing the 'owner' of the knowledge to have a monopoly over his or her invention for a designated period of time, during which no one else may use the invention except on payment of a royalty to the owner.

In situ *conservation:* 'on-site' conservation: the conservation of bio-diversity within the natural environment.

Jumping gene: a mobile section of DNA that can 'jump' from one gene to another, thus serving as an agent of change. Also called a 'transposon'.

Landrace: a variety developed over many plant generations, some-times encompassing thousands of years, by farmers selecting plants with desired characteristics. Landraces are usually more genetically diverse than modern farm varieties and are often adapted to specific local environments. Sometimes called 'peasant varieties' or 'primit-ive cultivars', they are looked down on by industrial agriculture, but are very valuable because of their diversity, survival qualities, adaptability and other characteristics.

Licence: a type of contract between an owner of intellectual property and another allowing the latter to use, manufacture or market the invention in exchange for a royalty.

Micro-organism: single-celled organism, often used as a vehicle, or mini-factory for the production of genetically engineered products, such as the sweetener thaumatin; or enzymes used in cheese mak-ing, which can be harvested from bacteria.

Miracle seeds: the so-called high-yielding varieties of the Green Revolution.

Non-governmental Organization (NGO): a non-profit group or asso-ciation organized outside of political structures to realize particular social objectives (such as environmental protection) or to serve particular constituencies (such as indigenous people). NGOs range from small groups within a particular community to national or international organizations.

Natural selection: the process by which the interaction between organisms and the environment leads to a differential rate of reproduction among genetic types in a population. As a result, some genes increase in frequency in a population, while others decline. Natural selection is one of the driving forces of evolution.

Neem: the neem tree *(Azadirachta indica)* has been used widely (particularly in Asia) for a variety of purposes: the leaves are used as a pesticide, its oil is used in candles, soap and a contraceptive, etc. Neem derivatives are now being patented and marketed by two US companies, and Southern farmers are outraged that their contribution to commercial neem's intellectual property is not being recognized.

Paradigm: a mutually-reinforcing pattern of concepts, values, beliefs, methods and behaviours.

Patent: a legal mechanism offering a temporary monopoly of rights which is awarded to an individual in respect of innovative processes or products that they have created.

Phenotype: the outward appearance, or physical and physiological characteristics, of an organism.

Plant Breeders' Rights (PBR): monopoly rights awarded to plant breeders and farmers. These differ from patents in that the monopoly is granted only for marketing a specific variety, not over ownership of the germplasm.

Polymorphism: the co-existence of two or more distinct forms of individuals bearing the same genes in a population.

Population: in genetics, a group of individuals which share a common genepool and can interbreed. Traditional planting materials used by farmers are usually referred to as populations because they are heterogeneous, as opposed to the pure lines produced by research centres or industry.

Prior informed consent: an agreement obtained following full disclosure of all relevant facts.

Polymerase chain reaction (PCR): a technique that has revolutionized molecular biology. PCR is a technique for amplifying DNA in the laboratory. Copies of DNA can be made from very small samples, even individual cells.

Public domain: everything that is known in the world that is not protected as intellectual property.

Racism: the belief in the superiority of certain races over others, combined with the power to act on that belief.

Racialism: the belief that humans are divisible into a finite number of types (races) and that individual biology and behaviour are explicable by race. Also called Scientific Racism.

Reductionism: the dominant approach to scientific method, which reduces organisms, and life itself, to their mechanistic parts and disregards the interconnections and dynamism between genes, physiological systems, organisms and their environments. cf. Systems approach.

Royalty: a payment, usually a fixed percentage per performance, broadcast or unit sold, to an intellectual property owner established by contract or other agreement. Royalties may also be payable, subject to a contract stating this, by a drug company to a supplier of biological matter if it contains a biochemical useful in developing a new drug product.

Scientific Racism: see 'Racialism'.

Selection: any process used to sift out certain genotypes rather than others.

Species: a population whose members are able to interbreed freely under natural conditions.

Species diversity: the variety and frequency of different species.

Sui generis *legislation:* a unique form of intellectual property protection, especially designed to meet certain criteria and needs. Because of its adaptability, *sui generis* protection is being considered by the Biodiversity Convention as an alternative to the universal blueprint protection that patents offer.

Sustainable development: development that meets the needs of the present without compromising the ability of future generations to meet their own needs; improving the quality of human life whilst living within the carrying capacity of supporting ecosystems.

Systems approach: looks at living organisms and living systems as interconnected and co-dependent entities, rather than as isolated, self-contained units. cf. Reductionism.

Trait: genetic predisposition for a physical characteristic, such as eye colour, pest resistance or drought tolerance.

Transposon: see 'jumping gene'.

Transgene: a gene transplanted from a dissimilar organism, or an artificially constructed gene introduced into an organism.

Transgenic organism: one that has been genetically engineered or that is the offspring of other transgenic organisms. Typically, a transgenic plant contains genetic material from at least one unrelated organism.

Variety: A group of plants within a species which share common characteristics. Usually refers to plants which have been selected by breeders to be distinct, uniform and stable.

Virus: the smallest known type of organism. Viruses cannot exist in isolation – they must first infect a living cell and usurp its synthetic and reproductive facilities. It generally causes disease in host organisms.

Organizations

European Campaign Against rBST
115 rue Stevin, B-1040 Brussels,
  Belgium
Tel: +322 230 0776 *Fax:* +322 230
  0348

The Greens in the European
  Parliament
Contact: Linda Bullard
Tel/fax: +322 284 2026
e-mail: epggeng@gn.apc.org

Genetics Forum
5–11 Worship Street, London EC2A
  2BH, UK
Tel: +44 171 638 0606 *Fax:* +44 171
  628 0817

Genetic Resources Action
  International (GRAIN)
Girona 25, pral., E-08010 Barcelona,
  Spain
Tel: +34 3 301 1381 *Fax:* +34 3 310
  5952
e-mail: grain@gn.apc.org

Indigenous Peoples Biodiversity
  Network (IBPN)
1 Nicholas Street, Suite 620, Ottawa,
  Ontario, K1N 7B7 Canada.
Tel: 1 613 241 4500 *Fax:* +1 613 241
  2292
e-mail: csl@web.apc.org

Intermediate Technology
  Development Group
Myson House, Railway Terrace,
  Rugby CV21 3HT, UK
Tel: +44 1788 560631 *Fax:* +44 1788
  540270
e-mail: itdg@gn.apc.org

Pesticides Action Network (PAN)
North America Regional Center
116 New Montgomery Street #810,
  San Francisco, CA 94105, USA.
Tel: +1 415 541 9140 *Fax:* + 1 415
  541 9253
e-mail: panna@igc.apc.org

PAN Europe
c/o The Pesticides Trust, 23 Beehive
  Place, London SW9 7QR, UK
Tel: +44 171 274 9086 *Fax:* +44 171
  274 9084
e-mail: pesttrust@gn.apc.org

*Contact either of the above for PAN
  in Asia/Pacific, Latin America,
  and Africa.*

Pure Food Campaign.
1130 Seventeenth Street, N.W., Suite
  300, Washington, D.C. 20036,
  USA
Tel: +1 202 775 1132. *Fax:* +1 202
  775 0074

Rural Advancement Foundation
  International
International Office
Suite 504, 71 Bank St., Ottawa,
  Ontario, K1P 5N2, Canada
Tel: +1 613 567 6880 *Fax:* +1 613
  567 6884
e-mail: rafican@web.apc.org

Swissaid
Jubiläumstrasse 60, CH 3000 Berne,
  Switzerland
Tel: +41 31 351 3311 *Fax:* +41 31
  351 2783
e-mail: swissaid@igc.apc.org

Third World Network
228 Macalistair Road, Penang 10400,
  Malaysia
Tel: +60 4 366359 *Fax:* +60 4 364505
e-mail: twn@igc.apc.org

Union of Concerned Scientists
1616 P Street, N.W., Washington,
  D.C. 20036, USA
Tel: +1 202 332 0900 *Fax:* +1 202
  332 0905

World Sustainable Agriculture
  Association (WSAA)
Los Angeles Office
8554 Melrose Avenue, West
  Hollywood, CA 90069, USA
Tel: +1 310 657 7202

World Wide Fund for Nature-
  International
Rue du Mont Blanc, CH-1196 Gland,
  Switzerland
Tel: +41 22 364 9111 *Fax:* +41 22
  364 4238

WWF-Switzerland
14 Chemin de Poussy,
1214 - Vernies,
Geneva, Switzerland
Tel: +41 22 939 39 84
Fax: +41 22 341 27 84